TO TRAIN HIS SOUL IN BOOKS

TO TRAIN HIS SOUL IN BOOKS

SYRIAC ASCETICISM IN EARLY CHRISTIANITY

EDITED BY

Robin Darling Young and Monica J. Blanchard

The Catholic University of America Press

Washington, D.C.

The paper used in this publication meets the minimum requirements of American National Standards for Information Science—Permanence of Paper for Printed Library Materials, ANSI Z39.48-1984.
∞

LIBRARY OF CONGRESS CATALOGING-IN-PUBLICATION DATA
To train his soul in books : Syriac asceticism in early Christianity / edited by Robin Darling Young and Monica J. Blanchard.
p. cm.
In English; 1 contribution in Spanish.
Festschrift for Sidney H. Griffith.
"Bibliography of the works of Sidney H. Griffith"—P.
Includes bibliographical references and index.
ISBN 978-0-8132-1732-1 (cloth : alk. paper) 1. Asceticism--History—Early church, ca. 30–600. 2. Ephraem, Syrus, Saint, 303–373. 3. Syrian Church—History. I. Young, Robin Darling. II. Blanchard, Monica J. III. Griffith, Sidney Harrison.
BV5023.T68 2011
248.4'709394309015—dc22 2011012797

To Sidney H. Griffith, S.T.

CONTENTS

PART III. AFTER EPHREM THE SYRIAN

ABBREVIATIONS

AB	Anchor Bible
ACMP	*Arabic Christianity in the Monasteries of Ninth-Century Palestine.* Sidney H. Griffith. Brookfield, Vt.: Aldershot, Hants, 1992.
ACW	Ancient Christian Writers, 1944–
BCTA	*The Beginnings of Christian Theology in Arabic: Muslim-Christian Encounters in the Early Islamic Period.* Sidney H. Griffith. Burlington, Vt.: Ashgate, 2002.
BHG	*Bibliotheca hagiographica graeca.* Brussels. 1977.
CCL	Corpus Christianorum Series Latinorum
COr	*Cahiers de l'Orient*
CSCO	Corpus scriptorum christianorum orientalium. Edited by I. B. Chabot et al. Paris, 1903–
DOP	Dumbarton Oaks Papers
GCS	Die griechische christliche Schriftsteller der ersten [drei] Jahrhunderte
HAT	Handbuch zum Alten Testament
HE	*Historia ecclesiastica*
HTR	*Harvard Theological Review*
HUAC	*Hebrew Union College Annual*
ICC	International Critical Commentary
JAOS	*Journal of the American Oriental Society*
JECS	*Journal of Early Christian Studies*
JEH	*Journal of Ecclesiastical History*
JJS	*Journal of Jewish Studies*
JNES	*Journal of Near Eastern Studies*

JSJ	*Journal for the Study of Judaism in the Persian, Hellenistic, and Roman Periods*
LXX	Septuagint
NJPS	*New Jewish Publication Society*
NPNF[1]	*Nicene and Post-Nicene Fathers,* Series 1
NPNF[2]	*Nicene and Post-Nicene Fathers,* Series 2
NTS	*New Testament Studies*
OCP	*Orientalia christiana periodica*
OLA	Orientalia lovaniensia analecta
OLP	Orientalia lovaniensia periodica
OrChrAn	Orientalia christiana analecta
PG	Patrologia graeca. Edited by J.-P. Migne. 162 vols. Paris, 1857–86.
PO	Patrologia orientalis
PS	Patrologia syriaca. Rev. ed. I. Ortiz de Urbina. Rome, 1965.
RAM	*Revue d'ascetique et de mystique*
REA	*Revue de etudes anciennes*
RSR	*Recherches de science religieuse*
SAD	*Syriac Apocalypse of Daniel*
SC	Source chrétiennes. Paris: Cerf, 1943–
SP	Sacra pagina
ST	*Studia theologica*
StMon	*Studia Monastica*
StPatr	Studia patristica
SVThQ	*St. Vladimir's Theological Quarterly*
TDNT	*Theological Dictionary of the New Testament.* Edited by G. Kittel and G. Friedrich. Translated by J. T. Willis, G. W. Bromiley, and D. E. Green. 10 vols. Grand Rapids. 1964–1976.
TDOT	*Theological Dictionary of the Old Testament.* Edited by G. J. Botterweck and H. Ringgren. Translated by J. T. Willis, G. W. Bromiley, and D. E. Green. 8 vols. Grand Rapids, 1974–
TU	Texte und Untersuchungen
VAG	Vita Athanasii graeca
VAS	Vita Athanasii syriaca
VC	*Vigiliae christianae*

INTRODUCTION

This volume of essays, a collection of studies on the work of Ephrem the Syrian and subsequent developments in Syriac-speaking asceticism, is a small sign of the respect and fondness its authors share for Professor Sidney H. Griffith. Some of the authors have worked with Sidney as his students, and others began as colleagues and are grateful to call themselves his friends. Compiling this volume in celebration of Sidney's scholarly work and in view of his approaching seventieth birthday, they also know that they are representing many other scholars and friends who gladly would add their tributes to the life and work of this remarkable man.

Sidney H. Griffith is well known among scholars as both a pillar of the international world of Syriac and early Arabic Christian studies, and of the Department of Semitic and Egyptian Languages at the Catholic University of America in Washington, D.C. His many friends know him as a scholar, as a priest, as an indefatigable traveler, as a devoted son, brother, and uncle, and as a lively and engaging conversationalist. The many students who have sat in his classrooms—principally around the broad tables of the library of the Institute of Christian Oriental Research at the Catholic University of America—know him as a kind but exacting teacher, and as one whose patience with a text and its students extends from week to week, and year to year. His natural environment is the classroom and the lecture hall, where he proceeds with stately leisure to discuss his discoveries or to respond to questions, and in this climate he radiates contentment. To students in at least one class—weary at the end of a semester—he was heard to wish fervently that the class would simply continue indefinitely, without respect to the inconveniently seasonal calendar of the university.

Sidney is a bookman, an admirer of ancient librarians and interpreters, and a man profoundly at home around books. Those who meet Sidney in his office, in the northwest corner of the basement of Mullen Library at Catholic University, cannot miss his devotion to books. By the window is his desk, surrounded and surmounted with overflowing bookshelves. The surface of the desk itself is covered with papers—Syriac or Arabic texts he is currently reading, letters from correspondents and his own compositions. Like a wall, a tall bookshelf of the *Corpus scriptorum christianorum orientalium* volumes show their spines to any visitor, and obscure Sidney from sight. In front of that shelf are an ell made of two more desks, jammed against a row of filing cabinets. A visitor may be invited to sit for discussion at one of the chairs beside this public desk, but risks tripping over the library book truck, full of texts for the current seminar, between Sidney's office and the seminar room next door. Even his jacket pocket holds a book—usually a paperback, and often a current novel. He has been an eager trader of recent books, swapping them with numerous friends.

If anyone has lived with books, it is Sidney, and this love of books must have blossomed in childhood; more than one friend knows his delight in the used and new bookstores of Washington, D.C., Princeton, Cambridge, Chicago, and Oxford (to begin with). But even the very tools of writing can still make him happy—like many of his scholarly comrades of a certain age, he can still admire the rows of fresh notebooks, pens, and pencils in a local pharmacy, arrayed fresh and new for the new school year. As with his life in the church and in the priesthood, his life in books expresses Sidney's stability—settled in the church, specifically, the Roman Catholic Church in the vicinity of Washington, he is also settled into the world of the university and the life of the mind. His frequent travels serve only to accentuate his love of home.

Sidney was born on December 21, 1938, the first of the five children of the Griffith family of Gaithersburg, Maryland. He is a native Marylander, and has lived in the state of Maryland and the city of Washington, D.C., for most of his life. On both sides he is descended from old Maryland families—through his father, the Griffiths; through his mother, the Sappingtons. Through his father's family his roots are to be found in Baltimore; through his mother's family he represents the English Catholic community of Southern Maryland. Sidney's openness to scholars and thinkers of other religious communities recalls the peaceful outlook that distinguished a previous representative of the same community. John Carroll was a much earlier representative of English Catholicism; as the founder of Georgetown University, he also became a promoter of Catholic-Protestant cooperation in the newly founded capital city of the young United States, and later as archbishop of Baltimore.

Sidney attended the elementary school of his family's parish in Gaithersburg, St. Martin's, and he has happy memories of the days of his grammar schooling and of serving as an altar boy at another local church, St. Rose's. When he entered high school in 1952, however, he rode the train all the way from what was then a small country town in the farming country into Washington to attend the one-year-old John Carroll High School on Taylor Street, near Catholic University.

In his junior year of high school, Sidney left Carroll and entered the novitiate of a religious congregation, the Missionary Servants of the Most Holy Trinity. This congregation was one of the foundations established by Fr. Thomas Augustine Judge (1868–1933), who as a Vincentian living in a period of missionary fervor, saw the need to provide for underserved Catholic populations in the South; a century of Catholic immigrant history demonstrated that they could likely leave their tradition for other churches. Thus Father Judge sponsored a movement of lay people to address the problem; soon this foundation led to two new congregations of religious sisters and priests who worked in Mississippi and Alabama for the better part of the twentieth century as internal missionaries.

Attracted to this congregation, and drawn like many young Catholics to a life of missionary service with a highly structured community life, Sidney overcame the reluctance of his fond parents and traveled south to Holy Trinity, Alabama for the minor seminary. Here, seminarians—gathering in cassocks for the monastic horarium and assembling in workclothes for farm work—lived a community life envisioned by Father Judge when he built the first wooden chapel and residence there. The group of young men Sidney joined, overseen by their teachers, not only completed high school coursework but also worked clearing underbrush as well as assisting at Masses on the weekends. The congregation's most well-known chronicler describes the place in this way:

> The rural deep South was an unlikely spot for a 14-year-old to take up studies for the Catholic priesthood. Holy Trinity had been an old plantation till the twenties. It stood twenty-three miles out from Phenix City, along the Chattahoochee River, past a rise in the road called Red Level. Russell County, Alabama, had red clay, sweet

pine, kudzu, and Baptists. DeSoto passed through in 1540 with 12 priests and four friars; it may have been the last time Catholics were chronicled. In 1957, the year before I came, the Ku Klux Klan burned a cross on the lawn. My freshman year a reporter came out from town, looked around, and wrote: "Spread out to the horizons are lush, green patches of spring wheat and oats and fat cattle grazing and tractors plowing in the black loam, for these are men and women of the soil as well as the spirit." Actually, the loam was pretty sandy. But you knew what he meant. Maybe 500 of us went through the place during the forties and fifties; maybe five percent are priests today (Paul Hendrickson, "Search for a Seminary," 1980).

After completing the curriculum in Alabama, Sidney returned to the Chesapeake Bay watershed, attending the Father Judge Mission Seminary in Monroe, Virginia, before coming to Catholic University. He was ordained a priest in 1965. At Catholic University, he gained a Licentiate in Sacred Theology (S.T.L.) in 1967. Fittingly for a bibliophile, he went on to earn a graduate degree in library science. That Sidney had joined a missionary congregation presaged his later, and well-known, love of travel; his library degree was foreshadowed by his intense love of books and reading—a love that led him as young man to be the custodian of the congregational library and permitted his indulgence in the bibliophile's delight, reading after curfew, under the covers, with a flashlight. If these books were sometimes prisoners of the *Index Librorum Prohibitorum,* a penitentiary now happily closed, so much the better—Sidney learned from them, too, before they had to return to their cells in the morning.

Sidney had emerged from the Trinitarians' institutions as the church, along with American culture, underwent the upheavals of the period. He knew the Latin Mass, and had learned theology from the manuals. But the Catholic world was changing rapidly, and along with others in the archdiocese, Sidney welcomed the vernacular Mass and eagerly attended to the new directions in theology by his prodigious reading and in all the *fora* of the university and the city that offered occasions for intense discussion as old forms of Catholic life and thought gave way—for a time—to the new. Within this period—the late sixties and most of the seventies—Sidney was forming the habits of a scholar and a teacher that have made him an institution in the world of national and international scholarship among scholars of Syriac, Christian Arabic, and early Christianity more broadly.

These were the years of Sidney's study in the Department of Semitic and Egyptian Languages and Literatures, into which he settled as a permanent home.

At this university, founded in 1887 by the American Catholic bishops, the Semitics Department was one of the earliest foundations. Unlike many Catholic colleges, founded by religious orders to equip first-generation collegians for a life in the American professions, the Catholic University of America was to be a graduate, research institution, where devoted scholars would pursue the highest level of scholarship in an institution that could eventually stand alongside its older, established European counterparts where the intellectual life had thrived since the High Middle Ages. As Sidney himself has often pointed out, if the American bishops were often distracted by more pressing material needs of their dioceses, and were unable to provide sufficient funds for their university, the scholars of Catholic University nonetheless could devote themselves to the life of the mind in a setting where, within certain limits of their religious obedience, the rigors of scholarship were unquestionably more precious than the collegiate atmosphere and athletic rivalries of other Catholic institutions of higher education.

As a graduate student in the doctoral program of the Semitics Department, Sidney joined a group of energetic young scholars who could draw on resources accumulated since the founding of the department by Fr. Henri Hyvernat (1858–1941), himself a scholar of all the languages of the ancient and modern Near East and an indefatigable traveler, collector, and bibliophile of a kind not uncommon in the late nineteenth century. Hyvernat's personal library, including manuscripts in many of those languages, is the core collection of the Institute of Christian Oriental Research whose library surrounded and supported the Department of Semitics. His successors added to the collection, and the names of Arthur A. Vaschalde and Romain Butin are still known by contemporary scholars of the late Ancient Near East. From these roots came the Semitics Department's co-sponsorship of the *Corpus scriptorum christianorum orientalium,* which it publishes jointly with the Catholic University of Louvain.

In the mid-twentieth century, of the prominent scholars at Catholic University, two in particular worked in the Semitics Department and taught Sidney there. By enrolling in the Semitics Department, Sidney began training in a highly specialized area of scholarship in a period of great activity at Catholic University. Not only had Joseph Fitzmyer, S.J., joined the Department of Sacred Scripture (later, Biblical Studies) in the newly formed School of Religious Studies; Patrick Skehan, trained in Semitics at Catholic University, had joined the department in 1939, and by 1951 was leading the Department of Semitics and at the same time engaging in groundbreaking text-critical work, including early work on the Dead Sea Scrolls. Skehan had himself been trained by Henri Hyvernat. But Skehan's cooperation with the biblical and Ancient Near Eastern scholars of Johns Hopkins University and the Pontifical Biblical Commission gave the Semitics Department a lively connection both with the international community of scholars and with scholars throughout the church, at a time when the Church had opened itself to critical biblical scholarship and the excitement of an entire generation of scholars was still at its height.

Thus Sidney joined a line of scholars who were both trained in the scholarly institutions of the Catholic Church and were conversant with scholars throughout the world, in both ecclesiastical and secular institutions. Parochialism and religious isolation among American Catholic scholars had ebbed in the period after World War II and from the sixties through the seventies; scholars at Catholic University were the beneficiaries of their careful training in Catholic scholarship and of the cooperation between Catholics, non-Catholics, and secular scholars in scholarly enterprises. Not only did Fr. Skehan participate in the initial teamwork on the Dead Sea Scrolls; he also supervised the translation of the Old Testament for the New American Bible (1970) that replaced with philologically based scholarship the Douai edition as the approved Bible for use by English-speaking Catholics in the United States. Catholics had been encouraged to read the Bible in the vernacular; it was Fr. Skehan's intent that they read it in a reliable translation based on solid, rigorous scholarship.

To this tradition of scholarly Catholic work Sidney has continued to contribute, even as he became a kind of ambassador for the Semitics Department by representing its works at international conferences and by welcoming students from other countries to be trained in the department. Remaining in the Semitics Department, founding the Early Christian Studies program, and directing both for extended periods of time, he has at the same time continued the investigations he began as a graduate student, and trained other scholars in Syriac and in Christian Arabic—but not merely training them in the necessary disciplines of their particular field; he has also encouraged them with the broad-minded generosity of learning that is his hallmark, and that makes him a catholic in the undivided sense. The honors of his fellowships at the Hebrew University of Jerusalem and at the Dumbarton Oaks Center for Byzantine Studies, along with an offer of a fellowship at the Institute for Advanced Studies, are eloquent indications of the estimation in which he is held among various constituencies, and of his ability to converse genuinely, and without cant, across the borders of differing cultures.

In his research, Sidney has devoted continuous attention to the life and teaching of Ephrem of Nisibis (d. 373), the most famous biblical interpreter and Christian thinker of Mesopotamia during the entire period of late antiquity. Translating Ephrem's *memrē* and *madroshē* is a notoriously difficult process, but as translations have become available, a wide audience has recognized the depth and art of Ephrem's compositions and has learned from Sidney's exposition of various themes in Ephrem's works. In addition, the earliest Christian theologians writing in Arabic have also absorbed his attention; his contributions to the study of their work are represented in the two volumes of collected essays that represent groundbreaking research into this little-known era of Muslim and Christian dialogue. Other authors have also received his attention—the mystically inclined Louis Massignon and his subject Al-Hallaj, the Islamic mystic, are a continuous interest for Sidney, as is the contemporary monastic author Thomas Merton.

Finally, Sidney has accompanied his scholarship and his teaching with charity toward the ecclesiastical reality that is charity's harshest test. He has continued to work for his religious congregation, both in its remaining parishes and foundations in the South, and during the time in which it became a constituent part of the Washington Theological Union; he has participated for over twenty years in the Eastern Orthodox–Roman Catholic dialogue and has taken an interest in Christian-Muslim dialogue as well; and he has celebrated with graciousness, warmth, and humor various baptisms, weddings, and funerals for the family members of his friends who knew they could rely on his generosity—and for the children of the friend who writes this essay, whose younger son is his godson. For a quarter of a century, he has counted on the assistance of his colleague Monica J. Blanchard, herself a graduate of the Semitics Department and a scholar publishing in the fields of Syriac, Armenian, and Georgian languages and cultures.

A list of Sidney's publications follows the essays in this book, and there is no need to duplicate that in this brief introduction. A glance at his *curriculum vitae* confirms that he has continued to develop his interest in the theologians of

Christianity who wrote in Arabic; thus his dissertation (1977) became, in 1997, *A Treatise on the Veneration of the Holy Icons Written in Arabic by Theodore Abu Qurrah, Bishop of Harran,* published by Peeters Press. His articles on Arabic and Syriac Christianity have been collected and published in the Collected Studies series of Variorum Reprints, and his many articles on Ephrem the Syrian are reflected in his Marquette Lecture, published as *"Faith Adoring the Mystery": Reading the Bible with St. Ephraem the Syrian* (1997). Sidney continues to write on the same subjects to which, by his lectures and articles, he has drawn numerous other scholars.

The essays in this volume are, by intention, representative of only one of Sidney's pursuits. With the appearance of the critical editions and German translations of the works on Ephrem the Syrian has come increasing popular and scholarly interest in Ephrem and in the Syriac-speaking Christianity he helped to shape. Geniuses in theology are rare in any age, but Ephrem by universal agreement was a genius of the Syriac language and its world in late-ancient Mesopotamia; thanks to his intelligence, his perceptions, and his written expression, he has now attracted followers among both those who read ancient Syriac and those who do not. In the United States, as well as in Europe, Sidney has been a chief expositor of the thought of Ephrem. Thus these essays reflect that interest and offer further scholarship on the work, and the world, of the saint and upon the corps of intensely devoted followers of the Christian path to which he belonged—the sons and daughters of the covenant—and for whom, among others, he wrote.

The first part of the volume consists of two essays dedicated to Ephrem, both by students who wrote doctoral dissertations with Sidney. The first, "Syriac Strophic Poetry: Intercalated Psalms," looks at the way in which biblical interpretation follows from the text of the Syriac Bible itself in its ritual use; Javier Martinez follows with a translation into Spanish of the first three of Ephrem's famous *Madroshē* [usually translated "Hymns"] *on Virginity.*

The second part, "Texts, Terms, Metaphors," explores the themes of human sinfulness as shaped by Aramaic and Syriac terminology (Gary Anderson); a proposal that the *Syriac Apocalypse of Daniel* comes from a monastic setting (Alexander Golitzin); Michael Hollerich's study of the Syriac Life of Athanasius shows the Syriac tradition's admiration for the Greek-speaking monastic promoter of Egypt. The ideal in early Syriac Christianity of radical renunciation of the standard comforts of human life on the part of ascetics, summarized by the term *msarrqûtâ,* by Sebastian P. Brock, and an exploration of the idea of housekeeping as an ascetic theme in late antiquity, and particularly in the Syriac realm (Susan Harvey).

The final part, "After Ephrem the Syrian," contains two essays. The first is an examination of the legacy of the Greek monastic Evagrius in the works of a later Syriac-speaking author, Philoxenos of Mabbug; and finally, from later in the Syriac-speaking monastic tradition, an exploration of a favorite goal of monks, "purity of heart." This essay is by Sidney's student and colleague Monica Blanchard, and concentrates upon the concept of purity of heart in the Discourses of Beh Isho' Kamulaya.

Each of these essays, and all of them together, are offered both to Sidney and to other readers as a sign of the friendship and admiration of those who have benefited from his work, and who in some way hope to extend it. All wish for a happy birthday for Sidney, and for many more years of scholarship and publication.

PART I

POETRY AND EPHREM THE SYRIAN

Joseph P. Amar

1. SYRIAC STROPHIC POETRY

Intercalated Psalms

Beginning with the New Testament itself, early Christian literature abounds with references to the use of the psalms in Christian worship.[1] Although the psalms were employed in a variety of ways, the evidence suggests that the simplest, and perhaps earliest, method of praying the psalms consisted of a soloist who chanted each verse of the psalm, to which the congregation then responded with a simple word ("Alleluia") or a phrase ("Glory to you") or a set psalm verse. From this basic "responsorial" pattern, there emerged the more highly developed "antiphonal" form of praying the psalms in which each verse of the psalm was followed by a liturgical composition which was inspired by the psalm verse which preceded it. For example,

Have mercy on me, O God, in your goodness; in the greatness of your compassion, wipe out my offense (Ps 51:1).

This contribution is intended to make available for the first time in English translation the proper variable texts of an hour of the Syriac Maronite Divine Office for the purpose of observing the use of intercalated psalmody in its full liturgical setting. To the best of my knowledge, none of the texts that appear here has been translated before into English. I want to express sincere gratitude for the generous help and guidance offered by Aelred Cody, O.S.B., and Robert Taft, S.J., when I first began research on this topic.

1. For the history of the use of the psalms in Christian worship, see Robert Taft, S.J., *The Liturgy of the Hours in East and West: The Origins of the Divine Office and its Meaning for Today* (Collegeville, Minn.: Liturgical Press, 1986). For what follows, see especially pp. 39–41, 48–55, 116–20, 123–30.

David, son of Jesse, said, "Have mercy on me" in his hymn inspired by the Holy Spirit; "for I have killed Uriah by deceit (Cf. 2 Sm 11:1–26) and I am marked with human blood." Sprinkle me with the hyssop of your mercy, alleluia, and wash away my impurity, O Jesus, Savior of the world.[2]

Although this elaborate and time-consuming antiphonal pattern was often modified so that the antiphon was chanted only at the beginning and end of the psalm, as in the case of the Roman Divine Office, the ancient pattern survived more fully in the West Syriac family of churches where the antiphons are called *'enyōnô* (pl. *'enyōnê*), "responses."[3] The *'enyōnê* are early examples of the Syriac genius for liturgical poetry modeled on the psalms, a genius already well developed in *The Odes of Solomon,* arguably the earliest extant work in Syriac. The *Odes,* with their pseudonymous attribution to a biblical author, represent a continuation of Jewish psalmic poetry in a Christian liturgical (baptismal) context.[4]

Among the Syriac Orthodox, the psalms are not entirely intercalated with *'enyōnê*; either *'enyōnê* will accompany only the initial verses of a psalm, or several *'enyōnê,* usually between six and eight, will be gathered at the end of a psalm to be chanted together, and are not intercalated with psalm verses. It is impossible to say to what extent intercalating verses of a psalm might have been present originally and were then reduced at a later time. However, according to the liturgical tradition of the Syriac Maronite Church, psalm verses are always entirely intercalated with *'enyōnê* which are chanted according to a specific *qōlô* or "melody."[5]

The renaissance in Maronite studies that has taken place in recent times allows us to view that tradition with greater clarity than was heretofore possible.[6]

2. Maronite *š^eḥīmtô* (Daily Office), *ramšô* (Vespers) for Thursday.

3. It could be argued that *'enyōnê* are not, strictly speaking, antiphons, if by antiphon one means to refer to identical words that are repeated after each psalm verse. Although some *'enyōnê* in the present translation are similar, no two are identical. For a general introduction to the subject, see Anton Baumstark, *Liturgie Comparée: Principes et Méthodes pour l'étude historique des liturgies chrétiennes,* Collection Irénikon, ed. Dom Bernard Botte, O.S.B. (Paris: Éditions de Chevetogne, 1953), 102–16. On the relationship between *'enyōnê* and verses intercalated with biblical odes in the Byzantine rite, see P. Odilo Heiming, *Syrische 'enyōnê und griechische Kanones: Die Hs. Sach. 349 der Staatsbibliothek zu Berlin,* Liturgiegeschichtliche Quellen und Forschungen 26 (Münster: Aschendorff, 1932).

4. See James H. Charlesworth, ed., *The Old Testament Pseudepigrapha,* 2 vols. (New York: Doubleday, 1985), 2: 726–71.

5. The Maronite musicologist, Louis Hage, O.L.M., has published extensively on the liturgical music of the Syriac family of churches. For complete bibliographies, see Louis Hage, *Musique maronite,* Bibliotheque de l'Université Saint-Esprit de Kaslik 43 (Kaslik, Lebanon: Université S.-Esprit, 2001).

6. For a general introduction, see Pierre Dib, *Étude sur la Liturgie Maronite* (Paris: P. Lethielleux,

Once dismissed as a Latinized variant of Syriac-Antiochian tradition, recent research has shown the Maronite Church to represent an independent synthesis originating among Syriac-speaking Chalecdonians in Syria who were able to establish themselves independently of the Greek-speaking coastal cities and thus preserve their Syriac identity.[7] In the tenth century, when most Syriac-speaking Chalcedonians adopted Byzantine usage, Maronite monks, who had taken refuge in the mountains of Lebanon early in the eighth century, maintained and developed their indigenous Syriac heritage. Beginning with the Crusades, the Maronite Church underwent progressive waves of Latinization; however, the Divine Office was not affected, and in recent times, steps have been taken to restore the *Qurbōnô* ("eucharistic liturgy") and *Rōzê* ("sacraments").

The Maronite Divine Office consists of the *Šᵉḥīmtô* (Daily Office)[8] and the *Fenqîthô* (Proper of the Saints) which was published in its entirety in two volumes in 1656 and 1666.[9] This is the only premodern edition, and the only one that preserves the full compliment of *ʿenyōnê* and other metrical compositions.[10] The text presented here is that of *ramšô*[11] ("vespers") of the feast of the Announcement to the Bearer of God, Mary,[12] which is the second of the Sundays of the Season of Announcement, the West-Syriac equivalent to Advent.

In the present text, the event of the Announcement to Mary by the angel Gabriel is recapitulated and enhanced in the *ʿenyōnê* by a creative use of the mi-

---

1919). For a more recent and critical survey, see Michel Hayek, *Liturgie Maronite: Histoire et Textes eucharistiques* (Paris: Maison Mame, 1964).

7. William F. Macomber, "A Theory on the Origins of the Syrian, Maronite and Chaldean Rites," *Orientalia christiana periodica* 39 (1973): 235–42.

8. For the structure of the Maronite office, see R. Taft, *The Liturgy of the Hours,* especially Part II, chap. 14, "The West Syrian and Maronite Traditions"; see also Jean Tabet, "L'eschatologie dans l'office commun maronite," *Parole de l'Orient* 2 (1971): 5–30; Tabet, *L'office commun maronite: Etude du lîlyô et safrô,* Bibliothèque de l'Université S.-Esprit (Kaslik, Lebanon: Université S.-Esprit, 1972).

9. *Officia Sanctorum juxta ritum Ecclesiae Maronitarum,* 2 vols (Rome: Typographia Propoganda Fidei, 1656–1666).

10. There now exist a range of adaptations of the *Fenqîthô* for popular use. For example, *The Prayer of the Faithful According to the Maronite Liturgical Year,* translated and adapted for use in the Diocese of St. Maron, U.S.A., from Butros Gemayel, ed., *Prière du croyant selon l'année liturgique maronite* (Brooklyn: Diocese of St. Maron, 1982, 1984, 1985).

11. For a general introduction to the history and structure of *ramšô* in West Syriac liturgical tradition, see Pierre Gemayel, "La Structure des Vêpres maronites," *L'Orient Syrien* 9 (1964): 105–34; and Juan Mateos, "Le ramšo maronite," *De officio matutino et vespertino in ritibus orientalibus* (Rome: S. Anselmo, 1968–69), 60–69. A more general discussion may be found in J. Puyade, "Les heures canoniales syriennes et leur composition," *L'Orient Syrien* 3 (1958): 401–28.

12. *Officia Sanctorum,* vol. 2: *Pars hiemalis,* 152–233.

drashic elements of dramatic, extra-biblical dialogue and exuberant imagery. These elements are seen not only in the similar, though never identical, words exchanged between Mary and the angel, but also in scenes which depict the charge given to Gabriel by God, and in the angel's dramatic descent through the spheres of heaven on his way to Nazareth. These *'enyōnê* in particular are reminiscent of the mystical spirituality related to the *merkabah* (Syriac: *markabtô*), the chariot which bears the throne of God, and which ascends and descends through the spheres of heaven.[13] Of course, *'enyōnê* also reflect traditional features of Syriac spirituality associated with the classical period. They abound with distinctive titles of Christ ("King of Kings," "Hidden One," Giver of Life," "Blessed Groom," "Heavenly Eagle") and of Mary ("Cherubic Throne," "Ark of blessings," "Heaven on earth," "Most blessed of the daughters of Eve," "Royal Lady," "New Sion," "Lofty Cedar"). The Virgin Mary, who is depicted at prayer in the temple, is spoken of as conceiving the Word through her ear.

The *'enyōnê* that we observe in the text translated here are strophic compositions of a set number of syllables which are sung according to a specific *qōlô* that accommodates the number of syllables in the *'enyōnê.* The psalm verses themselves are chanted very simply, and with little modulation. As a result, in the actual chanting of the office, the *'enyōnê* dominate the verses of the psalm. In fact, it is a characteristic feature of Syriac strophic compositions to overwhelm, and in some cases to displace, the biblical passages and related texts which they were intended to accompany. In the text translated here, this displacement can be observed in three metrical compositions: the *mazmûrô* which introduces the Gospel, the *Bo'ûtô,* the final changeable prayer of *ramšô,* and the *qōlô* of the *ḥûssōyô.*

The *mazmûrô,* or "psalm," always precedes the scripture readings in the Divine Office and in all the mysteries. As one can observe in the present text, the actual psalm verses which, at one time, were intercalated with the *'enyōnê,* have disappeared; all that remains are the liturgical responses that accompanied them. Nonetheless, the original designation "psalm" survives.

A further example of the tendency for liturgical poetry to displace what it originally was intended to accompany may be seen in the closing composition

13. Cf. Ezekiel 1; Isaiah 6. On the Christian appropriation of *merkabah* imagery, see now Timo Eskola, *Messiah and the Throne: Jewish Merkabah Mysticism and Early Christian Exaltation Discourse* (Tübingen: Mohr Siebeck, 2001).

of the office, the *Boʾûtô,* or "intercession." The intercessions which at one time were intercalated with the verses of this composition have disappeared. But, as in the case of the *mazmûrô,* the original title, *Boʾûtô* remains.

The third example of the displacement of psalm verses by their intercalated *ʿenyōnê* pertains to the liturgical unit popularly referred to in Maronite tradition as the *ḥûssōyô*[14] (pl. *ḥûssōyê*), the Syriac word for "forgiveness" or "absolution."[15] The *ḥûssōyô* is an elaborate penitential rite which has always been associated with the burning of incense. The *ḥûssōyô* is ubiquitous, and forms a basic component of the Liturgy of the Word in every hour of the office and in every mystery; there are *ḥûssōyê* for every feast and observance. The basic elements of the *ḥûssōyô* (*proemion, sedrô, qōlô,* and *ʿetrô*) are all found in the present text. It will be enough for our purpose to summarize the elements of the *ḥûssōyô* in order to focus on *ʿenyōnê* that form a constitutive element.

The earliest examples of the *proemion* (Greek: *prooimion*) are simple doxologies which expanded over time to accommodate the developing nuances of dogma until they became "mini"-catechisms of Trinitarian theology. The *sedrô* is divided into two parts. The first part is an *anamnesis,* or recollection of blessings, which follows the well-known *Paradigmengebet* pattern that recalls God's earlier blessings before the current requests are made. The name *sedrô* refers to the second part of the prayer, that is, to the "order" of the intercessions that follow. The chanting of the *sedrô* is a diaconal function.[16]

The *qōlô* ("melody") returns us to the subject of the *ʿenyōnê* with their proper

14. The earliest use of the term that I have been able to discover is most likely in the Peshitta of Exodus 25:17, where *ḥûssōyô* translates *kapporet* ("mercy-seat"). In Syriac Orthodox usage, the term *ḥûssōyô* appears as the title of the unit. However, the term never appears in Maronite liturgical books. Finally, the liturgical unit which is being spoken of here is not to be confused with *Taksâ d-ḥûssōyô,* the formal rite of absolution that takes place in both the East and West Syriac churches on Holy Saturday. For the Chaldean rite, see J. Isaac, *Taksâ d-ḥûssōyô: Le rite du Pardon dans l'Église syriaque orientale,* Orientalia christiana analecta 233 (Rome, 1989). For the West Syriac equivalent, see A. Mouhanna, "Le Rite du Pardon dans l'Eglise maronite," *Parole de l'Orient* 6–7 (1975–76): 309–24.

15. The early history and development of the elements of the *ḥûssōyô* have been researched by Juan Mateos in a series of articles. See Juan Mateos, "Sedre et prières connexes dans quelques anciennes collections," *Orientalia christiana periodica* 28 (1962): 239–87; Mateos, "Trois recueils anciens de Proemia syriens," *Orientalia christiana periodica* 33 (1967): 457–82; Mateos, "Prières syriennes d'absolution du VII–IXe siècle," *Orientalia christiana periodica* 34 (1968): 252–80. For a basic orientation to the *ḥûssōyô* in Maronite usage, see M. Hayek, *Liturgie maronite,* 158–59. It is my intention to publish new research on the *ḥûssōyô* in the near future.

16. It has been suggested that the *sedrô* represents an early form of the Byzantine diaconal litany in which the response ("Lord have mercy") that follows each petition has fallen away. See M. Hayek, *Liturgie maronite,* 158–59.

qōlô. In the case of the *ḥûssōyô,* the intercalated psalm verses have fallen away, but the strophic poetry meant to accompany them is all that has survived.

The *'etrô,* "sweet-smelling spices,"[17] usually contains a specific mention of the burning of incense,[18] and incorporates a reference to Numbers 17:11: "Moses said to Aaron, 'Take your censer ... and bring it quickly to the community to make atonement for them.'" In Maronite usage, incense is not burned at this point, as it is by the Syriac Orthodox, but at the beginning of the *proemion,* a custom which may reflect ancient practice, as some early manuscripts indicate.[19]

Announcement to the Bearer of God, Mary

Ramšô

Opening Prayers ܦܬܓܡܐ

Lord our God, make us worthy to praise you with the fiery angel who
announced your coming to the virgin daughter of David;
and to marvel at you with Joseph who perceived the mystery of your
conception;
and to extol you wondrously, and praise you purely, and worship you
solemnly

with the glorious Father who begot you
and the life-giving Spirit, forever. ⁘

Holy virgin, you received a holy announcement from a holy angel
and in your holy womb you bore the Lord of all holiness;
Now make us holy through your holy prayers
so that our voices may rise to the One who made you holy to
conceive him in the Holy of Holies,
to praise and make his name holy, with his Father and living Spirit of holiness,
forever. ⁘

17. The word is used in the Peshitta of Exodus 37:29.

18. In the present text, the *'etrô,* concludes the *ḥûssōyô.* However, according to Maronite usage, the *ḥûssōyô* may contain other elements including a *qûbōlô,* "Prayer of Acceptance," and *ḥûṭōmô,* "Conclusion."

19. See P. Gemayel, "Vêpres maronites," 120.

Psalmody

Psalm 51 ܡܙܡܘܪܐ ܢܐ

Qōlô: Lord, protect your Church.

ܪܚܡ Have mercy on me, O God, according to your goodness; and according to your great mercy, erase my sins.[20]

The archangel Gabriel came to announce your conception, Lord of all, to Mary your Mother. He greeted her: "Hail to you, perfect palace; the King of Kings dwells in your womb. I left him seated on a throne above, and now a virgin's womb holds the One who fills the cherubim with awe." And the Church rejoices in the birth of him who saves her children from the tyranny of sin.⁘

ܐܘܦܐ Completely wash me from my offense, and cleanse me from my sins. For I know my transgressions, and my sins are before me at all times.

The archangel Gabriel said to the holy Mother: "Hail, full of grace, most blessed of all women, the Lord is with you. You will have a wondrous conception, and give birth to a blessed child who will save creation. The Spirit of holiness will come upon you, and the power of the Most High will overshadow you."

Glory to the hidden One who willed to become human, and save the nations by his birth, and turn them from their aimless wandering to the path of life.⁘

ܠܟ Against you alone have I sinned, and performed evil before you. Indeed, you are justified in your sentence, and vindicated in your judgments. I was conceived in guilt, and in sin my mother conceived me.

The archangel Gabriel spoke to the virgin and said: "Hail to you, Mother of the One who fashioned Adam in his image.[21] From you will arise the Giver of Life. And he will return the lost children of Adam to their inheritance. The Word of the eternal Father will shine forth like the dawn from your womb. And he will save creation from the worship of idols."[22]⁘

20. The psalms are translated from the Peshitta Old Testament.

21. Gen. 1:26.

22. Rom. 1:23.

ܐܢܬ ܕܝܢ But you desire truth, and you have taught me the hidden secrets of your wisdom. Sprinkle me with your hyssop that I may be purified; purify me with it, and I shall be whiter than snow.

The archangel Gabriel brought a greeting to Mary. He saw how pure she was, and said to her: "Hail to you, full of grace. Our Lord is with you, most blessed of the daughters of Eve. You will conceive a wonderful child by the power of the Holy Spirit. He is my very Lord and God, the Savior of all creation. Glory to him and to the One who sent him to save the feeble race of Adam." ⁘

ܐܫܡܥܝܢܝ Fill me with your delight and your gladness, and my humbled bones will rejoice. Turn away your face from my sins, and erase my wrongdoing.

The watcher[23] descended from on high at the command of his mighty Lord. He came to the daughter of David and spoke to her: "Hail to you, Mother of the hidden One who sent me to greet your purity. He who fills heaven and earth, the seas and everything in them, wills to dwell in you, for he is the Savior of the children of Adam." He will unite all things in himself, and in him there will be peace and tranquility for both sides when he shines forth from your womb.[24] ⁘

ܠܒܐ Create a pure heart in me, O God;
 and an honest spirit renew in me.
Do not dismiss me from your presence,
 nor take your holy Spirit from me.

To a place high above the watchers, God summoned Gabriel and spoke to him carefully: "Take this letter written with fire and go to Nazareth, and say to the virgin Mary: 'The Lord wills to dwell in you to clothe himself with a pure and holy body from your womb. He will suffer and die in order to return Adam to the paradise he lost.'" ⁘

ܐܠܐ But return your gladness and salvation to me, and your glorious Spirit will sustain me. For I shall teach the evil your way, and sinners shall return to you.

The angel Gabriel descended with the announcement foretold by the prophets. He greeted her and said: "Hail to you, full of grace. My Lord is truly with you.

23. I.e., "angel."

24. Cf. Eph 2:15.

He shall shine forth from you to reign over the house of Jacob forever. He will save all nations from the worship of idols, and he will free the servants of his Father from slavery to death and Satan." ⁘

ܦܨܝ Deliver me from blood-guilt, O God, my God who saves me; and my tongue will sing your righteousness. O Lord, open my lips, and my mouth will proclaim your praises.

Let David rejoice today on high, for his hidden words are explained. God gave a message of hope with great power to Gabriel who brought it swiftly to the daughter of David, full of grace. He bowed his head in reverence to her, and greeted her: "Hail to you, royal Lady. From you will shine forth the mighty God whose name is before the sun, as it is written."[25] ⁘

ܡܛܠ For you do not desire sacrifices, nor are you pleased with burnt offerings. The sacrifice of God is a humble spirit; a simple heart, O God, you will not reject.

A letter of peace went forth, mystically written with fire by the Father, Son, and Spirit. He it is who gave the command to the watcher to take the letter of his Creator. The angelic spirit descended and saw the Mother of his Lord in prayerful praise. He greeted her: "Behold, Ark of blessings, you carry the Life of the world." ⁘

ܐܛܐܒ Show your bounty to Sion and to those who dwell in Jerusalem; then you will be pleased with true sacrifices and burnt offerings; then they shall offer bullocks on your altar.

Mary was startled as she continued in prayer, wondering at the words of the watcher. "How can it be that a virgin should give birth to a child when no man has ever known me in marriage or intercourse?" The angel replied: "The Spirit of holiness will overshadow you, and he who is too great for heaven and earth to contain, in your small womb will make a home." ⁘

ܫܘܒܚܐ Glory to the Father and to the Son and to the Spirit of holiness, now and forever, Amen.

25. Cf. Ps 110:3.

The prophets before the ages proclaimed that salvation
would come at last.
The apostles carried the news to the ends of the earth
and turned minds from ignorance to understanding.
The martyrs heard and prepared to suffer with joy, for the love
of the Only-Begotten, the First Born of the eternal Father.
Glory and worship to the Groom who betrothed the Church
and summoned prophets, apostles, martyrs, and the children of the kingdom to her wedding feast. ⁘

ܢܝܚܐ Grant rest to the faithful departed; and to you, O Lord, we sing glory.

O Son, who descended to the house of the dead and gave hope to those in the tomb; have mercy on the dead who clothed themselves in the robe of glory at baptism. They believed in your passion and resurrection, and confessed your Trinity. May they be refreshed by you and join the watchers above to raise their voices in praise to your Hiddenness, and in thanksgiving to your mercy. ⁘

Marmîtô ܡܪܡܝܬܐ

Glorious Ark, Light from Light wondrously dawned from you.[26]

Ask the eternal Light who dwelt in you to banish the nighttime of sin from us, and to fill us with the light of his goodness, so we may honor your feast with sincerity, and sing praises to the Light who dwelt in you.

Psalm 140 ܡܙܡܘܪܐ ܩܡ
Qōlô: To the limit of Faith.

ܡܪܝܐ Lord, to you I have cried out; hear and answer my words and accept them.

26. The *marmîtô* is a subdivision of the psalter for use in the Divine Office. The present pattern represents that usual sequence of three psalms and one verse from Psalm 166 following the *marmîtô.*

The archangel Gabriel carried the letter of his Lord to Nazareth in Galilee to a virgin named Mary. He said to her: “Behold, most blessed of all women.” Thus did the angel open the letter before her and begin to read. And as he did, the virgin grew fearful. “Hail, full of grace,” he said. “Hail, temple of the Spirit of holiness, alleluia, the King now dwells with you.” ⁘

ܨܠܘܬܝ My prayer is like incense before you; the raising of my hands like the evening offering. Lord, set a guard at my mouth, and a guard for my lips, so that my heart may not turn away to an evil word and I should do the deeds of the wicked.

The angels and the fiery hosts were unaware that Gabriel descended to the virgin Mary. Through her ear he entered in purity, through the letter carried by the archangel. For nine months he dwelt in her. He who fashioned Adam from dust, fashioned a body for himself in her womb, and so was born with a body, alleluia, and she remained a virgin. ⁘

ܥܡ I shall not be a companion to impious men. Let the just One discipline and strike me. The oil of the impious shall not anoint my head.

Mary was frightened at the sight of the archangel. The chaste one began to inquire of him: “What kind of greeting is this? And what a strange message: that Mary, the virgin, shall have a son.” The angel answered: “The Spirit of holiness will overshadow you, alleluia, and you will bear a wonder.”[27] ⁘

ܡܛܠ Because of my prayer against their wickedness, their judges met their end among the rocks, and they heard how sweet my words were.

The overshadowing of Mary amazes us, for you diminished your glory so that human flesh could bear you.

O Mighty One who became small,
if you had not diminished yourself, creation itself would not have
been enough to contain your greatness;
if you had not put on a body from our race, earth and sky above

27. Cf. Isaiah 9.6.

would not have endured your glory;
if you had not clothed yourself with our humanity, all creation
would have been too small to hold you.
But behold, the overshadowing of Mary is vast, alleluia,
and sufficient to bear your greatness. ⁘

ܐܝܟ As when a plough scores the earth shall their bones be strewn at the mouth of Sheol. My eyes look to you, O Lord; I rely on you for help. Do not reject me.

The virgin was a child of Adam. With the announcement that the snake brought, death entered all his children. But new life entered all creation through the pure virgin, with the announcement that the watcher brought to her. Humans shed their glory in Eden, but Mary wove a robe of glory in her womb to cover their shame. Christ our King, through her prayer, clothe us with your hidden power, alleluia, that we may magnify the one who bore you. ⁘

ܛܪܢܝ ܡܢ Protect me from the hand of the boastful who have set traps for me.

The watcher left the ranks of angels to bring a letter of hope to all creation. He came to the daughter of David and spoke to her: "Hail to you, lofty Cedar. A heavenly eagle will descend to make a nest in your blessed branches, alleluia, and He is Lord and God of all. ⁘

ܢܦܠܘܢ The evil will fall into their own nets, while I escape.

The angel Gabriel left the vaults of heaven to prepare a way before the King. He soared above the walls of flame, past fiery ranks who ceaselessly praise. He parted the winds and commanded the air. He left angels and seraphim in his wake to come to Mary of Nazareth, alleluia, and deliver the greeting of his Lord. ⁘

Psalm 141 ܒܡܘܪܐ ܘܣܟܐ
Qōlô: (again) To the limit of Faith.

ܒܩܠܝ With my voice I cried out to the Lord. With my voice I entreated the Lord, and I raised my entreaty. And my distress I displayed before him. When my spirit is shaken, You know my paths.

Mary was amazed at the sight of the watcher clothed in fire. He greeted her with the announcement of her conception. She said to him: "But I am a virgin, and unacquainted with marriage. How can what you say happen?" But he answered her: "The Spirit of holiness will come and dwell in your womb, alleluia, and the One you bear will save the nations. ⁘

ܒܐܘܪܚܐ On the way that I walk, they laid a trap. I look to the right to see, but I know no one. There is no means of escape left to me. There is none to avenge my life. I cried out before You, O Lord, and I said, "You are my hope and my portion in the land of the living."

The sight of the fiery angel was fearsome, but he spoke to the virgin of Nazareth and calmed her fears: "Peace be with you, purest of Adam's race. The Son of God himself will descend and dwell in the palace of your body. He will reign over the house of Jacob, as it is written, and his kingdom will have no end," alleluia, now and for all ages.[28] ⁘

ܨܘܬ Answer my request, for I am very low. Deliver me from my persecutors because they are too strong for me. Remove me from this prison, and I will confess your name.

Word of God, you sent the archangel Gabriel with an announcement of joy and gladness for all creation. "Behold, my Lord is with you. He has sent me to announce to you that he who is without a body wills to become incarnate from the purity of your body," alleluia, and he will give life to all creation. ⁘

28. Cf. Luke 1:32, 33.

from Psalm 118 ܡܙܡܘܪܐ ܩܝܛ
Qōlô: (again) To the limit of Faith.

ܫܪܓܐ ܗܝ Your word is a lamp to my feet, and a light to my paths. I resolve and confirm that I will keep the decrees of your righteousness. I have been brought very low. O Lord, give me life according to your word. Be pleased with the words of my mouth, O Lord, and teach me your decrees.

A greeting was sent by the Father through Gabriel, chief among watchers and archangels. He came to that virgin, utterly filled with blessings, the bearer of God, Mary, of the same nature as her ancestor, Adam. The archangel greeted her: "Hail, full of grace, most blessed of women. From you will shine forth the One who set the stars in their place, alleluia, and who will save the nations." .

ܢܦܫܝ My life is in your hands at all times. I will not forget your law. Sinners have set a trap for me, but I have not turned aside from your commands. I have inherited your testimony forever, for it is the joy of my heart. I have turned my heart to do your commandments forever in truth.

Come, Mary, tell us; what did the archangel say when he came to greet you from the Father? Mary, the daughter of David, replied: "He brought me peace and serenity. From him I received peace and I returned peace to him." Peace took root in a pure temple, and behold, watchers and mortals alike proclaim, alleluia, glory to the One who sent Peace to Adam and his children. ∴

Psalm 116 ܡܙܡܘܪܐ ܩܝܘ
Qōlô: (again) To the limit of Faith.

ܫܒܚܘ Praise the Lord all you nations; praise him all you peoples. His goodness has prevailed on our behalf; truly the Lord is eternal.

Sûgîthô ܣܘܓܝܬܐ

ܐ The hidden Father willed to renew his fair image that became corrupt.[29]

ܒ He sent his Son out of love, who became mortal for the sake of mortals.

ܓ His birth was hidden from heavenly spirits, but he revealed it to the mere dust of the earth.

ܕ Watchers fear gazing on him, but at the appointed time, he descended to earth.

ܗ All that the Father willed on account of Adam, his Son accomplished.

ܘ When Adam went astray and fell from paradise, the Father grieved for his corruption.

ܙ Divine will set in motion the renewal of the children of Adam.

ܚ A single fiery being brought the announcement to Mary,
the daughter of David.

ܛ And the hidden Offspring flew like lightening and dwelt in the virgin without intercourse.

ܝ He entrusted his letter to one of the watchers who came to greet the blessed Lady.

ܟ He folded his hands and bowed before her as she prayed in the temple.

ܠ "I bow before you, blessed Lady, new heaven on earth."

ܡ "The Lord desires you to be the Mother of his Only-Begotten Son who will shine forth from you like the dawn."

29. The *Sûgîthô* is an alphabetic composition of twenty-four strophes. The present text has sixteen syllables per verse, divided into four groups of four syllables each. The *Sûgîthô* concludes the psalmody in *Ramshô, Lîlyô* (Compline), and *Safrô* (Matins).

ܠ “The living fire of divinity will dwell in your womb but you will not be consumed.”[30]

ܣ “Divine watcher, your announcement is very gentle, but I fear your words.”

ܥ “Divine watcher, how do virgins conceive without intercourse”?

ܦ The watcher of the Spirit of holiness replied: “He will dwell in your womb to sanctify you.”

ܨ “I also want to learn from you in what manner he will come.”

ܩ “I heard his voice and understood its meaning but I could not endure his sight.”

ܪ “He gave a sign and I understood quickly.” He said, “He is with you even now. Do not be afraid.”

ܫ “He left his glory behind with his Father to dwell in your womb in humility.”

ܬ Church of holiness, bless and worship the Father, Son and Spirit of holiness who makes you holy.

Ḥûssoyô ܚܘܣܝܐ
Rite of Pardon

Proemion ܦܪܘܡܝܘܢ

May we be worthy to praise, confess, and glorify
the true God who is confessed as one and acknowledged as three;

30. Cf. Ex 3:2–3.

the eternal One who is known in three persons and glorified in one being;
    one hidden Father sent new hope to Nazareth;
    one Son dwelt in the virgin and confirmed the hope;
    one Spirit of holiness who overshadowed the virgin and
    sanctified her to complete the wondrous event;
three holy persons who brought salvation to the world;
one true God who renewed creation out of love when it grew old.
To him is due glory forever.

Sedrô ܣܕܪܐ

Glory to you, exalted and sublime Lord, who left the hidden dwellings of the Father to dwell in the pure womb of the holy virgin.

When the exalted One willed to move among the lowly,
with a glance, he gave a sign to the Father in secret
and roused the archangel with wonder,
and sent him on his mission with awe,
to deliver the Word to the ear of the virgin.

The mighty One, with the whisper of his command,
    sent the archangel to meet his pure servant.
Heavenly tranquility commanded the watcher to take peace
    to the chaste virgin Mother;
The hidden One with his overshadowing
    sanctified the lodging of the holy virgin before his descent.

The eternal Word entered through the ear of the young girl
    to heal the ancient fall of her father, Adam.
But the Father of all tribes and nations, the power of the Most High,
    overshadowed a mystical mountain,
    and dwelt wondrously in the haven of the virgin,
    in a womb that never knew intercourse.

And he dawned from the holy virgin
    while abiding in nature with his holy Father.

And he was conceived in the daughter of David
while hidden mysteriously in the womb of the hidden Father.
And he formed him in nature and intelligence
in a womb that never knew intercourse.

He aptly depicted the image of marriage in the wombs of married women. And he became incarnate of the virgin in a human way,
acquiring a body with all its parts, he entered the world.
But she remained unchanged in her virginity
and he remained unchanged in his divinity.

To you, therefore, God the Word,
who willed to become incarnate from the holy virgin,
a daughter of our own nature,
we offer the fragrance of our incense with the fervent prayers and petitions we raise to the place of your divinity,
so that on this day of the announcement of your wondrous conception,
you might bestow on us mercy and compassion and spiritual gifts in abundance, with forgiveness of sins, and deliverance from danger.

Grant tranquility and peace to churches and monasteries everywhere,
honor to the priests,
reverence to the monks
purity to the deacons,
respect to the elderly,
discretion to the youth,
prudence to your people,
peace and safe lodging for travelers,
joy, satisfaction, and the fullness of blessings to those who help the poor and receive strangers,
a worthy reward to those who make offerings and give first-fruits and tithes in your church,
and blessed rest in your kingdom for the dead,
with a glorious place at your joyful wedding feast.

Qōlô: Lord, protect your Church ܩܠܐ

Today, through a watcher who was sent to Nazareth of Galilee, to Mary, daughter of David, the Lord let the news shine forth of salvation upon the house of Adam: Heavenly beings and mortals are now equal. While she stood before God in praise, he appeared before her like a blinding flash of lightning and said:

> Hail to you, full of grace : my Lord is truly with you; from
> your womb he will take flesh;
> Hail to you, cherubic throne; the chariot that was seen in the
> heavens[31] is no greater than you;
> Hail to you, portal that Ezechiel saw and through which God
> brought him;[32]
> Hail to you, and peace be with you; fiery ranks of heavenly
> beings also send peace to you and greet your purity.

And behold, now the Church and all her children petition you, our Savior: through the pure prayer of the one who bore you, forgive us and have mercy.

ʿEtrô ܥܛܪܐ

O light-filled Cloud, you sprinkled dew and sweet fragrance on Mary, your holy dwelling. You filled the mortal world with your immortal fragrance, and made Mary a sweet-smelling field. A fountain of blessings to water all creation came from her blessed womb.

Now, holy virgin, whose prayer is ever heard; pour forth on us the rich blessings of your prayers, and the sweet anointing of your intercession through this incense which we offer as we commemorate the announcement of your blessed conception.

And Lord, may this incense bring rest and gladness and remembrance to all the righteous and just, and to all who depart in your peace.

31. Ezek. 1.
32. Cf. Ezek. 10.

Office of Readings

Psalm ܡܙܡܘܪܐ

Peace to you, Mary; from you shall shine forth the Son of God who will save all generations from error.

Glory to the hidden One who came to Galilee in his goodness. From the womb of the blessed Lady, you willed to be born in the flesh.

You accepted the offerings made by the righteous before us; now, accept, Lord, our offering, comfort us and be attentive to our prayer.

Peace be with you.

And also with you.

Let us be attentive to the Gospel of Life as recorded by the Apostle Matthew.

Matthew 12:38–50

Bo'ûtô—in the meter of Mar Jacob of Sarug ܒܥܘܬܐ

The watcher descended while Mary was at prayer. He gave her the greeting sent to her by the Most High: "Hail to you, Mary. Our Lord is surely with you, most blessed of women. You will conceive and give birth to a son, and you will remain a virgin."

When she who is filled with mercies heard this, she wondered what the reason was for this unusual greeting, and she was astounded by the message. "You announce to me a son though I am innocent of any familiarity with a man."

The watcher answered: "Do not fear, full of mercies. God is mighty, and wills you to be the Mother of his Only-Begotten. Behold, even now you conceive him in holiness. You will give birth to a son whose kingdom will have no end.

Glory to the Father who sent his Son to the daughter of David; worship to the Son who shone forth from her in holiness, with the Spirit of holiness who purified her to prepare her, and then overshadowed her. And mercy upon us through her gentle prayer. Amen. Alleluia. Amen and Amen.

Francisco Javier Martínez

2. EFRÉN DE NISIBE, HIMNOS *DE VIRGINITATE*, I–III

Mi primer contacto con S. Efrén tuvo lugar en Jerusalén, allá por el año 1978, en el monasterio sirio ortodoxo de S. Marcos. La profesora que aquel curso enseñaba siríaco en L'École Biblique, Kathleen E. McVey, llevó a sus alumnos a participar en una liturgia de vísperas en el monasterio, famoso por aquel entonces debido al papel que había jugado en las peripecias de los primeros manuscritos hallados en Qumran. También fue con ella con quien, por primera vez, "intentamos" traducir un himno de S. Efrén. Y fue también ella quien primero me habló de Catholic University y de Sidney H. Griffith, que poco después habriá de ser mi maestro en Washington desde 1979 a 1985, y el director de mi tesis doctoral.

Considero el haber podido trabajar con el Profesor Griffith uno de los regalos grandes que el Señor me ha hecho en la vida. Por muchas cosas, por su saber, que siempre estaba dispuesto a compartir, y por su sencillez y su facilidad para dejar a personas muy distintas ser ellas mismas, para acercarlas entre sí, y para ilusionarlas con realismo por proyectos que valían la pena. Recuerdo especialmente los seminarios en que un excelente grupo de compañeros, entre los que estaban Monica Blanchard y Robin Darling Young (las dos editoras de este volumen), Joseph P. Amar y Edward G. Mathews, leíamos y comentábamos con él los himnos de S. Efrén. Con una gratuidad que no se puede dar por supuesta en la vida, y que era en buena parte fruto del modo de hacer las cosas del Profesor Griffith, buscábamos apasionadamente comprender el pensamiento del santo doctor de Nisibe, aprendíamos a ver la realidad con los "luminosos ojos" con que él la veía desde Cristo, y gozábamos inmensamente con la belleza de su palabra, y con la belleza del Misterio.

Naturalmente, si estoy agradecido a Sidney Griffith, entre otras cosas, por haberme introducido a S. Efrén, es porque el encuentro con S. Efrén ha sido para mí un bien muy grande. A pesar de la enorme distancia cultural, me es imposible no percibir en la obra de este hombre, de quien R. Murray decía que es "el poeta más grande del período patrístico, y acaso el único poeta teólogo a situar junto a Dante,"[1] la obra de un gran cristiano y un maestro de la fe.

Algunas de las verdades que S. Efrén tuvo que defender en los conflictos doctrinales en que intervino como pastor (*ʿallānâ*) y maestro (*mallpānâ*) de la Iglesia, a saber, en las polémicas con el arrianismo y el gnosticismo, tal como éstos existían en Nisibe y Edesa en el siglo IV, tienen un notable interés para nosotros hoy.[2] Acaso porque entonces como hoy el centro del debate está en si la cultura y la racionalidad dominantes han de ser el criterio discriminatorio de la fe, o si al revés, es el saber que se adquiere con la fe el que discierne lo que es valido en la racionalidad dominante. Pienso, por ejemplo, en la viva conciencia que tenía S. Efrén de los límites de la razón para comprender y decir el Misterio

1. Robert Murray, *Symbols of Church and Kingdom: A Study in Early Syriac Tradition* (Cambridge: Cambridge University Press, 1975), 31. En la tradición de lengua española, a la hora de mencionar poetas-teólogos, habría que incluir también al menos a S. Juan de la Cruz y a Calderón de la Barca. La cuestión de la deuda más que probable de la poesía teológica española para con la tradición cristiana oriental está aún esperando que algún estudioso le preste atención.

2. Sobre este aspecto del combate doctrinal en la obra de S. Efrén, cf. Sidney H. Griffith, "Setting Right the Church of Syria: Saint Ephraem's 'Hymns against Heresies,'" en William E. Klingshirn and Mark Vessey, eds., *The Limits of Ancient Christianity: Essays on Late Antique Thought and Culture in Honor of R. A. Markus* (Ann Arbor: University of Michigan Press, 1999), 97–114. S. H. Griffith ha ayudado a recuperar diferentes aspectos de la figura y de la obra de S. Efrén, cf. "Ephraem, the Deacon of Edessa, and the Church of the Empire," en Th. Halton y. J. P. Williman, eds., *Diakonia: Studies in Honor of Robert T. Meyer* (Washington, D.C.: The Catholic University of America Press, 1986), 22–52; "Images of Ephraem: The Syrian Holy Man and His Church," *Traditio* 45 (1989–90): 7–33; *"Faith Adoring the Mystery": Reading the Bible with St. Ephraem the Syrian,* The Père Marquette Lecture in Theology, 1997 (Milwaukee: Marquette University Press, 1997); "A Spiritual Father for the Whole Church: The Universal Appeal of St. Ephraem the Syrian," *Hugoye: Journal of Syriac Studies* 1, 2 (1998). Para una introducción a la obra de S. Efrén de carácter más general puede leerse Edward G. Mathews Jr., "General Introduction," en Edward G. Mathews, Jr. y Joseph P. Amar, *St. Ephrem the Syrian. Selected Prose Works,* ed. Kathleen E. McVey, The Fathers of the Church 91 (Washington, D.C.: The Catholic University of America Press, 1994), 3–56. Sobre la deformación de la biografía de S. Efrén en la tradición hagiográfica, cf. Edward G. Mathews Jr., "The Vita Tradition of Ephraem the Syrian, the Deacon of Edessa," *Diakonia* 22 (1988–89): 15–42; Joseph P. Amar, "Byzantine Ascetic Monachism and Greek Bias in the Vita Tradition of Ephrem the Syrian," *OCP* 58 (1992): 123–56. Para una presentación general de S. Efrén en lengua española, cf. J. J. Martínez, "Los himnos de S. Efrén de Nisibe y la liturgia de la Iglesia en lengua siríaca," en Asociación Española de Profesores de Liturgia, ed., *Liturgia y Padres de la Iglesia,* Culmen et Fons 2 (Bilbao: Grafite Ediciones, 2000), 125–217.

al margen o más allá de las cosas que Dios había revelado (*galyātâ*) en la creación y en la historia, y en su insistencia de cómo la única actitud legítima del hombre ante el Misterio que se revela es el silencio que adora o la palabra de gratitud y de alabanza. Pienso también en su afirmación constante de que Cristo es la clave interpretativa, no sólo de la historia, sino también de la creación, de la que S. Efrén decía que "llevaba en su seno los símbolos de Cristo, como María llevó los miembros de su cuerpo" (*Virg.* 6.7). O pienso en su aguda percepción de que la Iglesia es el lugar donde se prolonga en cierto modo en el tiempo la Encarnación del Verbo. O en su reconocimiento de la dignidad sagrada del cuerpo y de la carne, convertidos en morada de Cristo y destinados a la resurrección.

Todas estas verdades me parecen especialmente adecuadas para ser recordadas en este tiempo nuestro, cuando la demolición ilustrada de la propia Ilustración amenaza con arrastrar consigo a la Iglesia, en la medida en que ésta ha asumido para comprenderse a sí misma las categorías de una modernidad hoy agonizante. Es en momentos así cuando la Tradición se muestra como una saludable medicina. Encontrarse entonces con un cristiano grande y "no moderno," es decir, no comprometido con la "inevitable" tarea de "hacer creíble" la fe poniendo de manifiesto cómo la fe "contribuye" a la sociedad moderna o en el fondo coincide con ella, es sencillamente una bocanada de aire fresco. Lo es, no sólo para la Iglesia, sino también para esos ideales de la modernidad que los presupuestos de la modernidad han comprometido tan decisivamente.

A mi regreso a España en 1985, yo volvía cargado de proyectos de investigación sobre la tradición apocalíptica cristiana tardía en Oriente, que había sido el objeto de mis preocupaciones académicas al tiempo de mi trabajo doctoral. Pero el Señor tenía otros planes sobre mí vida, y aquellos proyectos tuvieron que ser aparcados. La responsabilidad de pastor de la Iglesia me alejó del mundo académico y de la posibilidad de dedicar un tiempo continuado a la investigación. Y sin embargo, el amor por S. Efrén y por su obra que había nacido en aquellos seminarios del Institute of Christian Oriental Research (ICOR), y también el amor a la porción de su Iglesia que el Señor me ha confiado, ha hecho que los tiempos de descanso de que he podido disponer en estos años los haya dedicado a traducir algunas de las obras de S. Efrén al español, un ámbito lingüístico en el que el Doctor de Nisibe es prácticamente desconocido. Por todo ello considero un privilegio participar en este homenaje, que me da la ocasión y la alegría de expresar mi gratitud al Profesor Sidney H. Griffith y a los demás profesores y compañeros del ICOR, y del Departamento de Lenguas Semíticas de la Catholic University of America. Lo que puedo ofrecer en él como trabajo es precisamente eso, la traducción al español de unos himnos de S. Efrén, en concreto, los himnos *De Virginitate* I–III.

Los Himnos *De Virginitate* I–III

S. Efrén habla de la virginidad consagrada en muy numerosas ocasiones, al hilo de otras reflexiones teológicas: así, por ejemplo, es un tema frecuente en la colección *Nat.* V–XX, en relación con María, que es vista siempre, como es habitual en la perspectiva de S. Efrén, como "tipo" de la Iglesia, y particularmente, de las vírgenes.[3] Igualmente, y también sólo a título de ejemplo, en la colección de himnos *De Paradiso,* hay referencias a la virginidad en *Parad.* 6, 12.24; 7, 7.15.18; 14, 11. En cualquiera de sus otras colecciones de himnos se pueden señalar muchos pasajes que aluden a la virginidad consagrada o hablan de ella. Ciertamente, los célibes y las vírgenes estaban muy cerca de él en su preocupación de pastor, y seguramente colaboraban con él de algún modo en su instrucción al pueblo por medio de los himnos. Pero sólo cuatro himnos en su obra publicada en siríaco tienen como tema explícito, señalado en los títulos que los introducen, la virginidad: son los himnos *Virg.* I–III, y XXIV.[4]

3. Todas las referencias a la obra de S. Efrén son a la edición de Edmund Beck, publicada entre 1955 y 1979 en diversos volumenes del Corpus scriptorum christianorum orientalium (CSCO) de Lovaina/Washington. Para una valoración del estado de los trabajos en la edición de las obras de S. Efrén, cf. J. Melki, "Saint Ephrem: Bilan de l'edition critique," *Parole de l'Orient* 11 (1983): 3–88; y para una guia completa de las ediciones y traducciones disponibles, cf. Sebastian P. Brock, "A Brief Guide to the Main Editions and Translations of the Works of St. Ephrem," *The Harp* 3 (1990): 7–29. Para los himnos *De Virginitate,* cf. Edmund Beck, ed., *Des Heiligen Ephraem des Syrers Hymnen de Virginitate,* CSCO 223–24 (Louvain: Peeters, 1962). De la colección entera existe hoy también una versión inglesa anotada, obra de Kathleen E. McVey, *Ephrem the Syrian: Hymns,* Classics of Western Spirituality (New York: Paulist Press, 1989), 259–468.

4. En la colección antigua de 51 himnos de s. Efrén que se conservan en armenio, los himnos II–IX constituyen una subcolección que versa sobre la virginidad. Dentro de la subcolección, los himnos IV y V son poemas de disputa entre la virginidad y la castidad, mientras que el himno IX es una disputa entre la virginidad y el matrimonio. El himno XLVI de esta misma colección armenia es un himno para la consagración de una virgen. Cf. L. Mariès y C. Mercier, eds., *Hymnes de S. Ephrem conservees en version armenienne,* PO 30.1 (Paris: Firmin Didot, 1961). Dos de estos himnos están traducidos al inglés, cf. Robert Murray, "'A Marriage for All Eternity': The Consecration of a Syrian Bride of Christ," *Sobornost* 11 (1989): 65–68; Edward G. Mathews, Jr. "Armenian Hymn IX, On Marriage, by Saint Ephrem the Syrian," *Journal of the Society for Armenian Studies* 9 (1996, 1997 [1999]): 55–63. Sobre los poemas dialogados en la literatura siríaca, llamados en siríaco *sûgyâtâ,* cf. especialmente Sebastian P. Brock, "The Dispute Poem: From Sumer to Syriac," *Bayn al-Nahrayn* 7 (1979): 417–26; Brock, "Dialogue Hymns of the Syriac Churches," *Sobornost* 5 (1983): 35–45; Brock, "Syriac Dialogue Poems: Marginalia to a Recent Edition," *Le Muséon* 97 (1984): 29-58; Brock, "Dramatic Dialogue Poems," en *IV Symposium Syriacum 1984,* OrChrAn 229 (Roma, 1987),

El texto de los himnos

Los himnos *De Virginitate* I–III abren la colección *De Virginitate* y le dan a toda ella su título.[5] Estos himnos han sido publicados por primera vez en la edición de Beck. El MS que sirve de base a esa edición, al que Beck de la sigla B (MS Vat. Syr. 111, del año 522 de nuestra era), y que contiene, por este orden, las colecciones de himnos *De Ecclesia, De Virginitate, De Fide, Contra Haereses y De Paradiso,* cayó al Nilo al ser trasladado del Monasterio de los Sirios en el Wadi 'n-Natrūn (la antigua Scetis) a la biblioteca Vaticana, y parte del texto del MS está dañado y se ha perdido. La colección *De Virginitate,* en particular, está seriamente dañada, y sobre todo al principio, por lo cual no fue tenida en cuenta por los autores de la *editio romana* de las obras de S. Efrén. Tampoco T. J. Lamy, que luchó por completar las lagunas de MS B para incluir la colección *De Virginitate* en su edición, pudo incluir estos himnos del comienzo.[6] Y

135–47; Brock, "Syriac Dispute Poems: The Various Types," en G. J. Reinink y H. L. J. Vanstiphout, eds., *Dispute Poems and Dialogues in the Ancient and Mediaeval Near East,* OLA 42 (Louvain, 1991), 109–19. La "castidad" a la que se refieren algunos de estos himnos (literalmente "santidad," con el término armenio correspondienta al siríaco *qaddîšûtâ*), designa el estado de vido de los *qaddîšê,* cf. la cita de Sidney H. Griffith a que hace referencia la nota 11.

5. Al menos, tal como lo formula al comienzo el MS B (Vat. Syr. 111, f. 22 v.a., línea 1). El MS E (British Museum, add. 17.141, f. 37 r., línea 9 desde abajo), introduce la colección como *madrāšê d' ʿal ʿedtâ w-da-btûlûtâ,* esto es "sobre la Iglesia y la virginidad"; y las dos *catenae* que se contienen en los MSS British Museum, add. 12.155 (f. 75 v.), y add. 17.194 (f. 34 r.), citan pasajes de esta colección introduciéndolos como men *penqîtâ d' ʿalʿedtâ,* "del volumen sobre la Iglesia." Aunque el título *De Virginitate* se ha impuesto, la lectura de estos tres MSS tardíos no es en absoluto a despreciar, y podría dar cuenta del hecho curioso de que las dos colecciones actualmente designadas con el nombre *De Virginitate* y *De Ecclesia* tengan el mismo número de himnos, a saber, cincuenta y dos. No deja de ser curioso, de paso, que la colección de himnos armenios sea también una colección de 51 himnos (¡y 51 dice también que tiene la colección *De Virginitate* en el colofón del MS B, tanto al final de la colección como al final del MS!). La denominación *De Ecclesia* (*d' ʿalʿedtâ*), además, no puede entenderse en modo alguno en el sentido moderno de una reflexión "sobre la Iglesia" como desde fuera, inconcebible en el mundo antiguo, sino más bien como una colección de himnos "eclesiásticos," es decir, de asuntos que tienen que ver con la vida "interna" de la Iglesia, con la vida cristiana. El colofón de la colección en el MS B describe así su contenido: *madrāšê d-ʿal btûlûtâ w-ʿal rāzay māran,* "himnos sobre la virginidad y los simbolos de Nuestro Señor." Ese es el título que ha adoptado McVey, y es uno que describe bien el contenido global de la colección.

6. Thomas J. Lamy, ed., *Sancti Ephraem Syri Hymni et Sermones,* 4 vols. (Malines: H. Dessain, 1882, 1886, 1889, 1902). Lamy publicaría en el vol. 2 de su edición (col. 773–881) fragmentos de los himnos *Virg.* I–X (en la edición de Lamy, numerados XXII–XXXI) o, y estrofas sueltas de otros himnos de la colección (en Lamy, XXXII–XXXIV), a partir sobre todo de MSS litúrgicos posteriores. Luego, en el volumen 4 (col. 497–670), Lamy publicó la colección *De Virginitate* a partir del himno IX, basandose en el MS B, y completando las lagunas (y añadiendo estrofas) a partir del *Breviarium Syrorum,* 7 vols. (Mosul 1889), cuyo testimonio por sí mismo no ofrece suficientes garantías. La edición de Lamy, por esto, porque tiene muchas lecturas equivocadas, y porque deja fuera muchos pasajes perfectamente legibles en el MS, no es suficientemente fiable.

la excelente edición de la colección *De Virginitate* de Ignatius Ephrem Rahmani en 1906, los contenía sólo muy fragmentariamente, dados los daños que el MS tenía en este lugar.[7]

Beck ha podido completar prácticamente todas las lagunas del MS B gracias a la aportación del MS liturgico de los siglos VIII ó IX que recibe en su edición la sigla E (MS British Museum, add. 17.141), y que en los ff. 37r–40v contiene *excerpta* de los himnos *De Virginitate* I–X, y sobre todo gracias al llamado *Sermo de Virginitate* atribuido a S. Efrén en el códice palimsesto British Museum add. 14. 623, que es casi idéntico a los himnos I–III tal como se conservan en el MS B. Este *Sermo de Virginitate* (*SdV*) había sido publicado por Mitchell, Bevan y Burkitt, junto con las otras obras de S. Efrén contenidas en la escritura antigua de este palimsesto, en sus *Ephraim's Prose Refutations.*[8] El texto del *SdV* pudo ser recuperado entero porque el monje Aarón, que en el año 823 borró la antigua escritura del MS, quiso incluir en la antología de diversos autores con que la sustituyó, también algunos pasajes de S. Efrén, y entre ellos el texto íntegro del *SdV*. Aunque Burkitt creyó que el texto del *SdV* debía ser original con respecto al de los himnos, Beck ha probado que el *SdV* es solo una transformación en prosa de los himnos, naturalmente retocándolos para hacerlos utilizables en la predicación.[9]

Los tres himnos tienen la misma melodía y la misma estructura estrófica, una de las más complicadas y menos claras de las que se encuentran en los himnos de S. Efrén. Es muy posible que los tres himnos hayan formado originalmente una unidad, o sean fragmentos de un himno más largo dedicado al tema, y recortado después por necesidades prácticas del uso litúrgico. Es casi seguro que faltan estrofas en el himno II, una serie de testimonios del AT sobre la violencia hecha a las mujeres, donde el comentario a la violación de Tamar por Amnón ocupa siete estrofas (II,1–7), mientras que solo en una estrofa (II,12) se hace una referencia a Susana sin nombrarla, de tal modo que el texto parece suponer que el episodio ha sido comentado antes.

7. I. E. Rahmani, *S. Ephraemi Hymni de virginitate quos e codice Vaticano III nunc primum edidit* (Scharfe, Libano: Typis patriarchalibus in Seminario Sharfensis, 1906). Esta edición es mucho mejor que la de Lamy, pues gracias a su conocimiento de la tradición litúrgica siríaca y a su meticuloso trabajo sobre el MS B, Rahmani pudo recuperar muchos pasajes y completar no pocas lagunas del MS. Pero tampoco en esta edición estaba completo el texto de los himnos I–III.

8. Cf. C. W. Mitchell, *S. Ephraim's Prose Refutations of Mani, Marcion and Bardaisan,* vol. 1 (London, 1912); E. A. Bevan y F. C. Burkitt, *S. Ephraim's Prose Refutations of Mani, Marcion and Bardaisan,* vol. 2 (London, 1921). El *SdV* se halla en el vol. 2, cf. 170–89 (texto); lxxx–xc (traducción).

9. Beck, *Des Heiligen Ephraem des Syrers Hymnen de Virginitate,* II–VI.

No forma parte de todo este conjunto, en cambio, el himno *De Virginitate* XXIV, al que el MS B antepone también un título propio, *'al btûlûtâ,* "sobre la virginidad." Este himno, muy mal conservado, tieno otro metro y pertenece a otro contexto, aunque se dan evidentemente conexiones temáticas con los tres himnos que presento aquí.

Los himnos en su contexto litúrgico e histórico

Como es habitual, los himnos dan poca información sobre las personas a las que iban dirigidos o el contexto litúrgico para el que han sido compuestos. Estos datos, así como la situación de la Iglesia que está en el trasfondo de estos textos, han de ser deducidos del texto mismo de los himnos y de otros pasajes paralelos que ayudan a comprenderlos. Ni hay que olvidar la posibilidad, ya mencionada, de que lo que tenemos en estos himnos sea sólo una selección de un himno más largo o de una colección de himnos más amplia, con lo que las estrofas seleccionadas pueden reflejar las preferencias de quienes han hecho la selección, y condicionar nuestra percepción de los destinatarios o del marco litúrgico.

Tal como los tenemos hoy, los himnos van dirigidos a personas que se han revestido "del hombre nuevo" en el bautismo (I, 1–2), y que están en peligro de volver a la vida del "hombre viejo." Esa vida del hombre viejo, instigada por Satán, que ya extravió al pueblo judío y a los gentiles (I, 3–5), se concreta pronto en el terreno de la castidad (ya en I, 2, y claramente, desde I, 6–7). Que ese peligro no es una imaginación del poeta lo ponen de manifiesto el tono preocupado y las advertencias de los himnos. Aunque en el comienzo del himno I, el poeta se dirige al "cuerpo," como si fuera una realidad personal (cf. I, 1. 2. 7, y luego también III, 3. 6–7. 10, donde el apelativo *ḥabbîb(y),* "amigo mío," de III, 6, debe referirse también al cuerpo), desde I, 9–10 es evidente que S. Efrén se está dirigiendo a mujeres, y que la cuestión central es precisamente la virginidad (I, 7–8. 10–11). En el himno II, el poeta se dirige claramente a una virgen desde la estrofa 2. Esa virgen es Tamar, la hija de David, pero el poeta está hablando a su auditorio a través de ella. También a las vírgenes se dirigen indirectamente las advertencias de II, 10–12. En II, 11 se hace patente que S. Efrén está hablando a vírgenes que han hecho un "voto." Las exhortaciones de II, 13–15 parecen encajar mejor si en el auditorio, junto a vírgenes consagradas ya desde hace un cierto tiempo (lo que viene sugerido por II, 13, y también luego por III, 16), hay jóvenes vírgenes, que acaso acababan de hacer su consagración. En II, 4. 8–9.

14, y en III, 2. 13, el poeta habla a la virginidad personificada. Las observaciones de III, 11, donde el poeta se dirige al ojo, y le pide que no "robe" la belleza en la que están ocultos los achaques de la vejez, pudiera dar a entender que en el auditorio había también hombres, pero probablemente se trata de un artificio literario para exhortar a las mujeres.

Tampoco los himnos dicen mucho sobre la ocasión de su composición o de su canto. En su forma actual, y dado que los destinatarios parecen ser exclusivamente mujeres, esa ocasión pudiera ser lo que hoy llamaríamos una "profesión," es decir, la celebración en el momento de hacer la consagración. Ahora bien, por lo que sabemos de otras fuentes contemporáneas, la consagración a la virginidad en las iglesias de lengua siríaca en tiempo de S. Efrén se realizaba en el marco de la liturgia pascual, al mismo tiempo que el bautismo.[10] Y aunque la relación entre consagración y bautismo no es promenente en estos himnos, ése pudiera ser su *Sitz im Leben* originario. Esa relación sólo se expresa en I, 1–2, que ponen en relación la virginidad con el revestirse del hombre nuevo en el bautismo. Es cierto que el termino "virginidad" no aparece en estas estrofas, pero el poeta se dirije al "cuerpo" porque está ya pensando en la santidad de la carne, como lo ponen de manifiesto las alusiones a 1 Co 6,19, donde el Ápostol habla del cuerpo como santuario del Espíritu Santo en contraposición a la fornicación. La ausencia de más motivos bautismales en estos himnos no es difícil de explicar, si lo que tenemos en ellos es la selección de una obra más amplia: esa selección puede haber sido realizada en función de unas necesidades litúrgicas y pastorales distintas de las que constituían el contexto original de la obra, tal vez una "profesión" en un monasterio de mujeres.

Precisamente para la comprensión de estos tres himnos es fundamental tener en cuenta el contexto de la vida consagrada en Siria y Mesopotamia en tiempos de S. Efrén. Ese contexto, sobre el que existe una abundantísima literatura, y no siempre bien fundamentada en el conjunto de los datos históricos, ha sido excelentemente descrito en fecha reciente y de modo sintético por S. H. Griffith, a quien remitimos aquí. En sus conclusiones se basa también el breve resumen que sigue.[11]

10. Robert Murray, "The Exhortation to Candidates for Ascetical Vows at Baptism in the Ancient Syriac Church," *NTS* 21 (1974–1975): 59–80.

11. S. H. Griffith, "Asceticism in the Church of Syria: The Hermeneutics of Early Syrian Monasticism," en Vincent L. Wimbush y Richard Valantasis, eds., *Asceticism* (New York: Oxford University Press, 1995), 220–45. Cf. también Griffith, "'Singles' in God's Service: Thoughts on the Ihidaye from the Works

Los célibes y las vírgenes en las iglesias en que vivió S. Efrén eran sobre todo los llamados "hijos (o hijas) de la alianza," *bnay qyāmâ o bnāt qyāmâ,* grupos de consagrados que podían vivir o no en comunidad, pero que en todo caso participaban muy activamente en la vida de la comunidad cristiana. En ese sentido, su forma de vida se distingue notablemente de la que sería el monacato posterior, tanto eremítico como cenobítico, y es mejor considerarla como pre-monástica. Otra denominación que se daba a los célibes y a las vírgenes en el vocabulario siríaco antiguo era el término de *'iḥīdāyâ,* "único" (en inglés "single"), que puede haber sido un antecesor del término griego *monachos,* pero que en la tradición siríaca antigua tenía también una fuerte referencia cristológica, entre otras cosas porque era también el término usado para designar al "Hijo Único (unigénito) del Padre," *monogenês,* en John 1:14–18; 3:16–18.

En tiempo de S. Efrén, cerca de los *bnay qyāmâ,* o formando parte de ellos, pero como verdaderos *'iḥîdāyâ,* había pastores, como es el caso del Obispo Abraham de Nisibe o el del mismo S. Efrén, y estos también podían vivir de alguna forma en comunidad, en "apriscos de pastores."[12] Por último, entre los consagrados de los que dan testimonio las obras de Afraat y S. Efrén en las Iglesias de lengua siríaca durante el siglo IV estaban "personas que pueden haber estado casadas, pero que posteriormente se habían consagrado a sí mismas de modo especial y vivían como célibes en la comunidad cristiana con el nombre de *qaddîšê,* los santos."[13]

"De la evidencia que poseemos"—escribe S. H. Griffith—"parece que, al menos a comienzos del siglo IV, tanto los hombres como las mujeres célibes eran libres para escoger dentro de las comunidades locales su modo de vivir. Por esa fecha todavía no se oye nada de personas o de comunidades de consagrados apartadas en el desierto o en las montañas. Esa moda ascética aparece en textos de Siria hacia el final de la vida de S. Efrén."[14] Por otra parte, S. Efrén conoce y alaba el nacimiento

of Aphrahat and Ephraem the Syrian," *The Harp* 4 (1991): 145–59; Griffith, "Julian Saba, 'Father of the Monks' of Syria," *JECS* 2 (1994): 185–216.

12. Del Obispo Abraham de Nisibe, S. Efrén dice que era el protector de los *bnay qyāmâ,* cf. *Carmina Nisibena,* CSCO 218–19 (Louvain: Peeter, 1961), XXI, 5; el mismo era un *'iḥîdāyâ* (*Carmina Nisibena,* XV, 9), y governaba su diócesis como pastor (*rā'yâ*) del rebaño (*mar'îtâ*) con la ayuda de lo que S. Efrén llama "un aprisco de pastores" (*dayrâ d-'allānê,* cf. *Carmina Nisibena,* XVII, 3), al cual el mismo S. Efrén pertenecía, cf. himnos *Contra Haereses,* CSCO 169–70 (Louvain: Peeters, 1957), LVI, 10. Más aún, S. Efrén da testimonio de que en torno a Nisibe había otras iglesias "filiales," cada una con sus propios *dayrātâ,* "apriscos," en los que residirían sus respectivos *'iḥîdāyê,* entre los cuales habría también pastores, presbíteros y diáconos, dependiendo del Obispo de Nisibe (*Carmina Nisibena,* XIV, 1). Cf. Griffith, "Asceticism," 237.

13. Griffith, "Asceticism," 223.

14. Griffith, "Asceticism," 237.

de las nuevas formas de vida ascéticas caracterizadas por la "retirada física, individual o colectiva, de la comunidad de los bautizados," esto es, el monasticismo propiamente dicho, pero en su tiempo "las nuevas y las antiguas formas de vida ascética y célibe convivían juntas."[15] En esto como en otras cosas, S. Efrén trataba de promover la comunión de las iglesias de Nisibe y Edesa con la Gran Iglesia, lo que significaba, en su contexto, con la Iglesia del imperio. Es en este contexto en el que hay que enmarcar los himnos *De Virginitate* I–III, y es en ese contexto en el que se sitúan algunos de los motivos y preocupaciones que se ponen de manifiesto en el texto de los himnos, y que pasamos brevemente a reseñar.

Por una parte, es claro que S. Efrén trata de corregir una cierta valoración de la virginidad que se daba en círculos gnósticos o influidos por el gnosticismo. Basándose en el desprecio del cuerpo y de la carne, y con excusa de una "instrucción doctrinal" (*tûlmādâ*) cuyo carácter y cuyo lugar en el desarrollo de la vida cristiana no me es posible precisar más, llevaba por una parte al desprecio del matrimonio, pero por otra daba lugar a una vida licenciosa, "con pretexto de la instrucción ... se avergüenzan de asumir el estado matrimonial," pero "caen en las trampas del pecado" (I, 6). La tendencia encratita de un sector al menos del cristianismo de lengua siríaca es conocida, y S. Efrén tiene que afirmar la pureza del matrimonio en otros pasajes (cf., por ejemplo, *De Virginitate* V, 14). Algunas de las severas advertencias sobre las condiciones de la virginidad que encontramos en los himnos pueden deberse al deseo de corregir la ligereza y la falta de realismo de estos círculos, o de personas o grupos influidos por ellos.

El cuidado de esas condiciones es la otra gran cuestión que preocupa a S. Efrén en estos himnos. La virginidad consagrada es un don "divino", "celestial" (cf. I, 7–8), que debe protegerse cuidadosamente. Tampoco aquí el poeta da muchos datos precisos, pero en los himnos hay suficientes alusiones a esta cuestión como para deducir que a S. Efrén le preocupa la fidelidad de las vírgenes a su voto (II, 11; III, 12–16), y que esa preocupación tiene que ver con la pretensión de vivir la virginidad sin cuidar del espacio humano que la hace

15. Griffith, "Asceticism," 237; cf. también Griffith, "Julian Saba, 'Father of the Monks' of Syria," especialmente pp. 215–16. Si Julián Saba representa en Edesa las nuevas formas de la vida ascética, Abraham Kidunaya (otro asceta en cuya alabanza se atribuyen himnos a S. Efrén) era más bien un representante del antiguo ascetismo sirio. Ambos fueron celebrados por S. Efrén a su llegada a Edesa, en los últimos años de su vida, aunque en las colecciones de himnos sobre estos dos ascetas atribuidas a él por la tradición se contienen himnos añadidos posteriormente. Cf. Beck, *Des heiligen Ephraem des Syrers Hymnen auf Abraham Kidunaya und Julianos Saba,* CSCO 322–23 (Louvain: Peeters, 1972). Sobre la autenticidad de estos himnos, cf. Griffith, "Julian Saba, 'Father of the Monks' of Syria," 198–203.

posible. La severidad serena de las reflexiones de S. Efrén hace pensar que los himnos afrontan aquí abusos graves que se habían dado en la comunidad. En el mismo sentido apuntan también las advertencias sobre el retorno del hombre viejo (I, 1–5), sobre el vino y el mal amor (I, 10–13), sobre las astucias del Maligno (II, 1–6; III, 2–7), o las reflexiones sobre el remordimiento y la penitencia (I, 3; III, 9–10. 15–16).

Podemos hacernos una idea de esos abusos en las iglesias de la Alta Mesopotamia, además de por las alusiones de estos himnos, por otros pasajes de las obras de Afraat y del mismo S. Efrén que S. H. Griffith ha puesto de relieve en su estudio sobre el ascetismo en la Iglesia de Siria. Así Afraat, en su *Exposición* VI, "Sobre los *bnay qyāmâ,*" escribe:

> Por eso, hermanos, si un varón, un *bar qyāmâ* o un *qaddîšâ* que ama la vida consagrada (*'iḥîdāyûtâ*), pero quere a una mujer, una *ba(r)t qyāmâ* como él, para que viva con él, sería mejor para él tomar a una mujer abiertamente, y no vivir en los excesos del deseo. Y lo mismo también una mujer, le conviene que, si no puede separarse del hombre, del *'iḥîdāyâ,* pertenecir al varón abiertamente.[16]

Y más adelante en esa misma *Exposición* VI, Afraat se detiene a dar un consejo conretísimo a una virgen:

> ¡Oh, vírgenes, que os habéis desposado con Cristo! Si uno de los *bnay qyāmâ* os dijera a una de vosotras: "Voy a vivir contigo, y tú me servirás," le responderás así: "Yo estoy desposada a un varón que es rey, y le sirvo a él. Y si dejo su servicio y te sirvo a ti, mi esposo se encolerizará conmigo, y me escribirá la carta de divorcio, y me echará de su casa. Si tú quieres recibir honor de mí, y que yo lo reciba de ti, sin que haya daño alguno para mí o para ti, no pongas fuego en tu interior, no sea que quemes tus vestidos. Más bien, permanece honradamente solo, y yo permaneceré sola honradamente. Y hazte con esas cosas que el Esposo quiere que estén listas para su eterno banquete de bodas, como con un regalo de boda, y prepárate a salir a su encuentro. Y yo prepararé el aceite para entrar con las prudentes, y no ser dejada fuera con las necias."[17]

En cuanto a S. Efrén, en una obra sólo recientemente publicada por S. P. Brock, la llamada *Carta a Publio,* en el contexto de una descripción de la otra vida, escribe:

16. Afraat, *Exposición* VI, 4. Cf. *Aphraatis Sapientis Persae Demonstrationes,* I. Parisot, ed., PS 1–2 (1894, 1907; reimpresión anastática, Turnhout: Brepols, 1993), 1:260.

17. Afraat, *Exposición* VI, 7 (ed. Parisot, 1:272).

Yo vi allí vírgenes puras que, como su virginidad no estaba adornada con el buen aceite de las obras virtuosas, su virginidad había sido rechazada.... Y vi allí también a las que no tenían el nombre de la virginidad, coronadas con sus obras victoriosas, pues que su vida santa (*dûbbārê*) ocupaba el lugar de la virginidad.... Y cuando vi estas cosas allí, me dije a mí mismo: "Que nadie ponga su confianza sólo en la noble reputación de la virginidad, si está privado de las buenas obras que son el aceite de las lámparas."[18]

La situación que suponen los himnos es la misma que puede deducirse de estos pasajes, y tal vez eso indica que nos hallamos en una fase temprana de la actividad poética de S. Efrén. Por eso, lo que se dice en III, 12, que la virginidad pertenece a los "mercaderes solitarios," aunque puede leerse como una invitación al eremitismo, en realidad trata simplemente, al igual que los textos de Afraat citados más arriba, de proteger las condiciones de vida que hacen posible la virginidad. Así lo expresa muy claramente la estrofa II, 8:

Tanto en la alcoba como en el campo,
están a tú acecho,
virginidad;
pues si entras en la alcoba,
el astuto Amnón robó tu riqueza;
pero si saliste al campo, si te refugiaste en el desierto,
Siquem, el ladrón, saqueó tu tesoro.
¿Adónde irás entonces, paloma solitaria,
cuando por todas partes tantos son tus cazadores?

S. Efrén, pues, aunque es plenamente consciente de la necesidad de unas condiciones de vida determinadas para vivir la virginidad consagrada, no piensa en una forma concreta de vida como solución a los problemas que afronta. Al menos en estos himnos (o en lo que tenemos de ellos), no pone su confianza en la "retirada al desierto," o en la vida común, o en la observancia de una regla, como si esas "fórmulas" fueran la garantía de la virginidad. Lo que S. Efrén propone es una llamada a la libertad responsible (I, 9; III, 8), sobre la base de una conciencia más rica del significado cristiano de la virginidad (cf. I, 2; II, 11. 12. 15; III, 14-16): la virginidad como pertenencia plena a Cristo, esposo de las vírgenes, que mora en ellas. Lo que se pide a la auténtica virgen en II, 15 es sobre todo que su vida sea el reflejo y la imagen de su Señor. En cuanto al modo

18. Sebastian P. Brock, "Ephrem's Letter to Publius," *Le Muséon* 89 (1976): 261–305. Para el texto citado, cf. los nn. 15–16, en las pp. 286–287.

de vida que se propone (limosnas, visitas a enformos), la imagen que resulta de esa estrofa es poco compatible con el monacato.

Ciertos rasgos de los himnos pueden resultar chocantes para la sensibilidad del lector moderno. Su percepción del amor y de la pasión, llamada algunas veces "mal amor," *ḥûbbâ sanyâ* (cf. I, 12), *reḥmtâ snîtâ* (III, 3),[19] no ha pasado ni por el libertinaje ilustrado, ni por el *revival* romántico y deformado del amor cortés, difundido después por todo el mundo desde Hollywood en una versión vulgarizada, ni por la reacción puritana de la moralidad victoriana. Por antiguos y por cristianos, estos himnos pertenecen, pues, "a otro mundo." Y, sin embargo, la realidad cada vez más cotidiana de los abusos sexuales y de los malos tratos a la mujer en nuestra sociedad puede, tal vez, permitir que se valoren de nuevo algunas de las indicaciones de estos himnos—escritos ciertamente en un mundo culturalmente muy alejado del nuestro—como un signo de la defensa que la fe cristiana hace de la mujer y de su dignidad.

El Himno I

Con la melodia de: "La esposa del Rey."[20]

1. ¡Despójate, cuerpo, del hombre viejo,[21]
todo él detestable,
para que no desgaste otra vez la novedad

19. Aunque la distancia cultural que hay entre el siglo IV en la Alta Mesopotamia y la Castilla del siglo XIV es muy grande, un lector español no puede oír estas expresiones sin reconocer en ellas un precedente, al menos remoto, de la que da lugar al título de la obra del Arcipreste de Hita, *El libro de buen amor.*

20. La indicación melódica cita el *incipit* de una estrofa cuya melodía era conocida por los cantores, e indica la estructura estrófica del himno. La indicación "la esposa del Rey," *kallat malkâ,* vale para los himnos *Virg.* I–III. La misma indicación melódica se halla en los himnos *Carmina Nisibena* XXXIV y *De Crucifixione* IV–VI. La estructura de la estrofa no es nada clara. Beck la divide en seis líneas de verso, señalando otras indicaciones de división de verso de los MSS. G. Bickell, en su edición de los *Carmina Nisibena* (Leipzig: F. A. Brockhaus, 1866), había dividido la estrofa en trece versos, y Lamy en nueve, siguiendo la forma de presentación del *Breviarium Syrorum* (cf. Lamy, vol. 4, 492). Nosotros seguimos el texto de Beck, pero dada la incertidumbre respecto a la partición de la estrofa en muchos puntos, y las numerosas irregularidades métricas, la presentamos en nueve líneas, dividiendo aleatoriamente, según el sentido, los versos excesivamente largos (que no son siempre los mismos). La verdad es que las dos primeras líneas de Beck son a veces tan largas que parecen perder la condición de verso, y tampoco tienen una métrica regular. El resultado para nuestra versión se traduce en estrofas de nueve líneas, de verso irregular, y en las que la distribución de las sílabas en los versos puede ser diferente para cada estrofa. Esta presentación no pretende representar o recomponer la división original de la estrofa: sólo ofrecer un texto que no pierda la condición de poesía en español.

21. Cf. Col 3:9.

que revestiste al bautizarte!
Sería lo contrario de un pago justo[22]
si después de haber sido renovado, viene otra vez a desgastarte.
¡Escucha, cuerpo, mi consejo!
Despójate de él con una vida santa,[23]
para que no te revista él a ti con las malas costumbres.

Responsorio: ¡De todos los santos, en la tierra y en el cielo,[24]
Gloria al Padre, y al Hijo, y al Espíritu Santo!

2. Nuestro Señor, en efecto, ha renovado
tu vejez con el bautismo:
el Constructor de la vida, que por medio de su sangre,[25]
ha ideado y se ha construido
un templo para su morada.[26]
No permitas, pues, que en lugar suyo,
habite en el nuevo templo el hombre viejo.
¡Cuerpo, si reservas tu templo para Dios,[27]
también tú serás su palacio real!
3. La Escritura que enseña, y la naturaleza que proclama,
ambas reprenden al hombre.[28]

22. La expresión siríaca no es del todo clara. El texto dice, literalmente: "Sería lo contrario del pago de su deuda." La idea se ilumina con el verso siguiente: sería contradictorio, "no sería un pago justo," que el hombre viejo (que debe ser el sujeto de *'etḥaddat*), después de haber sido cambiado en el bautismo, vuelva a envejecerte.

23. "Con una vida santa," *dûbbārê.* Literalmente, *dûbbārê* significa sólo "modos de vida, comportamientos." Pero el uso elíptico del plural *dûbbārê,* por *dûbbārê 'allāhāyê,* "modos de vida divinos," es frecuente en la literatura siríaca, y se refiere especialmente a la vida ascética.

24. "Santos," *qaddîšîn,* tiene en siríaco una especial connotación alusiva a la castidad, cf. Murray, *Symbols,* 12–16. No parece que el término *qaddîšîn* tenga aquí el significado técnico de los *qaddîšê,* de que se habla más arriba (cf. la cita a que hace referencia la nota 11), aunque no los excluya, naturalmente.

25. "El Constructor de la vida." El término *naggārâ* significa *faber,* es decir, "obrero," "constructor," y especialmente "carpintero." Pero hace referencia a la construcción de casas, y podía equivaler a "arquitecto." El *SdV,* en todo caso, tiene el termino siríaco para "arquitecto:" *'ardîklâ.*

26. El texto siríaco dice para "templo" *nawsâ,* la transcripción siríaca del griego ναός, que es el término empleado por San Pablo en 1 Cor. 3:16s; 6:19. En cambio, la Peshitta en estos pasajes, tradue ναός por *hayklâ,* que San Efrén usa en el último verso con el sentido de "palacio."

27. Literalmente: "si dejas habitar a Dios en tu templo."

28. La "Escritura" equivale aquí a la "Ley (judía)," cf. *infra,* estrofa 5. El tema de la unidad entre Escritura y naturaleza, con resonancias antignósticas, es frecuente en Efrén. Cf. los himnos *De Fide,* CSCO 154–55 (Louvain: Peeters, 1955), pp. LXV, 2; *De Paradiso,* CSCO 174–75 (Louvain: Peeters, 1957), pp. V, 2; *Contra Haereses,* CSCO 169–70 (Louvain: Peeters, 1957), XXVIII, 11s. Aquí, tanto la Escritura como la naturaleza acusan y reprenden la iniquidad del hombre. En otros pasajes, las dos conducen a Cristo, y le dan a conocer mediante sus símbolos y sus esbozos.

Su maldad está puesta entre las dos:
para que, si ella hace pecar a uno que no tiene la Ley,
le reprenda la naturaleza;
y si hace pecar a uno de la Ley,
le corrija la Escritura.[29]
Satán hiere, y ellas nos curan:
tras la maldad entra el remordimiento.

4. Ellas despreciaban al rebelde, curaban al que hacía penitencia,
y declaraban justa la sentencia del Juez.[30]
También hoy reprenden a los rebeldes, pero sanan al penitente.
Permanecen en el tiempo, igual que ese Maligno,
que rejuvenece en cada generación, y acompaña a todo hombre,
y está siempre haciendo daño.
Así también ellas accompañan a todos,
y se rejuvenecen en cada generación,
y se encuentran a todas horas.

5. Escucha cómo la naturaleza y la Ley[31]
relatan sus perniciosas maldades:[32]
la nación judía
fue adultera teniendo la Ley;
sin la Ley, las naciones
trastocaron su naturaleza,
y sin la naturaleza han sido renovadas.[33]
Naturaleza y Ley presentan sus demandas contra él,
porque el Agitador ha pervetido el orden de ambas.[34]

29. Cf. Rm 2, 14. Aunque San Efrén no emplea el concepto de "ley de la naturaleza," o "ley natural," el texto lo supone. Pero hay que guardarse de comprender esa ley natural en las claves del pensamiento moderno.

30. "El Juez" se refiere a Dios, cuya sentencia han confirmado (= han declarado justa), *zaddeq(w),* tanto la Escritura como la naturaleza. Rm 2, 2. 5–6. 16 también menciona el juicio de Dios. Los verbos en perfecto pudieran indicar que S. Efrén se está refiriendo a un acontecimiento del pasado, acaso al rechazo de Cristo por una parte del pueblo judío y a la conversión de los gentiles. La expresión "también hoy," al comienzo del verso tercero, es una glosa del traductor para poner de relieve el contraste de los tiempos en el texto siríaco, a la luz del pensamiento del verso 4.

31. "La Ley," *nāmûsâ,* ilumina el sentido del termino "Escritura," *ktābâ,* en las estrofas anteriores. En realidad, toda la estrofa parece inspirada en las ideas de Rom. 1:18–2:16.

32. El texto no da el referente de "sus perniciosas maldades," que ha de ser masculino y singular. Beck cree que "sus" sólo puede referirse al pueblo judío, y que esa referencia es decisiva para la interpretación de la estrofa, que él traduce de un modo diferente. En mi interpretación, el referente es Satán.

33. "Trastocaron su naturaleza", cf. Rom. 1:26–27. "Sin la naturaleza han sido renovadas," es decir, por obra de Cristo. Mi traducción difiere aquí también de la de Beck.

34. De nuevo, a mi juicio, aquél contra el que la naturaleza y la Ley presentan sus demandas es Satán, lo que permite comprender el último verso mejor que si se refiere a la nación judía. Prefiero en ese verso

6. El Maligno ha robado el matrimonio a los sencillos
con el pretexto de la instrucción.[35]
Y cuando estaban a mitad del camino,
puso a sus espaldas la vergüenza de la ofensa,[36]
y ante sus ojos puso la hermosura,
que es la trampa del mal deseo.
Mientras se avergüenzan de asumir
el estado matrimonial,
caen en las trampas del pecado.
7. ¿Por qué persigues, cuerpo,
a la virginidad, que ha descendido a nuestra tierra,
y habita entre nosotros como una forastera?[37]
Si uno la persigue y arranca su nido,
como no puede volver a construirlo,
su ala la transporta rápidamente a la altura.[38]
Es un ave de lo alto,
que envejece en un solo nido,
y si se va y lo abandona, es para siempre.
8. Y cuando la amiga de los ángeles ha levantado el vuelo,[39]
entra la compañera de los demonios:
la pasión, enemiga de la virginidad,[40]
que José perseguía.[41]

---

la variante de E, que lee el singular, *šāgûšâ,* en vez del plural, y permite comprender el sufijo de *ṭûkāshûn* como referido a la naturaleza y a la Ley.

35. "Instrucción," *tûlmādâ,* puede referirse a la instrucción catequética que se recibía antes del bautismo, o a una instrucción esotérica especial dada por grupos gnósticos. No hay que olvidar el parentesco de *tûlmādâ* con el término rabínico Talmud, o con el siríaco *talmîdâ,* "discípulo." Toda la estrofa tiene una intención anti-encratita, y polemiza con comunidades o grupos que probablemente exigían la virginidad para acceder al bautismo.

36. "Puso a sus espaldas": leo con Beck la variante del *SdV.* El MS B lee, aquí y en el verso siguiente el plural, "pusieron." Al leer el singular, el sujeto sigue siendo "el Maligno," lo que parece más apropiado en el contexto.

37. "Perseguir" la virginidad tiene aquí el sentido negativo de "buscarla para cazarla," como más abajo en II, 1, donde se habla también del nido, aunque no se emplea el verbo "perseguir." En cambio, en el verso 4 de la estrofa 8, "perseguir" tiene inequívocamente el sentido positivo de "buscar para si," "proponerse."

38. "La altura," "lo alto," indica el cielo, que es el lugar al que pertenece la virginidad.

39. "Los ángeles" traduce *'îrê,* literalmente "los vigilantes" (es decir, los que no duermen). El término *'îrê* es una antigua denominación aramea de los ángeles, cf. W. Cramer, *Die Engelvorstellungen bei Ephräm dem Syrer,* OChrAn 173 (Roma: Pontificio Istituto Orientale, 1965), pp. 11–14, 97–99, 105–7, 152–55.

40. Traduzco aquí *regtâ* por "pasión" en vez de por "deseo," que es su significado proprio, porque "pasión" es femenino en castellano. El término *regtâ* es femenino en siríaco, y por eso Efrén puedo oponerla a la virginidad, *btûlûtâ,* que también es femenino. En cambio, en otros lugares, empleo "deseo" para traducir *regtâ.* Cf., por ejemplo, II, 2–3.

41. Alusión a la historia de la mujer de Putifar, cf. Gen. 39:1–19. La afirmación de que José "perseguía"

La virginidad, en efecto, ama a los ángeles,
y si huye, es para ascender a las alturas angélicas.
¿Quién no llorará?
Que en lugar de la que daba sosiego,
ha entrado allí a vivir la que hace arder.[42]

9. Si un raptor te viola
y avergüenza tu modestia en el campo,
la violencia del impuro
probará que tú eres casta,
como también Sara
fue casta en el seno del faraón,
pues que no adulteró por su propia voluntad.[43]
La voluntad viene a ser un sacerdote, que con su hisopo
purifica a los que son mancillados con violencia.[44]

10. Teme al vino, que expuso las vergüenzas
del noble Noé, el vencedor en su generación.[45]
El que había podido dominar las aguas del diluvio,
fue dominado por una pizca de vino;
el diluvio de fuera no había podido con él,
y pudo con él el vino de dentro.
Si a Noé, cabeza de los linajes,[46]
pudo el vino arrojarle desnudo al suelo,
¿cómo no va a poder contigo, solitaria?[47]

11. Que te infunda temor a los jóvenes
la pasión del vino,
que despojó a Lot en la vejez.[48]

---

la virginidad sólo puede significar aquí que la quería seriamente para sí, como un propósito suyo. La pasión (el deseo) de la mujer de Putifar era enemiga del propósito de José.

42. "La que daba sosiego," "la que hace arder." Se refiere de nuevo a la virginidad y a la pasión (= el deseo). En siríaco hay un juego de palabras por el parecido entre *mšayyentâ* y *mšaḥḥentâ.*

43. Cf. Gen. 12:10–20. "Casta" es aquí *qaddîšâ,* literalmente "santa." Cf. supra, la cita a que hace referencia la nota 11. Sobre la violación de una virgen en el campo, cf. Deut 22:25.

44. Cf. infra, III, 8, y las referencias citadas en la nota 99.

45. Cf. Gen. 9:20–27. "El vencedor," es decir, en este contexto, el hombre más justo, el que se había preservado del pecado del resto de los hijos de Set.

46. En los *Sermones de Fide,* CSCO 212–13 (Louvain: Peeters, 1961), III, 52, S. Efrén llama a Noé *rîšâ da-trên,* cabeza "Segunda" (se entiende, "cabeza de la humanidad," después de Adán).

47. "Solitaria," *mšawḥadtâ.* El autor parece dirigirse a la virginidad personificada (cf. II, 8). En III, 12 se dirá con el mismo término que la virginidad "pertenece a los mercaderes solitarios." El término *mšawḥadtâ* es de la raíz *yḥd,* la misma de la que se deriva *'iḥîdāyâ,* "único," "Unigénito." Sobre este último término, y sus resonancias cristológicas para el ascetismo antiguo en las Iglesias de lengua siríaca, cf. Griffith, "'Singles' in God's Service," 223–29. Mas abajo, en II, 11, el término *'iḥîdāyâ* se usa referido a Cristo.

48. Alusión al episodio de las hijas de Lot, cf. Gen. 19:30–38. En la primera frase, el pronombre

El vino llevó a cabo cosas bien arduas,
Que con él las mujeres robaron el quedarse encintas.
¡Cuánto más no hará lo que es sencillo,
que los hombres, con él, roben la virginidad!
Unas muchachas pudieron saquear el tesoro del anciano,
¡guarda tú tu tesoro de los jóvenes!
12. El que está ebrio de vino es más tolerable
que el ebrio de mal amor.
Los lazos más firmes son frágiles para él;[49]
el cetro, despreciable,
y débil el palo.
Castigo y reprensión
pasan por sus oídos como si fueran cuentos;
el reproche le resulta una broma,
y un salivazo en la cara le parece rocío.
13. La senda de las voces que llaman a sus oídos
no llega hasta su corazón,
pues las puertas de sus oídos
están abiertas la una para la otra:
la palabra que entró por un oído
ya ha salido por el otro oído de enfrente.
Y mientras su maestro piensa que le atiende,
no percibe que está derramando fuera su advertencia,
porque no hay sitio en su corazón para recibir nada.
14. El seno espacioso, en efecto,
de aquella mente suya
esta lleno, apretado, abarrotado,
de una gota de amor que destiló,
y que se ha convertido en un mar grande.
Los pensamientos se hunden y vuelven a salir a flote
como el barco roto de un marinero.[50]

---

reflexivo "te," que no tiene correspondiente en el texto siríaco, trata de explicitar el sentido de un texto que, sin ese añadido, sería ambiguo. La idea, en efecto, no es que los jóvenes deben temer la pasión del vino, sino que la pasión del vino debe hacer que las vírgenes teman a los jóvenes.

49. Traduzco este verso de manera diferente a McVey. El participio activo *p'l* del verbo *rpâ* no parece haberse usado, y por lo tanto la traducción "firmes lazos le debilitan" no parece posible, y oscurece a mi juicio el sentido del contexto.

50. Los dos verbos "hundirse" y "salir a flote," *'mad* y *nbag*, aparecen juntos también en los himnos *De Fide,* CSCO 154–55 (Louvain: Peeters, 1955), V, 9; en los himnos *De Paradiso,* CSCO 174–75 (Louvain: Peeters, 1957), pp. X, 8; y en el *Sermo de Domino Nostro,* CSCO 270–71 (Louvain: Peters, 1966), XXIX, *in fine* (p. 27, lineas 9–10).

El pensamiento va a la deriva en las olas de los placeres,
Como un barco cuyo timonel lo ha abandonado.

El Himno II

Con la misma melodía[51]

1. Con el disfraz de cordero,
el astuto Amnón
se aproximó a aquella oveja,[52]
y planeando seducirla con lo que era propio de ella,
se salió con la suya.[53]
El enfermo se levantó rápidamente para acudir a la lucha,[54]
y obtuvo una corona que resultó en vergüenza suya.[55]
Al ver que la virginidad estaba segura en su nido,
la trajo con engaño a su guarida, y así la capture.[56]

Responsorio: De todos los santos, ¡Gloria al Santo,
que ha dado la virginidad a las naciones![57]

2. Tu cazador, virgen, es astuto,
y tú, en cambio, una inocente;
pues Amnón, que te quería a tí, fingió querer comida,
el muy ladino, sin quererla realmente,
y por el alimento del que no tenía hambre,
servía al deseo carnal,
del que sí estaba hambriento.

51. El MS E lee: "Segundo del mismo (himno), con la misma melodía."

52. Cf. el episodio de la violación de Tamar por su hermano Amnón en 2 Sam 13:1–22.

53. "Lo que era propio de ella," "de él." Leemos *dîlāh, dîleh.* McVey supone un sustantivo derivado del *pa'el* de *dwl,* que significa "servir" y traduce por "su servicio," aunque esa formación no está atestiguada en los diccionarios. Beck traduce "ihr Werk," "sein Werk." "Lo que era propio de ella" aludiría en todo caso a la atención a su hermano enfermo. El verso cinco dice literalmente en siríaco,"asi llevó a cabo lo que era (propio) de él." La expresión idiomática española tiene una indeterminación analoga a la del siríaco, y representa bien el sentido de la frase.

54. McVey traduce *da-twah* por "laid low." Pero *twah* traduce en la versión *Vetus syra* de John 11:31 ταχέως ἀνέστη, "se levantó rapidamente."

55. En la metáfora del combate de los gladiadores que emplea S. Efrén, Amnón vence y se lleva la corona, pero es una corona que resulta vergonzosa.

56. "A su guarida." Leemos, con Beck, la variante del MS E. El MS B lee "a su nido."

57. Sobre la connotación de "santo(s)" en este contexto, cf. supra, la nota al Responsorio del himno I. La conexión entre la virginidad y las naciones contiene una nota polémica con el judaísmo.

¡Falso, que fingía querer algo que no quería,
para encontrar lo que quería con esa excusa!
3. Le pidió tortas de corazones.[58]
¡Ay, qué lista que fue,
que le llevó los corazones
al que no tenía corazón![59]
Él era una serpiente, que en su perfidia
se había disfrazado de la enfermedad,
para que su mano no la reconociese, y así poder herirla.[60]
Como el deseo mancilló con engaño a la virginidad,
la ira, con engaño, destruyó el deseo.[61]
4. Tamar rasgó sus vestidos,
al ver que había perecido su perla.[62]
En lugar de su túnica, podía adquirirse otra,
pero no recuperar su virginidad,
pues, una vez robada,
no puede recuperarse de nuevo.
¡Ay, virginidad!
Tu destrucción es sencilla para todos,
pero crearte sólo le es fácil al Señor de todo.

58. "Tortas de corazones," *lebbawwātâ*. Es la palabra que emplea la Peshitta par denominar los pasteles que Amnón pide que le traiga Tamar, 2 Sam 13:5, 6, 8, 10. Pero *lebbawwātâ* es también el plural de *lebbâ*, "corazón," y tal vez se usaba para designar ese tipo de pasteles por su forma, o porque eran especialmente dulces, o apreciados. Efrén juega con el doble sentido del término. La versión trata de mantener el juego de palabras, pero es una glosa. Literalmente, podría traducirse: "Le pidió los corazones," "le llevó los corazones," sabiendo que "corazones" indica tanto un tipo de pasteles como el órgano que en el mundo semita se consideraba como la sede del pensamiento y de la actividad espiritual.

59. "Al que no tenía corazón," literalmente "carente de corazón," *šqîl lebbâ*. Traducimos así para conservar el juego de palabras del original. Pero la expresión siríaca no significa lo que "carente de corazón" sugiere en el español actual, esto es, "sin entrañas," "sin misericordia." Mas bien, teniendo en cuenta que el corazón era considerado como la sede del pensamiento, "carente de corazón" equivalía a "falto de razón," "loco." Tiene que ver, pues, con el término *šāṭyâ*, "loco," "fuera de sí," que la Peshitta emplea en 2 Sam 13:13.

60. La mención de la "mano" aquí llama un poco la atención. Dado que en el contexto se usa la palabra "serpiente," *ḥewyâ*, podría ser una alusión a Isa 11:8, que en la versión de la Peshitta dice: "Jugará el niño de pecho con la víbora, y el recién destetado extenderá su mano en la hura del áspid (aunque el vocabulario para "víbora" y para "áspid" es diferente en la Peshitta). Pero también en 2 Sam 13:5, 10, Amnón insiste en "comer de la mano" de Tamar.

61. La expresión no es del todo clara, sobre todo por la insistencia en que la ira destruyó con engaño el deseo. Si no fuera por esta referencia al engaño, podría pensarse que el texto alude al aborrecimiento que Amnón tuvo por Tamar tras haber abusado de ella, cf. 2 Sam 13:15. Pero la mención del engaño hace pensar más bien en la venganza de Absalón, hermano de Tamar, que invita a Amnón a un banquete para matarlo, cf. 2 Sam 13:23–29.

62. Cf. 2 Sam 13:19.

5. Tamar tenía temor de callar,
pero también hablar le daba vergüenza;
y como no podía callar,
ni tampoco hablar,
rasgó sus vestidos, para que los jirones visibles
gritasen en silencio que habían sido forzadas
sus señales ocultas de la virginidad.
Las muchas perlas que llevaba puestas no podían consolarla
de aquella sola perla, mayor que todas las demás.
6. La muchacha era una princesa,
y sus miembros llevaban toda clase de gemas;[63]
persó su virginidad, siendo sólo una,
les sobrepasaba a todas.
Por eso el impuro despreció las gemas,
y aró los sellos;[64]
desestimó las piedras preciosas, y robó las señales de la virginidad.
El ladrón conocía tu valor, virginidad;
Tú, en cambio, no te diste cuenta de lo preciosa que eras.
7. Él era un gladiador,
y al ver que no podía derribarla estando en pie,
se apresuró a echarse a tierra, para así derribarla.[65]
Rompió el yugo del matrimonio, y se abalanzó a la fornicación.[66]
Y la maldad que había sembrado en la alcoba,
la cosechó en el campo.[67]
La espada destruyó al que había destruido la virginidad,
y el que se había salpicado con la sangre de ella,
se bañó en su propia sangre.
8. Tanto en la alcoba como en el campo,
están a tú acecho,
virginidad;

63. "Gemas," literalmente, *berûlê,* "berilos." Y lo mismo más abajo, en el verso cinco.

64. "Aró los sellos," naturalmente, los "sellos" de la virginidad, en paralelismo con *btûlê,* "las señales de la virginidad" en el verso siguiente. Beck traduce de otro modo: "Darum verachtete der Unreine die Kleinode und verschmähte die Juwelen."

65. "Gladiador," *ʾatlîṭâ.* Efrén retoma la imagen del combate, a la que ya había recurrido en la estrofa 1, para describir la lucha desigual entre el raptor y la virgen. Sin duda el texto describe una estratagema de los gladiadores, pero aquí alude a la mentira de Amnón, que se echa en cama como si estuviera enfermo para atraer a Tamar.

66. Tamar, en 2 Sam 13:13, le suplica a Amnón que le pida al rey David en matrimonio, pero Amnón rehusa. Aunque *gawrâ* significa normalmente "adulterio," ése no puede ser aquí su sentido.

67. Nueva alusión a la venganza de Tamar por Absalón, que invita a Amnón a un banquete en el campo con motivo del esquilado de las ovejas, y le mata, cf. 2 Sam 13:23–29.

pues si entras en la alcoba,
el astuto Amnón robó tu riqueza;
pero si saliste al campo, si te refugiaste en el desierto,
Siquem, el ladrón, saqueó tu tesoro.[68]
¿Adónde irás entonces, paloma solitaria,
cuando por todas partes tantos son tus cazadores?

9. Mira, pudorosa: los cazadores que te cazaron
han sido a su vez cazados, y han recibido al revés su paga.
Al impuro Siquem, que te asaltó y te capturó en el campo,
lo mataron en su casa;[69]
y en cuanto a Amnón, que te dio caza emboscado en la alcoba,
lo destrozaron en el campo.[70]
Los que te destruyeron han sido destruidos,
y en ellos se dibuja un paradigma:[71]
que aquel que te destruye es destruido.

10. A la hija de Jefté,
que ofreció su cuello a la espada,
la consoló su perla,
que había escapado de todos los peligros,
y permanecía con ella.[72]
Pero a la que en esta vida pierde su perla,
la tristeza será su compañera a la hora de su muerte;
y en el día de la resurrección, también habrá temor
ante el Juez, aunque haya hecho penitencia.

11. La hija de Jefté
quería morir
para que se cumpliera el voto de su padre.

68. Cf. la historia del rapto y la violación de Dina, hija de Jacob, por Siquem, en Gen. 34:1–5. El texto bíblico no dice expresamente que el rapto tuviese lugar en el campo, pero sí que Dina "salió una vez a ver las mujeres del país" (v.1). El v. 5 informa, sin embargo, que cuando Jacob tuvo noticia de lo sucedido "sus hijos estaban con el ganado en el campo."

69. Cf. Gen. 34:25 s.

70. Cf. 2 Sam. 13:28 s.

71. "Paradigma," literalmenta *ṭûpsâ*, τύπος. Pero no parece oportuno traducir aquí *ṭûpsâ* por "esbozo." "Modelo" podra ser también adecuado.

72. Cf. Jc 11:29–40. Jefté hizo voto de ofrecer en holocausto a Yahveh, si le concedía la victoria, la primera persona de su casa que encontrase. Y a quien encontró fue a su hija virgen, su única descendencia. La hija se ofrece al sacrificio, pero pide "dos meses para ir a vagar por las montañas y llorar con mis compañeras mi virginidad," cf. v. 37. En Israel, morir sin descendencia era visto como una desgracia. La interpretación de S. Efrén supone una valoración distinta de la virginidad. "Peligros," en el verso 4, es *qent)în,* que vuelve a aparecer en el verso 8 en singular, y allí lo traducimos por "temor". El término tiene los dos significados, cf. Brockelmann, *Lexicon Syriacum* (1928, repr. ed. Hildesheim: Olms, 1982), 676.

No hagas inválido con tus ojos[73]
el voto que prometió tu boca.
Jefté derramó la sangre de su hija.
Como tu Esposo ha derramado su sangre por amor a ti,[74]
la sangre del Unigénito ha comprado[75]
esa otra sangre con la que tu puerta está sellada.[76]

12. La mujer casada también quería morir
para que no se consumase el adulterio.[77]
La virgen murió
para que se cumpliera el voto de su padre.
Si la madre de una prole legítima
quería morir
para no recibir una semilla robada, cuyo sembrador es maldito,
¡que la virgen no robe ocultamente una semilla impura,
pues es un niño puro el niño que está en su seno![78]

13. No concluyas tu carrera, mujer honorable,
en el desierto sin fin de los malos deseos,
para que tu vejez no sea objeto de burla
porque en tí ha trabajado tu enemigo,
te ha quitado tu fuerza,

73. Para la relación entre los ojos y la pureza, cf. himnos *De Ecclesia,* CSCO 198–99 (Louvain: Peeters, 1960), XXXIII, 1.

74. "Tu Esposo," es decir, Cristo. La idea de que Cristo es el esposo de las vírgenes es frecuentísima en S. Efrén. Cf., por ejemplo, los himnos *De Nativitate,* CSCO 186–87 (Louvain: Peeters, 1959), IV, 132; VIII, 21–22; XI, 2; XII, 6–5, 9–10; etc. También se halla en estos mismos himnos, más abajo, en III, 14–16.

75. "Unigénito," *'iḥîdāyâ.* Este término se uso en siríaco también para quienes habían escogido la virginidad a imitación de Cristo. Hay, pues, una correspondencia entre el "Unigénito" y la persona que ha consagrado a Dios su virginidad, y eso explica el uso de este título de Cristo en este contexto. Sobre el uso de este término en siríaco, cf. especialmente Griffith, "'Singles' in God's Service," 223–29.

76. La sangre de la menstruación. Cf. imágenes similares en los himnos *Contra Haereses,* CSCO 169–70 (Louvain: Peeters, 1957), XLVII, 1; *De Nativitate,* CSCO 186–87 (Louvain: Peeters, 1959), XIV, 12 y, sobre todo, *infra,* el himno *De Virginitate,* III, 14. *SdV* glosa y lee *dmâ btûlâ,* "la sangre virginal."

77. Se refiere a Susana, cf. Dan 13:1–64, especialmente v. 43. "También" es una glosa del traductor, sin correspondencia en el texto, para subrayar el paralelismo entre el comienzo de esta estrofa y el de la anterior.

78. La referencia es a Cristo, que mora en las vírgenes como en María, cf. además de las referencias a los himnos *De Nativitate* que se dan más arriba, en la nota 74, los himnos *De Virginitate,* CSCO 223–24 (Louvain: Peeters, 1962), XXV, 10 y los *Carmina Nisibena* II, CSCO 240–41 (Louvain: Peeters, 1963), XLVI, 1. McVey refiere el texto de estos dos últimos versos a la madre de Jesus, y ve en ellos una polémica contra quienes objetaban al nacimiento virginal de Jesús: "The Virgin [Mary] will not steal a defiled seed in secret, lest the pure Infant inside her be a lawless one." Sin duda McVey ha vocalizado *'awwālâ,* que en inglés puede ser traducido por "lawless," la primera de las dos veces que el texto consonántico tiene *'wl.* Aún con esa vocalización, la traducción parece imposible sintácticamente. A mi juicio, es preferible leer *'ûlâ,* "feto" (en la versión, "niño").

y ha vaciado tu fuente.[79]
Con tu mala carrera has guardado la vergüenza para tu vejez:
¡Juventud, aligera tu marcha en la competición,[80]
para que la corona adorne tu vejez!

14. Cuando uno envejece y se vuelve deforme
las gentes recuerdan sus nobles caminos de juventud[81]
y aunque aborrecen su vejez
por causa de los achaques que lleva consigo,
le quieren, a él y a los achaques de su cuerpo,
porque ven los ornamentos del Espíritu
ocultos en su alma.
¡Plasma tus proezas, virginidad, en tus miembros,[82]
para que seas honrada por ellas cuando hayas envejecido!

15. Que la modestia esté pintada en tus ojos,
y en tus oídos el sonido de la Verdad;
marca tu lengua con la Palabra de Vida,
y pon en tus manos toda clase de limosnas;
marca tus huellas visitando a los enfermos,
y que la imagen de tu Señor esté pintada en tu corazón.
Si los dípticos son honrados[83]

79. Los versos 3–6 están cambiados de orden en la versión española para que aparezca con más claridad el flujo del pensamiento. La mujer es comparada a un campo, como lo había sido ya en la estrofa anterior: la imagen es tradicional. En la que se ha dejado llevar por sus malos deseos, ha trabajado su enemigo, esto es, Satán. Él es quien "te ha quitado tu fuerza," quizás la de la virginidad, "y ha vaciado tu fuente," quizás la de la menstruación. "Para tu vejez," en siríaco, *lāh,* "para ella." El antecedente es *saybûtâ,* "vejez," en el verso anterior. En toda esta estrofa, nuestra comprensión del texto difiere de la de McVey.

80. "Competición" traduce *'agûnâ,* retornando a la imaginería de las estrofas 1 y 7, aunque aquí tiene el término tiene un sentido y un contexto distintos.

81. "Las gentes" es una glosa para explicitar el sujeto de los verbos que siguen, implícito en el texto siríaco: "recuerdan," "aborrecen," "le quieren," "ven."

82. "Plasma," literalmente, "pinta," "dibuja." La estrofa siguente explicitará cómo las "proezas" de la virginidad "están pintadas" en los miembros del cuerpo. Las metáforas de la "pintura" y la "imagen" son muy queridas de Efrén, que recurre a ellas con frecuencia, cf. Sidney H. Griffith, "The Image of the Image Maker in the Poetry of St. Ephraem the Syrian," en *Studia Patristica* XXV (Louvain: Peeters, 1993), 258–69. En cuanto al término *regšê* significa, literalmente, "sentidos," pero con frecuencia hay que traducirlo por "miembros," cf. E. Beck, *Ephräm des Syrers Psychologie und Erkenntnislehre,* CSCO 419 (Louvain: Peeters, 1980), 18–20. De hecho, la estrofa no menciona tanto los sentidos propiamente dichos cuanto los órganos en que tienen los sentidos tienen su sede: el ojo, el oído, las manos y la lengua, sede del sentido "logikon" o la capacidad de hablar. En cuanto a los pies, no son sede de ninguno de los sentidos clásicos, pero sí miembros en paralelismo con las manos del verso anterior.

83. "Los dípticos," *dappê,* propiamente "tablas pintadas." Se refiere, casi con seguridad, a los llamados "dípticos imperials," cf. H. Leclercq, "Diptyques (archéologie)," *Dictionnaire d'archéologie chrétienne et de liturgie,* vol. 4.1 (Paris: Letouzey et Ané, 1920), 1094–170; A. Cutler, "Diptych," *The Oxford Dictionary of*

Por la imagen del rey que hay en ellos,
¡cuanto mas aquél cuyo Señor está pintado en todos sus miembros![84]

El Himno III

Con la misma melodía[85]

1. La juventud se parece
a la rama de un árbol frutal,
gloriosa en el verano,
pero despreciada una vez despojada de sus frutos.
Todos vuelven la cabeza ante ella,
y a todos los parece fea
la que antes era deseada por encima de todo.
Muchacha, no muestres a los extraños tu belleza,
para que quienes la ven no la desprecien cuando esté desfigurada.[86]

Responsorio: De todo el que ha luchado y conservado su virginidad,
¡alabanza a ti, Señor, y a tu Cristo!

2. ¡Qué livianas son tus alas, virginidad,[87]
que han alcanzado a tu Señor!
Huye del consejo de tu enemigo,
cuyo capital ha hundido a los que negociaron con él.[88]
El arruinó los tesoros del gran Adán,[89]

Byzantium, 3 vols. (Oxford: Oxford University Press, 1991), 636–37. Si esta interpretación es correcta, no sólo tendríamos aquí la única referencia literaria que conocemos a los dípticos imperiales, sino también la mas antigua a dípticos de cualquier clase: las otras dos referencias literarias antiguas que menciona Cutler son a S. Juan Crisóstomo, *Homiliae VI in illud: Vidi dominum* (Isa 6:1), cf. *PG* 56.110, por lo tanto, ligeramente posterior a S. Efrén, y a Quodvultdeus, *De gloria regnoque sanctorum,* 16, cf. CCL 60 (Turnhout: Brepols, 1976), 220:32–35, por lo tanto, en Cartago del siglo V.

84. De nuevo, "miembros" traduce *regšê,* como en la estrofa anterior. Cf. supra nota 82.

85. El MS E lee: "Tercero del mismo (himno), con la misma melodía."

86. Los dos últimos versos son una invitación a ocultar la belleza, tal vez mediante el uso del velo y de la modestia en el vestir. "Extraños," literalmente, "a los de fuera." Probablemente son llamados así por contraste con Cristo, que el final del himno presenta como el verdadero esposo de las vírgenes.

87. Leyendo con el MS E. El MS B lee: "virgin." En la observación del verso 2, de que la virginidad "ha alcanzado a su Señor," puede haber, a la luz del contexto que sigue, una alusión a la falsa promesa de Satán en la tentación del Paraíso: "Seréis como dioses," cf. Gen. 3:5.

88. "Tu enemigo" es Satán, representado aquí como un prestamista que parece ayudar, pero arruina a los que acuden a él.

89. La "grandeza" de Adán es descrita en términos de realeza en los himnos *De Paradiso,* CSCO 174–75 (Louvain: Peeters, 1957), XIII, 3–4.

que gracias a él se ganó una carga de miserias.
No le pidas prestado,
pues aunque presta sin reclamar la deuda,
le arruinas si le devuelves su dinero.
3. A sus malos deseos les acompañan
vergüenza y temor grande,
y dan inquietud y tristeza
a quienes los ponen por obra, para toda su vida.
Claros y puros, en cambio, son los rostros
de los castos, que se abstienen de todo mal deseo.
No te dejes cautivar, cuerpo,
por el mal amor,
que, aunque su obra está ya muerta, su ansiedad vive.[90]
4. El Maligno es astuto en su enseñanza,
para hacerse, él también,
todo con todos.[91]
El derrama su don sobre los miembros:[92]
soborna al vientre y el vientre se deja sobornar por él;
al ojo, para que aparte la mirada; a la boca, para que calle;
al oído, para que deje pasar sus feas historias.
Su silencioso vino se hace locuaz en quienes lo beben;
y canta canciones de borrachos en vez de las de su Señor.[93]
5. En su astucia, pone por delante,
a la boca de su trampa, cebo para la presa;
su amor va por delante de su odio,
como en Judas, que primero besó y luego mató.[94]

90. "Su obra está muerta." La expresión *'bādāh mît* recuereda a "las obras muertas," *'bādê mîtê,* de Heb. 6:1; 9:14. Allí se refiere a las "obras" que provienen del pecado y conducen a la muerte. El contexto, sin embargo, da aquí un matiz diferente a la expresión. La idea parece ser que, aunque la "obra," el poner por obra los deseos carnales, haya acabado, la ansiedad y el temor que le siguen permanecen.

91. "El Maligno," es una glosa mía para explicitar el sujeto. La construcción del segundo verso es idéntica a la que la Peshitta emplea en 1 Cor. 9:22: "me hice débil con los débiles," *hwît 'am krîhê 'a(y)k krîhâ.* El Maligno se presenta, pues, como un ministro y un apóstol, un auxilio aparente para el hombre, pero que en vez de auxiliarlo, lo destruye.

92. "Los miembros," conjetura de Beck sin apoyo textual, probablemente en función del contexto y de un cierto paralelismo con II, 15. El texto, tanto en el MS B como en *SdV* lee: "derrama su don sobre los buenos (*ṭābê*)," lo que obviamente ha de ser un error. El texto siríaco que supone la conjetura es *regšê,* "sentidos," "miembros," en lugar de *ṭābê* (sobre el sentido de *regšê,* cf. supra, nota 82). En todo caso, el Maligno es aquí pintado en cierto modo como imitador de Dios, que también "derrama su don (= su Espíritu)," pero los frutos son diferentes.

93. La frase final no es del todo clara. El texto siríaco dice simplemente "canta las canciones de ellos." Pero parece que ese "ellos" debe referirse a "quienes lo beben" del verso anterior.

94. Cf. Matt. 26:47–50, para el episodio del beso de Judas.

El Puro besó al impuro Judas,
para proclamar, por medio de Judas, al Maligno:
aunque sus seducciones son dulces,
como lo era el beso de Judas,
la muerte, ocultamente, está mezclada en ellas.

6. Así es éste: si él se levanta en tí,
con lo que puede pagarte es con una caída,
pues en cuanto él se levanta, te tira a tí por tierra.
Su deseo está muerto, amigo mío,
pero tu carne es capaz de darle vida
y de resucitarlo;
y, tan pronto como vive en ella, se revuelve y la mata.
Cuerpo, si tú das vida a su muerte,
también él será la muerte de tu vida.[95]

7. Que sea para ti un ejemplo el fuego:
está enterrado y muerto en el leño,
pero la fricción de un leño con otro
le da la vida, y así perecen los dos.[96]
Cuando ha revivido, en efecto,
se revuelve para quemar
la sustancia que le hizo revivir con su contacto.
¡Qué imagen! El leño se ha hecho sepultura para el fuego,
pero si el fuego es reavivado, el leño se consume con él.[97]

8. Nuestra libertad es, pues, como un alma[98]
para los malos deseos, y viven gracias a ella;
pero si ella los rechaza, se quedan como muertos.

95. Toda la idea de la estrofa es que el Maligno, y el mal deseo que el pone en el hombre, están como muertos, pero si reviven, es para matar al hombre. Si él se alza, es para derribar al hombre. La imaginería de la estrofa siguiente ilumina sobre todo la frase "su deseo está muerto," que es la que resulta menos clara. Probablemente hay que entenderla en un doble sentido: por una parte, se trata de un deseo "de muerte," es decir, que nace de la muerte y conduce a la muerte. Por otra, es un deseo "muerto," que sólo revive si lo resucita la libertad del hombre.

96. Para esta imagen, cf. los himnos *De Fide,* CSCO 154–55 (Louvain: Peeters, 1955), LXV, 8.

97. En el último verso, la traducción explicita los sujetos implícitos en el texto siríaco, muy elíptico, pero que en siríaco no ofrece dificultad, ya que "leño" es masculino y "fuego" es femenino, de modo que las formas verbales expresan el sujeto. Para la segunda parte del verso, "éste es consumido por él," sigo el texto del *SdV,* que parece más coherente. En la variante del MS B, el sufijo (en el que se ha omitido el punto indicativo del femenino) parece indicar que es el fuego el que se consume "por" o "con" el leño, lo cual no da un sentido satisfactorio.

98. "Alma," *napšâ.* La imagen se explica porque el alma es el principio de vida, y sin ella el cuerpo muere. Pero también porque *napšâ* designa originalmente el "aliento," el "soplo de vida." El término se deriva de la raíz *npeš,* que significa "respirar." Así la imagen continua en cierto modo la de la estrofa anterior. También el fuego se atiza "soplando."

Ella es la que gobierna;
que por su voluntad permanecen las culpas,
y por su voluntad caen los pecados.
Ella es como el Altísimo,
cuyo poder sostiene el universo,
y si Él lo retirara, todo se vendría abajo.[99]

9. Nuestro Juez, en efecto, es muy justo,
pues no nos reclama nuestras deudas al momento,
y precisamente por eso viene el remordimiento.[100]
Si el hombre hizo penitencia, el remordimiento borró su iniquidad;
pero si se resistió,
entonces le quitó su posibilidad de excusa.
Por ello, en todas nuestras culpas[101]
está el remordimiento observando,
para llevar al tribunal su testimonio.[102]

10. Hazte con la penitencia, que es estable,
y no con ese remordimiento que sobreviene a todas horas;
pues la penitencia
cura nuestras llagas con su constancia,
mientras que el remordimiento tiene la propiedad
de estar siempre construyendo y destruyendo los dolores.
Si te habituas, cuerpo,
a arrepentirte y a volver a pecar,
el sello de tu cuenta será el remordimiento.[103]

99. "Las culpas," *ḥawbê,* literalmente, "las deudas," en arameo, una imagen habitual para "los pecados." El término está, pues, en paralelismo con *ḥṭāhê,* "pecados," en el verso siguiente. El fuerte subrayado del poder de la libertad (cf. también *supra,* I, 9) procede de una teología anterior a la controversia pelagiana, y es también coherente con la defensa de la libertad que S. Efrén tiene que hacer frente a las doctrinas gnósticas, cf. T. Bou Mansour, "La liberté chez Saint Ephrem le Syrien," *Parole de l'Orient* 11 (1983): 89–156; 12 (1984/1985): 3–89; "La défense éphrémienne de la liberté contre les doctrines marcionite, bardesanite et manichéenne," *OCP* 50 (1984): 331–46; "Aspects de la liberté humaine chez Saint Ephrem le Syrien," *Ephemerides Theologicae Lovanienses* 60 (1984): 252–82.

100. "El remordimiento," *twāt napšâ.* S. Efrén lo distingue aquí de la penitencia, *tyābûtâ,* que designa probablemente la institución penitencial de la Iglesia. El remordimiento puede conducir a la penitencia, y entonces es reparador, pero si no lo es, se vuelve un testigo que acusa al hombre de su pecado. Cf. infra, estrofa 10. Sobre el remordimiento pueden verse también los himnos De Paradiso VII, 24 y XIV, 14.

101. En vez de "nuestras culpas," *ḥawbayn,* literalmente, "nuestras deudas" (cf. supra, nota 99), puede leerse también simplemente "las culpas," *ḥawbîn.*

102. El tribunal es el del juicio tras la muerte del hombre, al que se está refiriendo toda la estrofa. Es esa perspectiva la que explica los perfectos de los versos 4–6, porque en el juicio la vida del hombre se contempla en pasado.

103. "Tu cuenta," *'eštārāk,* literalmente, "tu documento," pero se refiere claramente al *'eštār ḥawbê,* a la "nota de cargo" de nuestras "deudas," es decir, de nuestros pecados. Es la misma expresión que usa la

11. Guárdate, ojo, de robar
una belleza en la que están ocultos los achaques de la vejez;
los miembros de una joven, en efecto,
tienen un hermoso aspecto,
pero la vejez los castiga,[104]
pues sólo una belleza prestada vivía en ellos;
una belleza que, aunque pone su morada
en el rostro de la juventud,
enseguida alzó el vuelo y se fue.

12. Tu perla se pierde volando
también entre dos ladrones,
pues pertenece a los mercaderes solitarios;[105]
y cuando se han mancillado, los dos han perdido
el tesoro que es mayor que todo.
Pero el necio le ofrece al ladrón
ese tesoro con sus propias manos.
¡Ay, perla, que si su dueño la pierde,
tampoco se queda en el tesoro del ladrón!

13. Cuando una virgen es deshonrada en el campo,
Moisés habla en su favor,
si la joven llamó a gritos
y no pudo hallar auxilio.[106]
Pero en favor tuyo, virginidad,
¿quién se pronunciará,

Peshitta en Col 2:14: Cristo "canceló *la nota de cargo* que había contra nosotros ... clavándola en la cruz." Aquí, en cambio, la idea es que el remordimiento sin penitencia lo que hace es "sellar" la nota de cargo, de forma que no pueda ser alterada, y que testifique contra nosotros en el juicio final.

104. "Los castiga" es un intento de traducir *makksâ,* que resulta un término un poco extraño en el contexto. Pues *'akkes* tiene el sentido de "acusar," "reprobar," y no se ve con claridad qué quiere decir que la vejez "reprueba" los miembros jóvenes. Se está tentado de leer *maksyâ bhûn dên hî saybûtâ,* "pero está oculta en ellos la vejez," lo que supondría una mínima corrección al texto consonántico siríaco. Cf. el participio *kseyn,* "están ocultos," en el verso 2 de la estrofa.

105. La primera parte de la estrofa, donde se dice que la virginidad "pertenece a los mercaderes solitarios," podría entenderse en el sentido de una invitación a la vida eremítica, al estilo del monacato posterior. El *SdV* glosa el termino "solitario," *mšawḥdâ,* con el de *'iḥîdāyâ,* término que en la literatura siríaca antigua designaba a los célibes, pero que con el tiempo vino a ser sinónimo de μοναχός. Cf. supra, nota 47. Y es muy probable que quienes han transmitido el texto lo hayan entendido precisamente así, como una invitación a la vida solitaria, apartada del "mundo" de la comunidad cristiana. Aunque es evidente que la estrofa debe leerse en el contexto de los abusos que S. Efrén quiere corregir, el texto no necesita ser entendido como propuesta de una forma de vida, sino que es más bien un reclamo a las condiciones que permiten vivir la virginidad, y más en concreto a evitar la convivencia de célibes de ambos sexos. En todo caso, el énfasis de la estrofa está sobre todo en la afirmación de que también quien "roba" la virginidad la pierde.

106. Cf. Deut. 22:25–27.

si fuiste cautivada en la tierra habitada y callaste?[107]
No te entreges a la cautividad en la tierra habitada,
para que la tierra habitada no te acuse en el juicio.
14. Está escrito que si un hombre calumnia a la mujer,[108]
el padre de ella debe sacar las señales de su virginidad.[109]
Como tu Esposo es el Altísimo,
que ve en lo secreto,
¡muestra en lo secreto a tu Señor invisible
las ocultas señales de tu virginidad,
no en un paño, sino en tu cuerpo!
Las mujeres calumniadas mostraban las señales en un paño,
¡muestra tú misma a tu Esposo las señales de tu virginidad![110]
15. Cuídate de no perder a tu Esposo,
para ir a ganarte un esposo falso en su lugar.[111]
Por más que digas para consolarte:
"he perdido uno, pero he encontrado otro,"
su amor es engañoso y fraudulento,
y va de flor en flor.
No puede acompañarte.[112]

107. "Fuiste cautivada": para obtener el sentido pasivo, el único que admite el contexto, hay que vocalizar leyendo el participio pasivo de *šbâ* con el pronombre enclítico de segunda persona femenino singular, *šābeyk.* Así lo entiende también el *SdV,* que glosa con el participio del *'etp'el,* y lee *meštbyat(y).* "La tierra habitada" es *šaynâ,* que en siríaco tiene el doble sentido de "tierra cultivada" y de "paz," por oposición al desierto, tierra de desolación y de destrucción (*ḥûrbâ*). S. Efrén, en el verso 1, no emplea para desierto *ḥûrbâ,* sino *dabrâ,* que significa también "desierto," pero tiene más bien la connotación de "campo abierto." Pero el poeta juega en la estrofa con los dos sentidos del término *šaynâ,* ya que es una paradoja ser cautivada "en el lugar de la paz." El juego de palabras es imposible de traducir al español.

108. Se entiende que quien calumnia a la mujer es su marido, que tras casarse con ella la acusa de que no ser virgen al serle entregada.

109. Cf. Deut. 22:14–17.

110. La valoración de las pruebas de la virginidad—la sangre de la menstruación—en este pasaje, lo mismo que más arriba en II, 11 o en el himno *De Nativitate* XII, CSCO 186–87 (Louvain: Peeters, 1959), refleja la sensibilidad tradicional del mundo judío, conservada tal vez en las comunidades cristianas de Mesopotamia. Con todo, Efrén apunta a una interiorización de esta vieja prescripción: lo importante es que Dios, que ve en lo oculto, tenga conocimiento de la virginidad.

111. Las reflexiones de esta estrofa son unas advertencias a las vírgenes, esposas de Cristo (cf. supra, estrofa 14; y también II, 11 y la nota 74), que ponen en peligro su virginidad, y son infieles a su voto. El trasfondo es el mismo al que S. Efrén parece haberse estado refiriendo a lo largo de los himnos: vírgenes que convivían con personas de otro sexo, bien seglares o célibes también, y que por ello terminaban abandonando su voto.

112. "Va de flor en flor" traduce *šaken 'al koll,* literalmente, "se posa en todo." La traducción es una conjetura del probable sentido de la expresión siríaca. Esta lleva consigo la connotación de algo pasajero, como la abeja "se posa" en las flores momentáneamente. La idea aparece subrayada en el verso siguiente con el verbo *lwâ,* "acompañar": "No puede acompañarte," tal vez en el sentido de que "no permanece contigo

Y entonces aumentará en ti el remordimiento,
cuando hayas sido abandonada por las dos partes.
16. Has sido abandonada por el Fiel[113]
porque tú le abandonaste a Él,
y el engañoso te ha dejado tirada,
extraviada por los caminos.[114]
¿Adónde se volverá ahora tu mirada,
paloma que desmanteló su nido
y se fue por amor a la serpiente?
No hagas también tú el descubrimiento de Eva,[115]
que no encontrarás en él sino pesadumbre.[116]

Fin de los tres himnos sobre la virginidad.

---

para siempre," a diferencia del Señor. O tal vez simplemente S. Efrén supone que el falso esposo, posiblemente ligado por otros vínculos, no podrá ser fiel.

113. "Fiel," o "Verdadero," *šarrîrâ*. Se refiere a Cristo, el verdadero esposo de las vírgenes.

114. "En los caminos," *bêt 'ûrḥātâ*. La misma expresión se halla en *De Nativitate* IX, 13, para referirse al lugar en que Tamar salió al encuentro de Judá, cf. Gen. 38:14, 21. Indica, pues, el lugar de las prostitutas.

115. Se refiere, naturalmente al descubrimiento de que el pecado no conduce a ser como dioses, sino a la tierra de las zarzas y las espinas, y a los dolores de parto, y a la desnudez del vestido de gloria que Adán y Eva tenían en el Paraiso, y que perdió con el pecado. Cf., por ejemplo, el himno *De Paradiso* III, 6–10; XII, 3. Hay en siríaco un juego de palabras entre *ḥewyâ*, "serpiente," y *ḥawwâ*, "Eva."

116. "Pesadumbre" traduce aquí *twāt napšâ*, que en el resto del himno hemos traducido por "remordimiento."

PART II

TEXTS, TERMS, METAPHORS

Gary A. Anderson

3. REDEEM YOUR SINS THROUGH WORKS OF CHARITY

In the fourth chapter of the Book of Daniel, King Nebuchadnezzar has a dream and the prophet Daniel is summoned to give an interpretation. In this dream, a tree, abundant in foliage and rich in fruit, rises up in the midst of the earth, providing shade to the animals below and a domicile for the birds above. But then, quite abruptly, a Holy Watcher descends and announces that the tree is to be torn down, and only a stump left in its place. The king is to be fettered to it and spend such time as it would take for his mind to leave the realm of the human and enter the domain of the animal. This punishment is to last for "seven seasons" in order to teach Nebuchadnezzar that the "Most High is sovereign over the realm of man and He gives it to whom he wishes" (Dan 4:22).[1]

But the matter has not been irrevocably decreed. Daniel intervenes to add an admonition to the king that was not present in the dream: "Therefore, O king, redeem your sins by beneficence and your iniquities by generosity to the poor; then your serenity may be extended" (4:24). In this surprising line, Daniel

I offer this essay in tribute to Sidney Griffith in view of the numerous conversations we have had over the use of the root *ḥâb* in the writings of St. Ephrem in particular, but in Syriac Christianity more generally. There this root, which means "to fall into debt," is used to depict the state of fallen humanity. The robust development of this metaphor in Syriac thought would require a lengthy monograph. I hope that this essay will be a first step toward that end.

1. The numeration of the verses follows the order of the Masoretic text. For the most part the translations in this essay are drawn from the *NJPS*. Minor alterations have occasionally been introduced as needed.

offers the king the chance to forestall his appointed doom—redeem your sins by beneficence, he exhorts, and your imminent punishment can be kept at bay.

I

But what is meant by Daniel's offer of mercy to this haughty ruler? Or, more specifically, what have the "works of beneficence" to do with the power "to redeem sin"? James Montgomery, in his ICC commentary on Daniel, compared this verse with the "rough gospel of repentance" that Jonah offered the Ninevites.[2] But the differences are significant. First of all, Jonah makes no offer of repentance; his word is solely that of doom. Second, there is no attempt taken by the Ninevites to undo their sinful state; rather they don sackcloth and ashes in the *hope* (and no more than that) that God might relent and turn away from his wrathful intentions in spite of their sin.

Daniel, on the other hand, offers much more than just hope; his words are more like that of a promise: do acts of beneficence and your sins will be redeemed. As Montgomery notes, this startling formula has been a *locus classicus* between Catholic and Protestant interpreters over the centuries. As Matthew Pole put the matter in his own tart fashion in 1694: "*Pontificii* [i.e. Papists] *ex hoc loco satisfactiones suas et merita colligunt.*"[3] We can loosely translate: The Papists gather from this verse their notions of satisfaction and merits. In no small part the dispute has centered on two terms within this verse: *ṣidqâ* and *peruq.* Catholics have preferred to translate the former "almsgiving" and the latter, "redeem," whereas Protestants (going back to Calvin!) have tended to prefer "righteousness" and "break-off." In the course of this essay I hope to clarify what is at stake in the translation of the verb *peruq.* But to orient this discussion properly let us begin with the problem of *ṣidqâ.*

II

In 1950, Franz Rosenthal, the noted scholar of Aramaic, argued that the noun *ṣidqâ* in Dan 4:24 is best translated "almsgiving" and asserted that the

2. J. Montgomery, *Daniel,* ICC (Edinburgh: T. & T. Clark, 1927), 239.

3. As cited in Montgomery, *Daniel,* 239.

best evidence for this was the parallel term found in the same verse: "showing generosity toward the poor."[4] As such, Rosenthal observed, this was the earliest usage of the term in this way. In a more recent article, Avi Hurwitz has shown how this meaning emerged within the biblical corpus.[5] He begins his argument by surveying the peculiar use of the root *ḥ-n-n* ("generosity")—the term that stands in parallelism to *ṣidqâ* in Dan. 4:2—in a set of materials from Proverbs and Psalms:

> The wicked man borrows and does the repay;
> The righteous gives generously ... (*ḥônen we-nôten*). (Ps 37:21)
>
> He is always lending generously (*ḥônen û-malveh*);
> His children are held blessed. (Ps 37:26)
> May no one show him mercy;
> May no one be generous (*ḥônen*) to his orphans. (Ps 109:12)
>
> ... he is gracious (*ḥanûn*), compassionate, and beneficent;
> All goes well with him who lends generously (*hônen û-malveh*)
> (Ps 112:4–5)
>
> He who despises his fellow is wrong;
> He who is generous (*meḥônen*) to the lowly is happy. (Prov 14:21)
>
> He who withholds what is due to the poor affronts his maker;
> He who is generous (*ḥônen*) to the needy, honors Him. (Prov 14:31)
>
> He who is generous (*ḥônen*) to the downtrodden makes a loan to the Lord;
> He will repay him his due. (Prov. 19:17)

"The common point," Hurwitz writes, "amid all these texts is that the display of generosity is in reference to the poor, lowly, downtrodden, or orphans.... On these grounds it is clear that the generosity spoken of here is not merely the showing of mercy as it normally is in the Bible. Rather the emphasis is on material assistance to the poor."[6] It would be difficult indeed, to separate this specific set of usages of the root *ḥ-n-n* from what is documented in Dan 4:24 when Nebuchadnezzar is enjoined to be "generous toward the poor."

4. F. Rosenthal, "*Ṣedeḳah,* Charity," *HUCA* 23 (1950/51): 411–30.

5. Avi Hurwitz, "*Reshitam Ha-Miqra'it shel Munahim Talmudiyyim—Le-Toledot Tsemihato shel Musag Ha-'Sedaqah,*" in *Mehqarim be-Lashon,* 2–3 (Jerusalem: Center for Jewish Studies, 1987), 155–60 [Hebrew].

6. Hurwitz, "*Reshitam Ha-Miqra'it shel Munahim Talmudiyyim,*" 156–57.

And just as striking is the fact that another set of texts, again taken from the Psalms deploys the term *ṣedaqâ* in similar fashion. Indeed, to make precisely this point, the *NJPS* translation renders this term "benefience" a number of times.

> Wealth and riches are in his house,
> And his *righteousness* last forever. (Ps 112:3)
>
> He gives freely to the poor,
> His *righteousness* lasts forever. (Ps 112:9)
>
> Ill-gotten wealth is of no avail,
> But *righteousness* saves from death. (Prov 10:2)
>
> Wealth is of no avail on the day of wrath
> But *righteousness* saves from death. (Prov 11:14)

In all these texts the term *ṣedaqâ* has a striking overlap with its later Mishnaic sense of "almsgiving." Clearly there was a firm linguistic ground upon which the later usage was shaped. As Hurwitz explains, this phenomenon provides us with a witness "that in these two terms, a parallel semantic development has taken place which finds expression in the books of Psalms and Proverbs alone and does not include the Bible as a whole. Alongside this, the fact that this process is attested in Rabbinic literature clearly teaches us that we are not dealing with a matter of stylistic variation."[7] No longer can we see the use of *ṣedaqâ* in these texts as simply a matter of poetic license; what these texts provide is solid evidence of an emerging line of linguistic development.

One half of our puzzle has now been solved. Nebuchadnezzar is not urged simply to be a generous and righteous person. His task is far more specific: he must give alms to those less fortunate than he. But what then of the verbal element of this puzzle—*peruq*? Should we render it "to break off" or "redeem [one's sins by almsgiving]"?

III

To get a handle on this problem we must step back for a moment and consider how language for forgiveness works in the Bible. As Baruch Schwartz has documented, the Bible contains a rich font of metaphors for the notion of for-

7. Hurwitz, "*Reshitam Ha-Miqra'it shel Munahim Talmudiyyim,*" 159–60.

giveness.[8] Two of the most prominent in the First Temple period are those of sins as a stain from which one must be washed clean, and sin as a burden that one must carry around until God or an offended party removes it. Accordingly, the verbs that are deployed by Biblical writers to illustrate forgiveness resonate very closely with these underlying metaphors. Stains are not forgiven, they are "washed away" or "whitened." Burdens are not atoned for; they are "unloaded" or "carried into the wilderness."

In the Second Temple period—or better, perhaps already at the close of the First Temple period—the metaphor of sin as burden is replaced by another idiom altogether, that of sin as debt.[9] And it should occasion no surprise that this idiom of sin as debt and forgiveness as debt-release has left its footprint in the Targums. In this literature, everywhere we have the Hebrew phrase "to *bear away* a sin" in a context of forgiveness, we find the Aramaic idiom "to *absolve* a debt." The point to be emphasized here is that the most commonly used term in Aramaic for forgiveness (*š̌-b-q*) literally means "to absolve [a debt]."[10]

This linguistic move is not simply that of the Aramaic Targum; it is equally well-grounded in Rabbinic Hebrew. In the Mishnah one who is at fault is said to be *ḥayyaḇ,* that is, in possession of a particular *ḥob*—debt—that must be repaid by the sinner or remitted by the offended party.[11] Schwartz writes, "The sin-

8. Baruch Schwartz, "'Term' or Metaphor: Biblical *nasa avôn,*" *Tarbiz* 63 (1994): 149–71 [Hebrew]. Also see Schwartz, "The Bearing of Sin in Priestly Literature," in D. Wright, D. N. Freedman, and A. Hurwitz, eds., *Pomegranates and Golden Bells,* FS Jacob Milgrom (Winona Lake, Ind.: Eisenbrauns, 1995), 3–21.

9. The *TDNT* (5:561–62), though marred by overt anti-Jewish sensibilities, captures the shift well: "Later Judaism, which views the relation to God as a legal and business relation, often applies the metaphor of indebtedness to the ethical and religious relation between man and God.... Each transgression means indebtedness to the God who has given the Law. In heaven men's acts are entered into an account book and the final reckoning decides whether the fulfillments of the Law or the transgressions are in the ascendancy. "Because the individual is judged by the majority (i.e., of his works)..., man always appears to be in part righteous (*zakkay*) and in part guilty (*ḥayyaḇ*). If he keeps a commandment, well with him, for he has... inclined the scale on the side of merit." (T. Qid 1.14) It should be noted that what is said here is not only true for Rabbinic Judaism but also Syriac-speaking Christianity. The crucial variable in this new understanding of sin is not "Judaism" but rather Aramaic idiom.

10. Strikingly, the cognate verb in Rabbinic Hebrew, *m-ḥ-l* and its related noun *meḥilâ,* follows a somewhat similar semantic path. H. L. Fleischer suggested on semantic grounds that this word should be derived from a root *ḥ-l-l* meaning "to free or loose someone [from a debt or other obligation]." Fleischer's suggestion can be found in his additions to the dictionary of J. Levy, *Wörterbuch über die Talmudim und Midraschim* (Leipzig: 1876–79), 3:308. Kutscher (*Arke-Ha-Milon He-Hadash le-Sifrut Hazal* [Jerusalem: 1972], 1:5) later substantiated this hypothesis on more solid philological grounds

11. This verbal root, along with its nominal derivatives, probably derive originally from Aramaic.

ner is said to be *ḥayyaḇ,* that is, in a state of indebtedness in Rabbinic Hebrew, because he must repay. The one who owes a sin-offering or a reparation offering must pay with that form of sacrifice; the one who owes a beating must pay with a lashing of his body; the one who owes death must pay with his life; and the one who owes *karet* must pay after his death."[12] No doubt it is this image that informs the diction of the Lord's prayer ("forgive us our debts"), and the content of several parables in which Jesus compares the sinner to a debtor (e.g., Matt 18:23–35).[13] These images, which are the stock-in-trade of the Gospel narratives, are without parallel in the Hebrew of the First Temple period.

Given this background, it is hard not to place the usage of the root *p-r-q* within the realm of monetary obligations. As we noted above, the root could be rendered "to break off," but such a translation would be quite difficult to relate to the general tenor of almgiving that we documented in the books of Psalms and Proverbs and the tendency in the Second Temple period to frame the forgiveness of sin in terms of release from debt. On the other hand, if we translate the term "to redeem"—a meaning well attested for this root—the metaphor makes elegant sense of the diction in Dan 4:24. In this case, the sinner is given the chance to accumulate merits (what will be known as *zekût* in later Rabbinic parlance) and so "pay off" his indebtedness.[14]

Indeed, if this is the sense of the metaphor, then we have a nice counterpart

---

Indeed, the whole move toward such a commercial idiom is probably, at origin, the result of a borrowing from Assyrian-Aramean usage. On the influence of these words on Mishnaic Hebrew, see E. Kutscher, *Words and Their History* (Jerusalem: Kiryat Sefer, 1961) [Hebrew]. On the importance of Aramaic as a conduit of legal metaphors and their influence on Rabbinic religion, see Y. Muffs, *Love and Joy: Law, Language and Religion in Ancient Israel* (New York: Jewish Theological Seminary, 1992), 121–93.

12. Schwartz, "'Term' or Metaphor," 153.

13. Nearly all scholars would concede that this line of the Lord's Prayer makes best sense when we assume a Semitic background. Raymond Brown ("The Pater Noster as an Eschatological Prayer," in *New Testament Essays* [Milwaukee, Wis.: Bruce, 1965], 244) puts the matter thus: "The Matthean use of 'debts' has a Semitic flavor; for, while in secular Greek 'debt' has no religious coloring, in Aramaic *hoba* is a financial and commercial term that has been caught up into the religious vocabulary.... The idea of remitting (*aphienai*) debts which appears in our petition is also more Semitic than Greek, for 'remission' has a religious sense only in the Greek of the LXX, which is under Hebrew influence."

14. It is worth drawing attention to Matt. 6:1–3. Here Jesus warns against practicing one's piety before others (v. 1); such persons will be without reward. There seems little doubt that the piety being spoken of here is specifically that of giving alms (v. 2), an action that Jesus declares carries with it the possibility of reward if it is carried out properly. For later Syriac Christians, informed by the underlying Aramaic images of this verse, such good deeds constituted the wealth of good works that filled out one's treasure in heaven (Matt. 6:19–21). The deeds of the Saints were so numerous that those of more pedestrian piety could "draw on" their merits in order to counterbalance the debt of their sins.

to another means of imagining the forgiveness of sin in the late biblical period: that of paying off one's sins by undergoing bodily punishment. Whereas the meritorious behavior outlined in Dan 4:24 provides "redemption money" so that one's enslavement to sin can be paid off, in Lev 26 the punishment that Israel undergoes during the exile is convertible to a sort of currency that enables it to pay its term of sin in full:

For the land shall be deserted by them that it may *pay*[15] its sabbath debts during the period it is in desolation and bereft of them. But they, on their part, shall *pay* [the price of] their sin in full for the very reason that it is my rules that they have spurned and my laws they have loathed. (Lev. 26:43)

The point is made even more clearly in the early Rabbinic commentary found in the Sifra's commentary to this text:

"For the land shall be deserted by them": I told them that they could sow seed for six years and then leave the ground fallow for one. This was so that they would know that the land belongs to me. They, however, did not do this, but rather persisted in sin. So they shall be exiled from the land and it then will go fallow on its own for all years of fallowness that the *land owes* (*ḥayyebah*) me. For it is written: "For the land shall be deserted by them that it may be paid its sabbath years by being desolate without them."

"And they shall pay the debt of their sin in full." [This means,] did I *collect from them* full amount for full amount? Rather *I collected* only one hundredth of their sins before me.

In this text both the land of Israel and the Israelites themselves are in a state of debt (*ḥayyab*) requiring some sort of repayment. They can only extricate themselves from this indebtedness by paying it off through enduring the punishment of the exile.

For good reason scholars have compared the imagery of this text from Leviticus 26 with the famous exhortation Second Isaiah delivered to the exiles in Babylon:

15. On the translation of *rasâ* as "to pay off a debt" see S. R. Driver, *The Book of Leviticus in Hebrew* (Leipzig: Hinrichs, 1894), 102; Karl Elliger, *Leviticus,* HAT 4 (Tübingen: Mohr, 1966), 378; S. Luzzato, *Commentary to the Pentateuch* (Tel Aviv: Dvir, 1965), *ad loc*; J. Milgrom, *Leviticus 23–27,* AB 3B (New York: Doubleday, 2000), 2323–24. For a more comprehensive treatment, see Gary Anderson, "From Israel's Burden to Israel's Debt: Towards a Theology of Sin in Biblical and Early Second Temple Sources," forthcoming.

Speak tenderly to Jerusalem, and announce to her that her period of servitude is ended, that *her iniquity has been paid off* (*nirṣâ*),[16] that she has received from the Lord's hand double for all her sins. (Isa 40:2)

That Israel's penal service has come to an end is in keeping with her status as a disobedient servant who has served an allotted period of punishment. What is surprising is the way in which this penal servitude provides the background for new metaphoric conception of human sin and its rectification. Israel's accumulated sin resulted in a margin of debt she could not handle and so she was sold into bondage in Babylon in 586. Now, some decades later, Isaiah makes the bold prophetic claim that her forgiveness is at hand, for, during this period of servitude, she has "paid" double the price of what her former sins required.

Israel is not unlike the debt slave of Lev 25:47–52 who is allowed to buy himself out of his state of slavery should he prosper and come upon the money required to redeem himself. What is new is that this Levitical law for monetary debt has become a metaphor for Israel's state as a culpable nation. Not surprisingly, Isaiah becomes the first biblical writer to link the concept of "redemption" with the act of forgiving sin.[17]

IV.

This evidence I think suggests rather strongly the following translation for our text in Daniel: "Redeem your sins through almsgiving and your faults through generosity toward the poor." Or, to put the matter in more paraphrastic terms in order to bring out the full force of the metaphor: "pay down the accumulated debt of your sins by giving alms, and that of your faults by showing

16. On this meaning compare the commentary of the medieval Jewish commentator Qimhi on this verse: "*For her sin is repaid:* her period of punishment has come to closure, so Lev. 26:34, 'Then the land will repay its sabbaths.' So for 'her sins'; the term refers to her punishment as in: 'For the sin of the Amorites is not yet complete'; And Targum Jonathan translates, 'her state of indebtedness will be cancelled.'"

17. Elsewhere in Isaiah the linkage of redemption to sin can be found. In Isa 44:21–22 we have a very rare parallelism between forgiveness of sin to that of being redeemed ("I will wipe away your sins like a cloud; your transgression like mist; Come back to me, for I redeem you"), a parallelism that evokes what we have seen in Dan 4:24 and 11QMelkisedeq. And in Isa 50:1–2 we find Israel's status in Babylon compared to person sold into slavery because of their sins: "Thus said the Lord: . . . Which of my creditors was it to whom I sold you off? You were only sold off for your sins." Most explicit, and quite singular in the Bible is what appears to be the late (exilic?) addition of two final verses to Psalm 130: "O Israel, wait for the Lord; for with the Lord is steadfast love and great power to redeem. It is he who will *redeem* Israel from all their iniquities."

generosity toward the poor." Here the act of giving to the poor, who will never have the opportunity to repay the king in monetary terms, provides a different sort of reward. In rendering the verse this way, an understanding of human sin and its rectification emerges that fits quite well into the larger theology of sin that held sway in emerging Rabbinic culture. When transgressing against the divine command, individuals slowly accumulated a form of debt that, if left unpaid, would have to be collected in the form of punishment.[18] One means of averting this penalty was to act in a virtuous manner such that one's meritorious actions might tip the scales in favor of mercy.

18. It is worth noting that the standard term for "punishment" in Mishnaic Hebrew (and Aramaic) is *pûr'anût* which means literally, "a repayment [on a debt]."

Alexander Golitzin

4. A MONASTIC SETTING FOR THE *SYRIAC APOCALYPSE OF DANIEL*

Just over a year and a half ago as I write, Professor Matthias Henze of Rice University published an edition with text, translation, annotations, and introduction of a Syrian Christian pseudepigraphon, which he entitled the *Syriac Apocalypse of Daniel* (hereafter, *SAD*).[1] The document is preserved in a single manuscript, Harvard MS Syr 42, where it is placed toward the very end of a collection of ascetical literature dominated by a fairly complete assemblage of the works of John of Dalyatha (eighth century), and including brief selections from John bar Penkaye, Evagrius Ponticus, Basil the Great, Philoxenus of Mabbug, John Chrysostom, and the monks Gregory (of Cyprus?) and Simon (the Graceful?).[2] Ostensibly quite unlike the materials that precede it, the *SAD* claims to offer its readers additional information about the life and prophecies of the biblical Daniel from the prophet's own hand. Its first thirteen chapters, all in the first-person singular, combine narrative based on the canonical

1. Matthias Henze, *The Syriac Apocalypse of Daniel: Introduction, Text, and Commentary*, Studien und Texte zur Antike und Christentum 11 (Tübingen: Mohr Siebeck, 2001). I should like to take this occasion to thank Professor Henze for the gift of his book. The present essay is an expansion of the "response" I was asked to make to it for the "Christian Apocrypha Section," at the Society of Biblical Literature annual meeting, November 19, 2001.

2. I am correcting Henze somewhat, in *SAD* 1–2, on the basis of Robert Beulay's inventory over twenty years earlier of the same MS (then labeled Harvard Syriac 30) for his edition, *La collection des lettres de Jean de Dalyatha*, *PO* 39 (1978): 257–535, here 268–72. Henze's summary of the MS contents does not take sufficient account of the overwhelming presence of John of Dalyatha. Over 90 out of 127 folio pages are devoted to John's oeuvre.

book and focusing on the prophet's adventures in the court of Babylon, with legendary materials which describe his further experiences with the Persian emperors and which, among other things, display a lively interest in the fate of the cult objects and priestly vestments attached to the service of Solomon's Temple, together with that king's wonderful throne.[3] The last two thirds of the book, chapters 14 to 40, present a single, unbroken vision of the last things, which culminates first in the appearance of Antichrist (chapters 21–24), and then in the manifestation of God in Zion (25–29), the enthronement of Christ on the temple mount (30–33), followed by the resurrection, last judgement, and entry of the righteous into the heavenly Jerusalem (34–39), and concluding with the messianic banquet (40).[4]

Professor Henze's learned introduction and notes deal at some length—and chiefly—with the similarities to, and possible dependence of the *SAD* on, other works of apocalyptic literature from the late Second Temple era well into the centuries after Christ.[5] His discussion here, together with the many parallels or affinities he indicates between this literature and the *SAD,* serves to set the latter firmly in the genre of apocalypse. More specifically, it is an "historical apocalypse."[6] According to the categories established just over twenty years ago by John Collins and others in Collins's landmark edition of *Semeia,* this is a subgenre of apocalypse which does not focus primarily on an ascent to heaven, in the way of such pre-Christian and later, rabbinic-era apocalypses as *1* and *3 Enoch,* or of such Christian exemplars as the *Martyrdom and Ascent of Isaiah,* nor does it feature a heavenly ascent as part of the narrative, as in the canonical books of Daniel and Revelation, but instead, like the pseudepigraphical *4 Ezra* and *2 (Syriac) Baruch,* concentrates exclusively on the end times, in particular on the ultimate manifestation of God that will usher in the eternal reign of heaven.[7]

At this point, however, Henze arrives at a couple of curious details about the *SAD.* If we allow (and I have no reason to contest) his dating of the work to the seventh century A.D., and his argument for placing it in a West Syrian,

3. *SAD* 2 and 4–11; Syriac, 33–38; English, 65 and 67–74. See also Henze's comments, 24–26.

4. *SAD*; Syriac, 39–63; English, 77–118.

5. *SAD,* "Introduction," 6–22.

6. Ibid., 10–11.

7. See John Collins, "Towards the Morphology of a Genre," in Collins, ed., "Apocalypse: The Morphology of a Genre," *Semeia* 14 (1979): 1–20, esp. 14–15, distinguishing the various types of apocalypse encountered in the ancient texts: "historical," "heavenly journey," etc. See also Henze, *SAD,* 27-31, esp. 27, noting the unusually unified character of the *SAD*'s eschatological vision.

Melkite milieu, then we are first of all confronted with the very odd phenomenon of an "historical apocalypse" which displays little or no interest at all in the actual events unfolding outside the author's doors. Unlike, for example, the background of struggle with Antiochus IV Epiphanes reflected in Daniel, or the usual—though not uncontested—setting of the Revelation of John against the persecutions of Domitian, or *4 Ezra*'s and *2 Baruch*'s obvious concern with the aftermath of the Roman destruction of the Second Temple, nothing of the epochal shifts and attendant catastrophes of the seventh century are reflected in the *SAD*'s concluding twenty-seven chapters devoted to the vision of the last things.[8] Yet those shifts and catastrophes were spectacular indeed, whether the massive and devastating invasion of Sassanid Persia early in the century, or the ensuing, decades-long war of recovery pursued by the armies of the emperor Heraclius, or the sudden and triumphant irruption out of Arabia of the hosts of the Prophet. This absence is all the more striking when compared with at least one contemporary work, the apocalypse and *Reichseschatologie* of the Pseudo Methodius, which reads these same events, especially the rise and lightning conquests of Islam, as indications of the last days.[9] Second, and I think relatedly, there is Professor Henze's puzzlement regarding the issue of theodicy in the *SAD* or, more precisely, its status as a non-question. The last judgment, he observes, is reduced "to a single line," while the work overall appears not to be concerned "about who is to be found guilty, let alone ... their future fate."[10] There are no fiery lakes of perdition, no chasms, no dividing into sheep and goats, no lengthy condemnations, and no catalogue of punishments whatever.

While Henze merely notes these oddities and modestly refrains from attempting an explanation, I should like to be a little more daring. In what follows, I venture the suggestion that what he finds puzzling about this composition would become much less so if one were to assume that the *Sitz im Leben* of the *SAD* is the monastery. I think that its author is a monk, and that he is paraphrasing the canonical Daniel, who himself was also traditionally an ascetic, in order to remind his fellow monks of the meaning of their vows, to encourage

8. Henze, *SAD*, 14 and 22.

9. As does the *SAD*'s contemporary twin, the apocalypse called *Der Junge Daniel*. For the latter, see Henze, *SAD*, 7–11, and on the Pseudo-Methodius, esp. Paul J. Alexander, *The Byzantine Apocalyptic Tradition* (Berkeley: University of California Press, 1985), 61–122.

10. Henze, commenting on chap. 38, *SAD*, 115, n. 256, and adding: "Our author does not feel compelled to come to terms with such issues as divine justice."

them to hold fast to their calling, and to counsel them about the nature—and dangers—of spiritual experience.[11]

Heavenly Fire as Cool Water: An Interiorized Theodicy

To begin with the two issues I singled out above, the lack of history in this "historical apocalypse" and the absence of theodicy, the apparent dissonance signaled by Henze is greatly reduced if we presume a monastic setting. To be sure, there were (and still are) Eastern Christian monks who sought to link the "signs of the times" with the biblical imagery of the "end of days," but the great, perhaps we might say the classical, monastic literature of the fourth century and afterwards is quite different. In the works of such Egyptian Desert Fathers as, for example, the *Letters* of Anthony or the oeuvre of Evagrius Ponticus, on the one hand, or, on the other hand, in the fourth-century Syrian ascetical writings of Aphrahat of Persia, Ephrem the Syrian, or the anonymous authors of the *Liber Graduum* and *Macarian Homilies,* one finds very little concern with philosophical-cum-theological questions of divine justice in the abstract, and no effort whatever to "connect the dots" of current events with the endtimes.[12] I can in fact think offhand of no examples of the latter in fourth-century ascetical writers, and next to none in the centuries following. Theodicy on the macrocosmic scale, so far as it is dealt with at all, and then usually in apologetic works directed to and drawing on the pagan philosophers, is a matter largely reserved for the preaching and occasional treatises of bishops and philosopher-theologians.[13] Monks, on the other hand, are focused on the affairs of the inner man, where the history of Israel and the salvation offered in the Church through Christ are to be discovered at the microcosmic level of the soul.[14] The civic piety which

11. So, canonical Daniel 1:8–17. On the ascetical portrait of the prophets generally, and of Daniel in particular, by the time of Christ, see the text and discussion of the (probably) first-century apocryphon, *The Lives of the Prophets,* in A.M. Schwemer, *Studien zu den frühjüdischen Prophetenlegenden: Vitae Prophetarum,* Band 1: *Die Viten der grossen Propheten Jesaja, Jeremia, Ezechiel, und Daniel* (Tübingen, 1995), esp. 296–370 on Daniel, with 296–98 for the Greek text and 303–8 on the ascetical features of the prophet's portrait.

12. Abba Sopatros seems to warn against such preoccupations, among other things, in the *Apophthegmata Patrum.* Asked for a "word" to live by, he replies: "Do not allow a woman to come into your cell and do not read apocryphal literature." Sopatros 1, *PG* 65:413A; ET: Benedicta Ward, trans., *The Desert Tradition: The Sayings of the Fathers* (New York: Constable, 1975), p. 225.

13. Sections of Origen's *On First Principles* spring to mind here, as does Augustine's *City of God.*

14. Though here, too, Origen was surely a leading influence. See the selections from, again, the

concerns itself with the sorrows of the world and the latter's affairs is neither really characteristic of apocalyptic literature itself, nor, *a fortiori,* of the monks. "Tell me," asks the hero of Jerome's admittedly romantic *Vita* of St. Anthony's legendary predecessor, Paul, "how fares the human race? ... Whose empire is it now that sways the world?"[15] Given the fierce concentration on inward matters pursued inside the hermit's cell or within the monastery enclosure, the macrocosmic motifs and foci of apocalyptic literature undergo a shift to the microcosm that produces the oddities which Dr. Henze wonders about.

This is not to say, however, that properly monastic literature is not eschatological in its orientation. To the contrary, meditation on the last things continues to be of direct relevance to, and at the very center of, classically monastic reflection. The great East Syrian hermit, Isaac of Nineveh, who died very old around 700 A.D.,[16] and whom I single out here because he was thus roughly a contemporary of the *SAD,* sums up the voice of prior generations of monks when he writes:

> The beginning of the renewal of the inner person consists ... in meditation and constant reflection on the things to come. By this means the person is little by little purified of customary distraction by earthly things.... Similarly, inasmuch as bodily thoughts ... diminish in the mind, accordingly reflection on things heavenly, and the gazing on things to come, increasingly spring up in the soul. Delight in the ministry [*teshmeshta*] of these things overcomes and proves stronger than the pleasure of bodily thoughts.[17]

De Principiis, as well as from his introduction to the Song of Songs and the *Homilies on Numbers* in the collection assembled by Rowan A. Greer, *Origen: An Exhortation to Martyrdom, Prayer, and Selected Works* (New York: Paulist Press, 1979), 171–269. For not dissimilar approaches in Ephrem the Syrian, see the essay by Sidney Griffith, *"Faith Adoring the Mystery": Reading the Bible with St. Ephraem the Syrian* (Milwaukee: Marquette University Press, 1997), esp. 32–37; and on the internalization of Israel's sacred history in the anonymous, Syrian author of the *Macarian Homilies,* see Alexander Golitzin, "A Testimony to Christianity as Transfiguration: The *Macarian Homilies* and Orthodox Spirituality," in S. T. Kimbrough, ed., *Orthodox and Wesleyan Spirituality* (Crestwood, NY: St. Vladimir's Seminary Press, 2002), 129–56, esp. 133 ff.

15. Jerome, *Vita Beati Pauli* VIII, cited in Helen Waddell, trans., *The Desert Fathers* (1937; rep. Ann Arbor, 1966), 14.

16. For Isaac's biography, see Dana Miller's "Introduction" to his translation, *The Ascetical Homilies of Saint Isaac the Syrian* (Boston: Holy Transfiguration Monastery, 1984), lxiii–lxxvi; and more briefly, Hilarion Alfeyev, *The Spiritual World of Isaac the Syrian* (Kalamazoo: Cistercian Press, 2000), 25–29.

17. Quoted by Alefeyev, *The Spiritual World of Isaac the Syrian,* 274, citing in turn from Sebastian Brock's translation of the long-lost second part of Isaac's homilies, *Isaac of Nineveh: "The Second Part," Chapters IV-XLI,* which Brock himself discovered, edited, translated and published in 1995 in CSCO 224 (the Syriac text) and 225 (the translation). This passage is from Chapter VIII.16, CSCO 225:30. I am entirely

One of the things Isaac is getting at in this passage, which in concert with the predecessors he dwells on frequently, is the process of an increasing, interior conformity to the world to come—the "new world," as he puts it often—which is to discover its confirmation and final expression in the eschatological transformation of the risen body.[18] I shall shortly come back to that note, and to what I take to be its relation to the theophanies and resurrection account in the *SAD,* but for now let me add a slight qualifier to Professor Henze's remarks on the last judgment, a qualification which I believe is directly relevant to this matter of the inside coming ultimately to match the outside. While he is correct that the picture of, and the term, "judgment," is limited to the one line he quotes in chapter 38, there is in fact a judgment that takes place a few lines later in chapter 39. The New Jerusalem is pictured as surrounded and guarded by divine "fire" and "sparks of flame." The righteous will pass through this barrier without difficulty:

> They will enter through her fiery walls,
> and on the sparks of fire they will set their feet.
> The fire will turn to dew under their feet,
> and the fiery sparks will become holy water.[19]

The fire which is felt as dew recalls first of all the episode of the three youths in the canonical book of Daniel. The flames of the furnace into which they are cast, according to the expanded version of the LXX, become a "moist wind."[20] Secondly, the association particularly of the baptismal waters with divine fire is long-established in Syrian Christianity, going back to "an ancient tradition that the Jordan went up in flames at Christ's own baptism"[21]—thus perhaps the "holy

---

indebted for my citations from Isaac to Alfeyev's choice of texts in the chapter, "The Life of the Age to Come," *The Spiritual World,* 268–97.

18. Alfeyev, *The Spiritual World,* 274–75; and for Isaac's use in particular of the phrase "new world," see Brock's annotation to Chapter V.5, CSCO 225:8, n. 4.

19. *SAD,* chap. 39, 116; Syr., 62. For the judgment, see chap. 38, 115 (Syr., 61): "The great Christ, the Son of Man, will sit on it [= the throne of righteousness] and will judge the peoples in righteousness and the nations in uprightness."

20. Daniel 3:50, LXX.

21. Sebastian Brock, *The Holy Spirit in the Syrian Baptismal Tradition* (Poona, 1979), 12, citing the materials assembled and discussed by Carl-Martin Edsman, *Le baptême de feu* (Leipzig: A. Lorentz, 1940), 182–90. Note also Brock's comparison of this idea (12) with "the eschatological imagery of the 'river of fire,' citing again Edsman, 57–63; and cf. my examples below from *3 Enoch, merkabah* literature, and the *Apophthegmata patrum,* together with nn. 23–25.

water" (*mayyê qaddîšê*) of the *SAD* which supports the chariot throne in God's ultimate manifestation?[22]—and the notes of holy fire mingling with the waters of the font and, indeed, of the three youths in the furnace, show up prominently in, among other places, the *Epiphany Hymns* ascribed to Ephrem the Syrian, which celebrate both the sacrament and, significantly enough, ascetical vows.[23] Thirdly, and somewhat in anticipation of what I shall have to say below about both the dangers of visionary experience and the matter of inner transformation, we might recall the angels' daily immersions in the fiery river flowing from the divine throne which feature in, for example, the rabbinic-era composition, *Sefer Hekhalot* or *3 Enoch*.[24] This example is perhaps particularly apposite, given the traditional identification of the monastic calling with the "angelic life," or, indeed, the belief, common to both Jewish *merkaḇah* mystics and Christian monks, that those specially favored may on occasion (albeit briefly) be transformed and so become like the angels, creatures of heavenly flame—a temporary angelomorphism that, as here in *SAD* 39, will be made permanent at the eschaton. Thus R. Akiba at one point in the *hekhalot* literature testifies to the *merkaḇah* adept as one "who walks through rivers of fire," and in another passage is himself described as ascending to heaven "on a chariot of fire." The following anecdote from the alphabetical collection of the *Apophthegmata Patrum* illustrates the same conviction:

Abba Lot went to see Abba Joseph and said to him, "Abba, as far as I can I say my little office, I fast a little, I pray and meditate, I live in peace and as far as I can, I purify my

22. *SAD,* chap. 28, p. 101: "Then Adonai Zeba'oth ... [will descend] from heaven, in majestic beauty, on clouds of light and on a chariot of holy water." Henze (101, n. 178) suggests that the phrase *markabtâ d-mayyê qaddîšê* represents a conflation of "the divine throne chariot ... and the sound of God's appearance 'like the sound of many waters,'" citing Ezek. 1:24, 43:2; Rev 14:2 and 19:6. See, however (or in addition), the texts cited below and nn. 23–25.

23. See esp. *Hymns for the Feast of the Epiphany* 8.4-8, here particularly stanza 5: "The famous three in Babylon / in the furnace of fire were baptized, and came forth; / they went in and bathed in the flood of flame, they were buffeted by the blazing billows. / There was sprinkled on them there / the dew that fell from heaven ..."; and stanza 6: "That visible fire that triumphed outwardly, / pointed to the fire of the Holy Ghost, / which is mingled, lo! and hidden in the water. / In the flame Baptism is figured, / in that blaze of the furnace ...," trans. J. Gwynn, *NPNF*[2] 13:277 (Syriac in Edmund Beck, ed., *Des heiligen Ephraem des Syrers: Hymnen de Nativitate (Epiphanie),* CSCO 186:169–70). On the link between baptism and ascetical vows in the early Syrian church, see Robert Murray, "An Exhortation to Candidates for Ascetical Vows at Baptism in the Ancient Syrian Church," *NTS* 21 (1974): 59–80.

24. *3 Enoch* 36:2, trans. P. Alexander, in *The Old Testament Pseudepigrapha,* ed. James H. Charlesworth (New York, 1983), 1:289. For the Hebrew text, see Peter Schäfer, *Synopse zur Hekhalot Literatur* (Tübingen: Mohr, 1981), 54; and cf. above and n. 21.

thoughts. What more can I do?" Then the old man stood up and stretched his hands towards heaven. His fingers became like ten lamps of fire and he said to him, "If you will, you can become all flame."[25]

For the unrighteous, on the other hand, the celestial city's walls remain impenetrable. They "cannot enter the fiery gate," and "gnash their teeth outside," for "the uncircumcised and unclean will not enter into her."[26] They are "unclean" and "uncircumcised" because, we may assume, they have not been transformed from within, and in consequence the heavenly fire remains fire. For them, it burns, and, rather ominously, we hear no more about them.

While chapter 39 thus clearly indicates a condemnation of sorts, it is not one which is imposed, so to speak, from outside onto the sufferers. Christ, the eschatological judge, does not condemn them. Rather, the *same* heavenly flame which burns them is experienced as "dew" and "holy water" by the righteous. Again, this is quite in accord with Isaac of Nineveh, for whom it is the same divine love which is at once the delectation of the saved and the bitter scourge of the condemned. As he puts it:

[That] love ... is given to all. But the power of love works in two ways: it torments sinners, even as happens here when a friend suffers from a friend; but it becomes a source of joy for those who have observed its duties. Thus I say that this is the torment of gehenna: bitter regret. But love inebriates the souls of the sons of heaven by its delectability.[27]

25. Joseph of Panephysis 7, *PG* 65: 229CD; ET: Ward, *Sayings of the Desert Fathers,* 103; and see also Arsenius 27 (96BC; Ward 13) and Sisoes 14 (396BC; Ward 215). For the *Hekhalot* texts on R. Akiba walking through fire and riding on fiery chariots, see Christopher R. A. Morray-Jones, "Transformational Mysticism in the Apocalyptic-Merkabah Tradition," *JJS* 43 (1992): 1–31, here 24, citing *Hekhalot Zutarti* (Schäfer, *Synopse* 349 and 366). Note also Enoch's spectacular transformation into the fiery Metatron in *3 Enoch* 15 (*Synopse* 19; ET by P. Alexander in Charlesworth, *Old Testament Pseudepigrapha* 1: 267), and for extended discussion of these and other, related texts in the *Hekhalot* materials, see James R. Davila, *Descenders to the Chariot* (Leiden: Brill, 2001), 136–55. On monastic life as eschatological anticipation and imitation of the angels, see Peter Nagel, *Die Motivierung der Askese in der alten Kirche und der Ursprung des Mönchtums* (Berlin: Akademie-Verlag, 1966), esp. 20–74; and P. Suso Frank, *Angelikos Bios: Begriffsanalytische und begriffsgeschichtliche Untersuchung zum "engelgleichen Leben" im frühen Mönchtum* (Münster: Aschendorffsche Verlagsbuchhandlung, 1964); for texts and discussion of the importance of heavenly fire in Syriac Christian literature, see Sebastian Brock, "Fire from Heaven: From Abel's Sacrifice to the Eucharist: A Theme in Syriac Christianity," StPatr 25 (1993): 229–43; and again, Brock, *The Holy Spirit in the Syrian Baptismal Tradition,* 10–14; and on the Second Temple and New Testament background for "angelomorphism" as a soteriological concept, see Crispin Fletcher-Lewis, *Luke-Acts: Angels, Christology, and Soteriology* (Tübingen: Mohr Siebeck, 1997).

26. Henze, *SAD*, 117, n. 263, citing Rev 21:27.

27. Alfeyev, *Spiritual World of Isaac the Syrian,* 280, citing Dana Miller's translation of Homily 28, *The*

In the words of John Climacus, a monastic contemporary of both Isaac and the *SAD* from the Greek-speaking side of the Fertile Crescent, one and the same divine fire "is that which consumes and that which illumines."[28] The final judgment is simply the revelation of what one has oneself already become. It declares or makes manifest one's measure of inward conformity to the transfigured body, and so to the attendant circumstances of the new creation. Thus, as Isaac warns elsewhere:

> Woe to that monk who has proven false to his vow [*qyāmeh*], who, trampling upon his conscience, stretches forth his hand to the devil! ... With what countenance will he meet the judge when his companions who have obtained purity will greet one another? For he had parted ways with them and walked the paths of perdition ... just as he has separated his path from theirs, so Christ will separate him from them in that day when the shining cloud will bear upon its back their bodies made resplendent by purity and carry them through the gates of heaven.[29]

Note that again, just as in the *SAD,* the mark of judgment is who will—or better, who *can*—enter the gates of the city. While it is Christ who appears to be doing the separating in this passage, He does so only because the monk has already separated himself. The Lord's judgment is merely the confirmation of this separation, or, put more exactly, its revelation.

Resembling the Kingdom of Heaven within as Fidelity to the *Qyāmâ*

Another and, I think, more obvious and important link between the *SAD* and Eastern Christian, especially Syrian monasticism lies in the word that Isaac uses above for "vow." *Qyāmâ* is usually translated as "covenant," and is a *terminus technicus* in Syrian Christian asceticism from at least as early as Aphrahat of Persia in the 330s, although the latter addresses the "sons" and "daughters of

---

Ascetical Homilies of St. Isaac the Syrian, 141; Syr. in Paul Bedjan, ed., *Mar Isaacus Ninevita, De Perfectione Religiosa* (Paris: Harrassowitz, 1909), 201–2.

28. John Climachus, *Ladder of Divine Ascent,* Step 28. *PG* 88:1137; ET: *The Ladder of Divine Ascent,* trans. Colm Liubheid (New York: Paulist Press, 1982), 280. Note that this remark occurs in the context of a discussion of the monk's "high-priestly" act of prayer, and the answering descent of the heavenly fire of the Spirit, and see above and nn. 3–5.

29. Alfeyev, *Spiritual World of Isaac the Syrian,* 275, citing Miller, Homily 9, *Ascetical Homilies,* 73; Syr. in Bedjan, *De Perfectione,* 114, esp.line 5 for the use of *qyāmâ,* and see my discussion below.

the covenant" (*bnay* and *bnāt qyāmâ*) as an already long-established institution. The "covenanters" of the Syro-Mesopotamian church have been at the center of a modest scholarly industry for the better part of a hundred years, from Burkitt and Conolly at the turn of the twentiethth century, to Arthur Vööbus, Robert Murray, Sebastian Brock in the 1960s through the 1980s, and most recently Sidney Griffith during the past decade.[30] In addition to "covenant," Griffith points to two additional resonances in the term *qyāmâ,* both of which have a certain relevance to, on the one hand, the ascetical life as understood by the Syrian Church, and, on the other, the subject matter of the *SAD*.[31] The radical, *qwm,* means "stand," and is in turn the root of the word for "resurrection," *qyāmtâ. Bnay qyāmâ* has thus at least an echo of the meaning "sons of the resurrection," or, given our subject here, perhaps we might better say, "sons of the eschaton." A second resonance lies in the notion of "standing" itself. For the devout ear, this word suggested a fundamental characteristic of the angels, the ministering spirits who "stand" continually before the divine presence.[32] Thus we have in this single term echoes of the ascetical vows taken in the ancient Syrian church at Baptism (and linked still to the latter ever afterward), of "covenant" with God, of the eschaton, and of the angelic life. For Isaac, then, to be false to one's "vow" was also tantamount to betraying the resurrection and the "angelic life," and so to becoming estranged from the world to come.

I trouble so much with this one word because it appears at a crucial point in the *SAD*. Chapter 13 of the apocalypse marks the transition from Daniel's narrative of his life in Babylon and Persia to his long, uninterrupted vision of the last things which occupies the remaining two-thirds of the book. The chapter concludes with the prophet directing his readers to the vision about to be described:

30. Sidney Griffith, "Monks, 'Singles,' and the 'Sons of the Covenant': Reflections on Syriac Ascetic Terminology," in *Eulogema: Studies in Honor of Robert Taft, SJ* (Rome: Centro Studi S. Anselmo, 1992), 141–60; Griffith, "Asceticism in the Church of Syria: The Hermeneutics of Early Syriac Asceticism," in Vincent L. Wimbush and Richard Valantasis, eds., *Asceticism* (Oxford: Oxford University Press, 1995), 220–45.

31. Griffith, "Monks, 'Singles,' and Sons of the Covenant," 147–52.

32. Ibid., pp. 149–50; see also Robert Murray, *Symbols of Church and Kingdom* (Cambridge: Cambridge University Press, 1975), 13. For "standing" as imitation of the angels in earlier Christian and Jewish sources, see April DeConick, *Seek to See Him: Ascent and Vision Mysticism in the Gospel of Thomas* (Leiden: Brill, 1996), 89–92; and, with respect to Jewish and Samaritan traditions of Moses' deification, Jarl Fossum, *The Name of God and the Angel of the Lord* (Tübingen: J. C. B. Mohr, 1985), 120–29.

Wondrous is the vision [*tmîh ḥezwâ*] which will be revealed at the end of days [*d-netglê b-šûlām zabnê*].... The wise [*ḥakkîmê*] and *those who keep the covenant* [*nātray qyāmâ*] will understand this book, and, at the end of ends, let them be moved [*nzû'ûn*] by it.[33]

Henze rightly notes this statement's parallels in older apocalypses, citing *4 Ezra* and *2 (Syriac) Baruch,* as well as the linkage between apocalyptic literature and the wisdom literature of Hellenistic Judaism and the Ancient Near East.[34] In view of our discussion on *qyāmâ,* we may surely add the echoes of their own vocation and, more specifically, of their vows which Syrian monks would have heard in these lines. Likewise, monasticism's own ties to wisdom literature have just begun to come into scholarly prominence.[35] The term "sage," *ḥakkima,* is the word that Aphrahat chooses to use for the ascetic holy man in an exceptionally important, if seldom noted, passage on mystical experience and transformation.[36] In Greek Christian literature, we find monks referring to their teaching as the true wisdom, while the description of the Christian ascetic as exemplary of the "philosophical life" is in vogue from at least as early as Eusebius of Caesarea.[37] What is less noted in contemporary scholarship, and which I hope to bring out in my own work, are the—to me—obvious ties between the concerns, imagery, and hopes of monastic literature, on the one hand, and the apocalypses of the late Second Temple era and early Christianity, on the other hand. Here we might recall the simple fact that we owe nearly all the materials in, for example,

33. *SAD,* 13 (Syr., 39; Eng., 75–76), emphasis added. Perhaps this is a veiled suggestion of the troubled times outside the monastery gates, i.e., an implied question: "Is now the 'end of ends'?" If so, however, the author's accents remain the same. One is to keep to the vows and to sobriety. See thus my conclusions below.

34. Ibid., 76, nn. 56–59. See also John Collins, *The Apocalyptic Imagination: An Introduction to the Jewish Matrix of Christianity* (New York: Crossroad, 1984), 19–31.

35. See, for example, W. Schoedel, "Jewish Wisdom and the Formation of the Christian Ascetic," in Robert Wilken, ed., *Aspects of Wisdom in Judaism and Christianity* (Notre Dame: University of Notre Dame Press, 1975), 169–99; and Antoine Guillaumont, "Monachisme et éthique judéo-chrétienne," *RSR* 60 (1977): 199–218.

36. See Aphrahat's *Demonstration* 14.35, PS 1, col. 661:9, and 664:10 and 18. For comment on the relationship of the whole of 14.35 to apocalyptic ascent and Jewish *merkabah* mysticism, specifically to *3 Enoch,* see Robert Murray, "Some Themes and Problems of Early Syriac Angelology," in René Lavenant, ed., *V Symposium Syriacum, 1988* (Rome: Pont. Institutum Studiorum Orientalium, 1990), 143–53, esp. 150–53.

37. Eusebius, *HE* 6.9.6–10, on the third-century bishop Narcissus going into the Judaean desert to live as a hermit as an example of the "philosophic life," cited in Karl Heussi, *Der Ursprung des Mönchtums* (Tübingen: Scientia Verlag, 1936), 74 and 84–86; and see also Gustave Bardy, "'Philosophie' et 'philosophe' dans le vocabulaire chrétien des premiers siècles," *RAM* 25 (1949): 97–108.

Professor Charlesworth's two-volume set of *Old Testament Pseudepigrapha* to the interests of Christian copyists and readers.[38] I rather think that, from the fourth century on, many if not most of those copyists and readers were monks.

In addition to *qyāmâ* and *ḥakkima,* there are four other terms in this passage which deserve our attention: "wondrous" (*tmîh*), "vision" (*ḥezwâ*), "to reveal" (*glâ*), and "to move" or "to stir" (*z'â*). All four, with the last in its substantival form, *zaw'â* ("impulse," "stirring"), once again appear prominently and often in my seventh-century anchorite, Isaac, for whom they serve as *termini technici* for, respectively, mystical ecstasy (wonder, *temhâ*), spiritual vision, revelation (*galyûtâ*), and the "impulses" or "stirrings" of the "new world" within the devout contemplative.[39] Daniel's preface to his vision is thus virtually monastic code, though hardly a secret code. Any Syrian monk of the era who was at all versed in the literature of his vocation would have surely have recognized it immediately, and in fact he was meant to do so, since it is these monks whom I take to have been the "learned and select core" to whom the *SAD* was addressed.[40]

The note of warning suggested at the end of chapter 13 becomes explicit three chapters later. At the end of chapter 16, after having described a number of the eschatological woes, the prophet asks:

> Who will there be in those days of the aforementioned wise men [*ḥakkimê*] and scribes who *will resemble the kingdom of heaven* [*nedmûnāh l-malkûtâ*]? This kingdom will be invisible to them!

Note here the use of *dmâ,* "to be like" or "to resemble." The sainted ascetic as an image of the Kingdom of God and restored humanity is another note that is long-established in the literature of Christian asceticism and later monasti-

38. There are, unfortunately, surprisingly few secondary works that I am aware of devoted to the role played by the OT Pseudepigrapha, or even by such Christian apocalypses as *Martyrdom and Ascension of Isaiah,* in monastic literature. See, however, Nagel, *Die Motivierung der Askese* (cited above, n. 25), together with the very preliminary remarks in R. A. Kraft, "The Pseudepigrapha in Christianity," in John C. Reeves, ed., *Tracing the Threads: Studies in the Vitality of the Jewish Pseudepigrapha* (Atlanta: Scholars Press, 1984), 55–86; and, more recently with respect to a medieval Byzantine author, Alexander Golitzin, "'Earthly Angels and Heavenly Men': Nicetas Stethatos, the Old Testament Pseudepigrapha, and the Tradition of 'Interiorized Apocalyptic' in Eastern Christian Ascetical and Mystical Literature," *DOP* 55 (2001): 125–53.

39. See Alfeyev, *The Spiritual World of Isaac the Syrian,* esp. 229–36 for "visions" and "revelations," and 241–48 for "wonder," which Alfeyev argues is the rough Syriac equivalent—at least for Isaac—of the Greek *ekstasis.* On Isaac's use of *zaw'â,* see Sebastian Brock, "Index 3," CSCO 225: 191–92.

40. So Henze, *SAD,* 76, n. 57: "The author ... sees apocalyptic literature, and specifically his own book, as primarily intended for a select circle.... Apocalyptic literature is a product of learned activity rather than of popular folklore."

cism.[41] In the Syrian monastic context of the *SAD,* one arrives at this resemblance precisely through fidelity to the *qyāmâ.* Not being faithful entails loss of the capacity even to perceive the world to come. Only those who resemble the Kingdom from within themselves, as a result of their fidelity, will be able to recognize the signs of its advent and ultimately, as we saw above, gain entry into it.

False Vision and Illusory Mystical Wonder: The Stature of Antichrist

Resemblances false and true are very much the subject of the rhetorical questions at the end of chapters 25 and 26 which herald God's eschatological epiphany: "who will there be on that day [*b-yawmâ haw*] to command, and who will be found ... ?"[42] The questions, I think, function as additional warnings to the writer's monastic readers. They follow not only the final woes (chapter 25) and the initial terror of the divine advent (chapter 26), but also, just before in chapters 22–24, the apparition of the Antichrist. The latter's description in chapter 22, together with the mode of his arrival, merit quoting at length:

> And these are his signs,
> And the awe-inspiring vision of his stature [*hezwâ d-qawmteh*]
> ....
> [a list of physical characteristics follow for several lines, then:]
> His figure [*hezweh*] is wrathful, stupendous [lit., "wondrous," *tmîh*].
> The figure of his stature [*hezwâ d-qawmteh*] is likewise stupendous [*tmîh*].
> He will appear like lightning [*'a(y)k barqâ*] in the sky,

41. *SAD,* 16 (Syr., 43; Eng., 84). For the hallowed ascetic as an "resembling the kingdom", see for example the portrait Aphrahat paints of the perfected sage in *Demonstration* 14.35, cols. 660:23–665:9, where the inner-being (*'ûbâ*) of the saint contains the world, the angels (who are worshipping him!), the thrones of judgement, and God Himself; and see the citations from John of Dalyatha and Macarius below. See also Ephrem the Syrian's *Hymns on Paradise* 6.8–14, esp. stanza 14, where the "victorious" ascetics have "adorned themselves / with the very likeness of Paradise; / in them is depicted/ the beauty of the Garden"; *Des heiligen Ephreaems des Syrers: Hymnen de Paradiso,* ed. Edmund Beck, CSCO 174 :21–22; ET: Sebastian Brock, *St. Ephrem the Syrian: Hymns on Paradise* (New York, 1990), 111–14, here 113–14; together with Abba Pambo in the following from the *Apophthegmata:* "They used to say that, just as Moses received the image of the glory of Adam when his countenance was glorified, so too with Abba Pambo, that his face shone like lightning, and he was as a king seated on his throne. And the same applied as well to Abba Silvanus and to Abba Sisoes." Pambo 12 (327A; Ward 197).

42. *SAD,* 25 (Syr., 47; Eng., 97–98).

and like a lamp [*lampîdâ*] in the camp.
With him [will be] fiery chariots [*markabtê d-nûrâ*] and war camps . . .
His stature [*qawmteh*] is great [*rabbâ*] and high [*rawmâ*]
and floats over the mountains [*l'el men ṭûrê*]
equal to the clouds in the sky . . . [lit., "with," *'am,* the clouds, *'nānâ ba-šmayyâ*][43]

Henze correctly observes that many of the signs "are modeled closely on the signs preceding the Second Advent of Christ, obviously in an effort to trick the human observer into thinking that the Antichrist is Christ."[44] I would like to add a few precisions that I think will lend greater force to his remarks. First, there are two terms I noted above, "vision" or "appearance" (*hezwâ*), and "wondrous," "awesome," or even "ecstatic" (*tmîh*). Second, we find another set of terms: "like lightning," "lamp," "chariots of fire" (*markabtê d-nûrâ*), and finally "stature" or "height" (*qawmtâ*). The Antichrist is huge, overtopping mountains, touching the clouds, and his size is thus cause for—mistaken—religious ecstasy or awe. This mention of enormous bodies and fiery chariots, third, should also recall not only biblical and para-biblical theophanies (cf. Ezek 4–28, Ps 68:17, Isa 66:1, Dan 7:9; *I Enoch* 14:19–22), but as well the Jewish *hekhalot* texts of rabbinic-era mysticism, which also are on occasion concerned with true and false visions, together with the descriptions of the *shi'ur qomah,* the "measure of the extent" of the divine body, which often feature in this literature.[45] *Qomah* in Hebrew answers, of course, exactly to the Syriac word, *qawmtâ,* which appears fully three times in this passage, and I for one have to believe that the repetition is not ac-

43. *SAD,* 22 (Syr., 47; Eng., 91-92).

44. *SAD,* 92, n. 133; citing esp. Matt. 24:27 (the lightning), together with Dan 7:13 (on the clouds).

45. For texts and discussion of the fiery—and lethally dangerous—environment of heaven, see again Davila, *Descenders to the Chariot,* 136–55. On the *shi'ur qomah,* see Gershom Scholem, *Jewish Gnosticism, Merkabah Mysticism, and the Talmudic Tradition,* 2nd ed (New York: Jewish Theological Seminary of America, 1965), 36–42; Scholem, *On the Mystical Shape of the Godhead: Basic Concepts in the Kabbalah,* trans. Joachim Neugroschel (New York: Schocken Books, 1991), 15–55; and for texts and translations, Martin S. Cohen, *The Shi'ur Qomah: Liturgy and Theurgy in Pre-Kabbalistic Judaism* (Lanham, Md.: University Press of America, 1983). On true and false visions in *hekhalot* and rabbinic literature, see the controversy over the appearance of Metatron, in particular the mistaken religious ecstasy of "Aher," and its relation to the "two powers" debate in rabbinic circles; for texts, see *3 Enoch* 16 (Charlesworth, *OT Pseudepigrapha* 1:268) and *b*Hag.15a; and for analysis, Alan F. Segal, *Two Powers in Heaven: Early Rabbinic Reports about Christianity and Gnosticism* (Leiden: Brill, 1977), 60–73; and Christopher R. A. Morray-Jones, "Hekhalot Literature and Talmudic Tradition: Alexander's Three Test Cases," *JSJ* 22.1 (1991): 1–39. My thanks to A. Andrei Orlov of Marquette University for directing me to this last point.

cidental. I think rather that the coming of Antichrist is presented here specifically as a false *merkabah* vision, and his enormous body thus a deceptive imitation of the divine body, gazing on which was the goal of the *hekhalot* mystics' ascent to God's chariot-throne, the *merkabah.*

Visions true and false were also a concern of early Christian and later monastic literature. Regarding the matter of the divine body of Christ and its wondrous size, we can find suggestions as early as the New Testament, for example in "the body of his [Christ's] glory" to which the believer is be conformed in Phil. 3:21, or "the measure of the stature [*metron tēs hēlikias,* the precise Greek equivalent of the Hebrew phrase *shi'ur qomah*] of his fullness" in Eph 4:13, together with the notes of the cosmic size of the Lord's body, combined often with suggestions of mystical vision, which occur in such early Christian works as the *Gospel of Peter,* the *Odes of Solomon,* the *Acts of John,* the *Gospel of Phillip,* and the late-fourth-century *Acts of Phillip.*[46] The same notes of ascent to heaven, converse with angels, and looking on the enthroned Glory which is Christ—all of them, I believe, related to the currents of Jewish mysticism touched on above (save, of course, the identification of the Glory with Jesus)—are far from uncommon in early monastic literature, either. One finds them thick on the ground, for example, in the turn-of-the-fifth-century *Historia Monachorum in Aegypto,* and also appearing on at least one occasion even in the markedly sober *Apophthegmata Patrum.*[47] As I have argued elsewhere, it is this archaic, Jewish-

46. Arguing for the presence of Jewish mystical ideas in early Christianity is a relatively recent phenomenon. See, with respect to the texts I cited, the following sampling: Segal, *Two Powers in Heaven,* 205–37; Segal, *Paul the Convert: The Apostolate and Apostasy of Saul the Pharisee* (New Haven: Yale University Press, 1990), 9–11 and 58–64; Jarl E. Fossum, *The Name of God and the Angel of the Lord* (Tübingen : J. C. B. Mohr, 1985), esp. 162–91, 213–20, and 292–321; Fossum, "Jewish-Christian Christology and Jewish Mysticism," *VC* 37 (1983): 260–87; Fossum, *The Image of the Invisible God: Essays on the Influence of Jewish Mysticism on Early Christology* (Freiburg, Switzerland: Universitätsverlag, 1995), esp. 71–151; Gedaliahu G. Stroumsa, "Form(s) of God: Some Notes on Metatron and Christ," *HTR* 76.3 (1983): 269–88; M. Fishbane, "The 'Measures' of God's Glory in Ancient Midrash," in Ithamar Gruenwald, Shaul Shaked, and Gedaliahu G. Stroumsa, eds., *Messiah and Christos* (Tübingen: Mohr, 1992), 53–74, esp. 70–72 (on Eph 4:13 and Phil 3:21); and Carey C. Newman, *Paul's Glory Christology: Tradition and Rhetoric* (Leiden: Brill, 1992), esp. 157–62 and 208–40.

47. See André-Jean Festugière, *Historia Monachorum in Aegypto: Édition critique du texte grec et traduction annotée* (Bruxelles: Société des Bollandistes, 1971), with trips to heaven in Patermuthis 21–22 (83-4); Sourous 5–7 (91–92); and Macarius 5–12 (125–26); angelic commerce with the monks in Apollo 5–6 (48–49), 38–41 (62–63), and 44–47 (63–65); Helle 1–5 (92–94) and 14–15 (96–98); and even a false *merkabah* vision, reminiscent of the *SAD*'s, in Or 7 (38). In the *Apophthegmata,* I am thinking of Abba Silvanus' ascent to heaven to "stand"—see above and nn. 31–32—before "the Glory of God" in Silvanus 3, PG 65:409A; ET: Ward, *Sayings of the Desert Fathers,* 222–23.

based mystical tradition which underlies the controversy around the Egyptian, monastic anthropomorphites in 399 A.D., whose dispute is echoed in many other places in the Christian world—effectively, from Roman North Africa to Persian Mesopotamia—at or around the same time.[48]

That there was a controversy indicates that this archaic, mystical-cum-theological current among some early monks was opposed, and opposed successfully, in the name of that stress on interiority which I touched on above in connection with "inner theodicy." Arguably, the stress on transformation from within is quite as old as the other current, to the extent that the two can be distinguished sharply (they seem to me to overlap a bit in St. Paul), but for my purposes here it is enough to note that the opponents of mystical anthropomorphism prevailed. These monastic opponents, however, were in fact no less "mystical" themselves. For them, too, the notes of vision and of mystical wonder or ecstasy were of central importance, save that their emphasis lay on beholding "the blessed light of the Holy Trinity" from within the soul, to cite perhaps their most important and influential spokesman, Evagrius of Pontus (d. 399). The latter takes specific aim at "mystical anthropomorphism" in the following passage from his justly famous, and hugely influential little treatise, *On Prayer*:

> When the intellect attains prayer that is pure and free from passion, the demons attack no longer with sinister thoughts, but with thoughts of what is good. For they suggest to it [i.e., the intellect] an illusion of the Glory of God in a form pleasing to the senses, so as to make it think that it has realized the final aim of prayer.[49]

Two features of this passage merit underlining. First, the vision of the Glory is assumed to be "the final aim of prayer." Evagrius shares this belief with his interlocutors. Second, however, to see that Glory in a form—or "shape" (*schēmatismos*)—that appeals to the physical senses is a sign not of the real thing, but of demonic delusion. This is exactly, I think, the message behind the "awe-inspiring" and "wondrous stature" of the Antichrist in the *SAD,* and the key to our apocalypse's so-to-speak "Evagrian take" on the false vision is, perhaps

48. See Alexander Golitzin, "'The Demons Suggest an Illusion of God's Glory in a Form': Controversy over the Divine Body and Vision of Glory in Some Late Fourth-, Early Fifth-Century Monastic Literature," *StMon* 44.1 (2002): 13–43, esp. 20–42. Note that the article's title features the citation from Evagrius quoted, n. 49.

49. *De oratione* 73. I am citing the text as given in the *Philokalia* of Nicodemus Hagiorites: *Philokalia tōn hierōn nēptikōn* (1783; rep. Athens:1957) 1:182; ET in Kallistos T. Ware et al., eds., *The Philokalia: The Complete Text* (London: Faber and Faber, 1979), 1:63.

more than anything else, the emphasis it places on terms relating to the vision's appearance and form, most notably Antichrist's *qawmtâ.* We shall find quite another set of terms in play when we arrive at the true manifestation of God and Christ in the apocalypse's concluding section.

I claim an Evagrian connection for the *SAD* for a couple of reasons. Evagrius was first of all influential not only in his native Greek, but throughout the world of Eastern Christianity. He was translated into all of the Eastern Christian languages, and most completely into Syriac, in which his influence was huge. He is just as important for an Isaac of Nineveh as for such of the latter's Greek-speaking contemporaries as Maximus Confessor (d. 662) and John Climachos.[50] There is, secondly, an even more specific reason for my assertion, one which relates to the *Lausiac History,* a collection of monastic stories edited and published in the 420s by one of Evagrius' closest disciples, Bishop Palladius of Helenopolis.[51] In the early seventh century, Palladius's book was included in *The Paradise of the Fathers,* the Syriac translation by Ananisho of a number of early monastic sources.[52] This compendium might have been available to the author of the *SAD.* In fact, it is not difficult for me to imagine that he had it in front of him, chiefly because we find the account of a false *merkabah* vision in Ananisho's rendering of Palladius which is functionally identical to what we saw above in our apocalypse's handling of the advent of Antichrist.

The story is included as an example of the dangers of overconfidence. A certain monk, named Valens, is fooled by his pride into trusting the demons that have been appearing to him in the guise of angels. Convinced of their heavenly origins, and arrogantly sure of his own judgment, he is ready for the ultimate delusion:

The devil went and made unto himself a form wherein he resembled [lit., "made himself resemble," *dammi napšeh*] our Redeemer, and he came unto him by night, to-

50. See Sebastian Brock, "Some Uses of the Term *Theoria* in the Writings of Isaac of Nineveh," *Parole de l'Orient* (1996): 407–19; and Brock, "Introduction," *CSCO* 225: xxiv–xxix and xxxviii–xl on Evagrius' presence in Isaac. For the Evagrian impress on John Climachus, see Kallistos T. Ware, "Introduction," *John Climachus: The Ladder of Divine Ascent,* 60–66.

51. Critical Greek text by Cuthbert Butler, *The Lausiac History,* vol. 2 (Cambridge: Cambridge University Press, 1903); ET by Robert T. Meyer, *Palladius: The Lausiac History,* ACW 34 (New York: Newman Press, 1964).

52. Critical text by René Draguet, *Les formes syriaques de la matière de l'Histoire Lausiaque,* vol. 2: *Éditions des chapitres 20–70,* CSCO 398 (1978); ET: Ernest A. Wallis-Budge, *The Paradise or Garden of the Fathers* (1907; repr., New York: Chatto and Windus, 1972).

gether with phantoms of angels in great numbers who marched along bearing lamps [*lampîdê*] . . . and they advanced with fiery chariots [*markabtê d-nûrâ*], as if that devil were Christ himself.

Valens is then summoned to come out and worship the seeming Christ:

Now therefore when Valens had gone forth and seen the ranks bearing lamps of fire, and Antichrist himself sitting upon a chariot of fire [*markabtâ d-nûrâ*]—now he was distant from him about a mile—he fell down and worshipped him.

The erring monk then runs off to the elders of Scete, interrupting their celebration of the Eucharist in order to tell them that he no longer needs the sacrament, "For this day I have seen Christ himself!" which is to say that he has no further need for the sacramental antitype of the divine body because he has seen the original itself. Needless to say, the old men are not impressed by this claim and promptly clap him in irons until he recovers his humility.[53]

Note here first the theme of "resemblance." To "resemble the Kingdom," as we saw earlier, is a mark of the "wise," while, conversely, here and in the *SAD*'s portrait of Antichrist (though in the latter instance without the use of the verb, "to be like"), we have a case of false resemblance. Second, the figure that Valens sees is more than a little reminiscent of the Antichrist of the apocalypse, and is also accorded the same title. Its great size is suggested by the fact that Valens recognizes—or rather thinks he recognizes—it from a mile away. While this is not quite on the same scale as the *qawmtâ* of the *SAD*'s Antichrist "overtopping mountains," I think it clear that we are nevertheless in the same ballpark. The "fiery chariots" of the fake angels, third, match those of the *SAD,* though here it is they who carry "lamps" while in the apocalypse it is Antichrist himself who is "like a lamp." Equally obvious and shared is, fourth, the demon's appearance as the object of a false *merkabah* vision, seated on a "chariot of fire" in imitation of the divine original. I also note, fifth, that it is Ananisho himself who introduces the specific term, "chariot." In Palladius's Greek original, the devil appears on a "fiery wheel" (*trochos pyrinos*), and Valens "recognizes" him from the distance of only a stade (600 feet).[54] Ananisho's rendering thus accentuates both the huge dimensions of the apparition, just as does the author of the *SAD,* and underlines

53. *Lausiac History,* 25.4–5; Greek in Butler, 79-80 (ET: Meyer, 85); Syriac in Draguet, 213–14 (ET: Wallis-Budge, vol. 1:133).

54. See Butler, 80, line 1, for *trochos pyrinos*; and Draguet, 213, lines 13–14, for *ʿal markabtâ d-nûrâ.*

the specific echo of *merkabah* mysticism. It is hard for me to believe that these parallels are accidental. If not a case of direct dependence, this is at the least evidence of a common set of concerns in the Syriac-speaking, monastic world of the seventh century, and it draws on an equally common set of replies.

The Real Thing: The Radiance of Christ Enthroned on the Temple Mount

In a recent essay on Byzantine eschatology, Nicholas Constas characterized the medieval Greek image of the world to come as "the inner life turned inside out and writ large upon the cosmos ... producing an alternative world through the subjective transformation of self."[55] The presentation of God's ultimate manifestation and the establishment of his eternal kingdom in the closing chapters of the SAD matches this description. It is nothing more nor less than exteriorized mystical experience, and as such squares with what I have characterized in this essay and elsewhere as the "interiorized apocalyptic" of Eastern Christian, monastic spirituality.[56] The climactic chapters of the *SAD* describe an environment where, for "the righteous" and "the wise," both the inside and the outside, the inner world and the outer, are at last established in perfect conformity. I shall cite selectively from the apocalypse's concluding chapters, then briefly examine some of the relevant vocabulary it deploys, and will conclude this section with the witness of three monastic writers, one from just after the period of the SAD and two from long before it.

The ultimate theophany begins in chapter 27 with echoes of God's appearance on Sinai as described in Exod 19: "darkness will cover the earth ... thick darkness the nations ... mighty thunders will abound, and fierce and awe-inspiring lightning."[57] Angels sweep across the skies in "swift chariots," reminiscent especially of Ps 68:17, and the "heart of all people will melt in fear and

55. Nicholas Constas, "'To Sleep, Perchance to Dream': The Middle State of Souls in Patristic and Byzantine Literature," *DOP* 55 (2001): 123. Perhaps I should add that possible links between even ancient apocalyptic literature and mystical experience are finding more sympathetic treatment by some modern scholars, e.g., Christopher Rowland, *The Open Heaven: A Study of Apocalyptic in Judaism and Early Christianity* (New York: Crossroad, 1982).

56. Golitzin, "'Earthly Angels and Heavenly Men,'" 141ff.

57. *SAD,* 27; Syr., 51–52; Eng., 99–100. Note the use of *'arpelê,* "dark clouds," on 52, line 7, and cf. Exod 20:21, together with the citation from John of Dalyatha and my analysis below and nn. 74–75.

trembling."[58] Then, in chapter 28, "Adonai Zeba'oth" appears "in majestic beauty, on clouds of light," and "on a chariot of holy water ... and with burning flame and a fiery coal." There follows an artful tapestry of psalm verses, borrowing especially, again, from Ps 68:17; 18:9; 77:16; 97:5; and 104:6—more clouds, in short, and "thick darkness," together with angelic chariots and the melting away of a terrified earth.[59] This is succeeded by the enthronement on Zion in chapter 29, which merits quoting at length:

> Adonai Zeba'oth ... will appear completely [*gmîrâ'ît*] on Zion ...
> He will set up a holy cherub on Zion,
> and the throne [*kûrsyâ*] of righteousness on the mountains of Jerusalem.
> Also the ... [*šekîntâ?*] of Christ the King will appear on earth ...
> Seraphim of splendor [*zîwâ*] will be standing [*qāymîn*] before him,
> and angels of reverence [lit.,"of glory", *'îqārâ*] will be ministering before him.
> He will let his Divine Presence [*škînteh*] abide on the mountains of
> Jerusalem ...
> It will abide [*naggen*] in Jerusalem and sanctify her ...
> and let the splendor of his countenance [*zîwâ d-parṣûpeh*] shine on her.[60]

Chapters 30 and 31 largely repeat the theophany of "Adonai Zeba'oth," save this second time around it is Christ who appears. Like "Adonai Zeba'oth," he comes surrounded by fire, cloud, and angels, though his mission in chapter 30 is specifically to break the "iron gates" and "cut off" the power of death. His

58. Ibid.; Syr., 52; Eng., 100.

59. *SAD,* 28; Syr., 53–54; Eng., 100–102. Henze's apparatus both here and in the preceding chapter (nn. 169–88) is very thorough, save the surprising absence of Ps 68 in his accounting of the *SAD*'s sources. This is all the more puzzling, given not only the psalm's express mention of angelic chariots (v. 17), smoke and melting (v. 2), earthquake and storm (vv. 8–9), but also—and most significantly, in light of the theophany and establishment of the throne on Zion in the following chapter of the *SAD*—God's movement from Sinai to the "holy place," i.e., to the temple on Zion, in vv. 18, and 24–35, where He is enthroned and receives the tribute of the nations. It offers a preview, in short, of the whole closing section of our apocalypse. Even more interesting, in light of the several instances above where I have had occasion to refer to Jewish *merkabah* mysticism, there is the key role this psalm played in the early rabbinic traditions of the synagogue, where it served to link together the Torah reading from the Sinai theophany of Exod 19, and the *haftorah* of the vision of the chariot in Ezek. 1, during the appointed liturgy for the feast of *shabu'ot.* On this exegetical and liturgical development, see David J. Halperin, *The Faces of the Chariot: Early Jewish Responses to Ezekiel's Vision* (Tübingen: J. C. B. Mohr, 1988), 16–18, 60–61, and esp. 141–48.

60. *SAD,* 29; Syr., 54; Eng., 102–3. Note the ellipsis and *škîntâ,* in parenthesis, on line 4 of the citation, and see Henze, 103, n.194, on an evident lacuna in the text, where the missing word takes a feminine verb (*tthz'*). *Shekinta* is my own conjecture and, though other terms are certainly possible, it seems to make sense: the divine Presence *both* appears (as it has in the past) *and*—a few lines later—is now allowed to abide forever.

splendor, *zîwâ,* is then in chapter 31 revealed with "great glory," *šûbḥâ rabbâ,* to all creation, which responds with abounding fertility and joy. The building of the New Jerusalem, echoing particularly Rev 21–22, comes next in the *SAD*'s chapter 33.[61] The general resurrection and last judgment follow (chapters 34–37), succeeded by the entry of the righteous through the "fiery walls" of the heavenly city, as we touched on the latter above, and the paschal feast (38–40). The following items are of perhaps special note: a) the "holy cherub" and "throne of righteousness" appear again (chapter 38); b) the "light of the Mighty Lord / and the splendor [*zîwâ*] of Christ" shine eternally over the new city in chapter 39 (cf. Rev 21:23); and, c) the rejoicing is an eternal "Paschal Feast . . . a banquet of peace" (chapter 40). To these we should add the *SAD*'s closing prayer:

> We beg from Christ our Lord that he deem us worthy to stand at his right side, and to mingle [*naḥlûṭ*] us among the company of his saints, among the ranks of his friends, those who have loved him and have kept [*nt)ar(w)*] his commandments.[62]

For our purposes here, I should like to underline the following: 1) the echo of the biblical theophany at Sinai; 2) the setting up of the cherubim throne on Zion; 3) an array of terms, some of them verging on *termini technici,* dealing with divine manifestation and light, notably *'aggen* (dwell or overshadow), *zîwâ* (radiance, splendor), *škînta* (presence, or glory), and *'îqārâ* (glory); 4) the paschal feast; 5) the plea to be "mingled" (*ḥlṭ*) with the holy ones (*qaddîšê*) and friends of God; who have 6) "kept" (*nṭr*) the Lord's commandments. Perhaps equally striking, in contrast with the chapters on Antichrist, is the absence of any description of either God the Father (presumably "Adonai Zeba'oth") or of Christ in terms of their physical appearance. There is no reference to the Lord's features, nor his *qawmtâ,* nor any words such as form (*ṣûrtâ*), likeness (*dmûtâ*), or shape (*'eskîmâ*), and here we should recall Evagrius's strictures against endowing the divine presence with form. What therefore remains is a language of divine abiding and light, the traditional loci of theophany at Sinai and the temple mount, together with the notes of the eternal feast, of "mingling," and of the "guarding" or "keeping" that we earlier saw urged on the members of the *qyāmâ.*

The last item clearly ties the concluding lines of the *SAD* to the note which

61. *SAD,* 30–33; Syr., 54–57; Eng., 103–8. See Henze's notes 218, 220, and 222–23 for the echoes of Revelation 21.

62. *SAD,* 34–40; Syr., 57–63; Eng., 108–18. The passage quoted from chap. 40 is in Syr., 63; Eng., 117–18.

its author sounded at the end of chapter 13 in his preface to the eschatological vision. The entirety of the latter is therefore bracketed by a call to fidelity. In between, in the extended account of the last things, we have as it were the raison d'être for that fidelity, both negatively, as in guarding against the illusory vision of Antichrist, and positively, as in looking forward to the vision of the true King enthroned. The other five elements I singled out for attention appear regularly and importantly in the liturgical and ascetical texts of Syriac writers. While I have no space to dwell on the liturgy here, its importance for the *SAD* should surely be assumed, especially given my argument for the apocalypse's monastic setting. In the regular offices and Eucharist of the monastery church, we must recall the daily image of the eschaton with which the apocalypse's author would have presumed his readers to be familiar. The Eucharistic meal in particular, as an icon and real anticipation of the messianic banquet, is a feature of Christian tradition which goes back to the latter's origins.[63]

Turning to the first four terms underlined, all play a central role in the ascetico-mystical literature of the East, with the fourth, the language of "mingling" (Syriac *ḥlṭ* or *mzg*), representing a peculiarly—though not quite uniquely—emphasized note in the lexicon of Christian Syriac. In the case of Isaac of Nineveh, for example, and as argued recently by Hilarion Alfeyev, the traditional language of "mingling" served to modify the strict dyophysitism of East Syrian Christology in such a way as to allow for a real participation in God or in other words, for what Greek-speaking Christians would refer to as *theōsis,* deification.[64] In his landmark study of the *Macarian Homilies,* Columba Stewart has done the same service, and at greater length, for the earlier, predominantly fourth-century sources of Syriac ascetical literature, notably Aphrahat of Persia, Ephrem the Syrian, and the anonymous *Liber Graduum.*[65] The SAD's use of the word is consonant with that background.

63. On the book of Revelation as itself liturgical in origin, see for example Pierre Prigent, *Apocalypse et Liturgie* (Neuchatel: Delachaux et Niestlé, 1964); and more broadly on liturgy and eschaton, Jean Daniélou, *Jewish Christianity,* trans. J. A. Barker (Philadelphia, 1964), 315–46, esp. 331–37 on the Eucharist.

64. Alfeyev, *The Spiritual World of Isaac the Syrian,* 56–58. On the importance of the idea of *theōsis,* if not the word itself, in early Christian Syriac literature, see Sebastian Brock, *The Luminous Eye: The Spiritual World Vision of Saint Ephrem the Syrian* (1985; rev. ed. Kalamazoo: Cistercian Publications, 1992), 148–54. Regarding the East Syrian ascetical writers' struggle with "Nestorian" school Christology, see also Robert Beulay, *La lumière sans forme: Introduction à l'étude du mystique chrétien syro-orientale* (Chevetogne: Éditions de Chevetogne, 1987), 188–97.

65. Columba Stewart, *"Working the Earth of the Heart": The Messalian Controversy in History, Texts,*

Perhaps even more important is the apocalypse's choice of the verb *'aggen* for the abiding of God's light and splendor. Sebastian Brock has devoted a pair of important articles to *'aggen* and its derivatives, noting its connection with Lk 1:35, the Lord's "overshadowing" of Mary at the time of the Annunciation, and further associations with the liturgy, the consecratory *epikleseis* over the baptismal waters and the Eucharistic elements, and with the "overshadowing" presence of God within the soul which appears often in Syriac ascetical literature. These, he further suggests, can be taken together with the term's ties to the divine protection extended to Israel at the Passover, and its association with the descent of the Presence at both the Sinai theophany and the Lucan Pentecost.[66] The common thread, Brock observes, is that "in each case" the verb signals "some dramatic form of transformation, what happens . . . when spirit clothes itself in body and what is created puts on the Spirit."[67] The several resonances of the word—especially Pascha/Passover, Sinai, and transformation—are of obvious relevance to the concerns of the *SAD.* In particular, the association of *'aggen* with divine overshadowing establishes an important link with the themes of tabernacle and temple, a linkage which could go back to the Third Evangelist himself, whose use of *episkiazo* in Lk 1:35 very possibly looks toward the LXX version of Exod 40:34, the *kavod YHWH* (*doxa* in the Greek) "overshadowing" the newly constructed tabernacle at the latter's consecration.[68]

The note of the Old Testament *kavod,* the Hebrew term par excellence for divine manifestation in the Priestly source of the Penteteuch, in Ezekiel, and in the Psalms, takes us to the several words used in our apocalypse for divine light, splendor, and presence.[69] All are familiar and in more or less frequent use

and Language to A.D. 431 (Oxford: Oxford University Press, 1991), 169–77 (on Macarius' Greek vocabulary of "mingling") and 188–203 (on its Syriac precedents).

66. Sebastian Brock, "Passover, Annunciation, and Epiclesis: Some Remarks on the Term *Aggen* in the Syriac Version of Luke 1:35", *NT* 24.3 (1982) 222–33; Brock, "*Magganuta:* A Technical Term in East Syrian Spirituality and its Background," *COr* 20 (Geneva, 1988): 121–29.

67. Brock, "Passover, Annunciation, and Epiclesis," 232.

68. See C. H. Hutcheon, "'God is with us': The Temple in Luke-Acts," *SVThQ* 44.1 (2000): 3–33, for a tentative exploration of Luke as advancing a "Glory" Christology, esp. 11–12 on Luke 1:35. For a more extended treatment along similar, though not identical, lines, see Fletcher-Lewis, *Luke-Acts: Angels, Christology and Soteriology.* On the importance of "Glory" language more generally in Jewish and Christian literature, both biblical and extra-biblical, see the works cited in nn. 46 and 69.

69. See the articles on "glory" in the OT and NT by, resp., M. Weinfeld, "*KBD,*" in G. Johannes Botterweck, ed., *TDOT,* trans. D. E. Green (Grand Rapids: Eerdmans, 1995), 7: 22–38; and G. Kittel, "*Doxa,*" in Gerhard Kittel, ed., *TDNT,* trans. Geoffrey W. Bromily (Grand Rapids: Eerdmans, 1964–74), 3: 233–53. For more on the OT *kavod* and, for our purposes perhaps even more importantly, on its context in the

in the ascetico-mystical literature of Christian Syriac beginning with the fourth century, if not before. In the 330s and 340s, Aphrahat of Persia uses *škîntâ,* the exact Aramaic equivalent of the rabbinic *šekinâ,* together with *zîwâ* and *'îqārâ,* for the radiance (*zîwâ*) of the *kavod* (*škîntâ*) that Moses sees on Sinai, as well as for the glory (*'îqārâ*) of the divine throne that the transfigured sage sees *within* his soul, and from whose radiance (*zîwâ*) the angels veil their faces—in the same way and, quite precisely and deliberately, with the same words that he uses elsewhere for the angelic response to the Sinai theophany.[70] Not long after Aphrahat, Ephrem employs *šûbḥâ* and, again, *škîntâ* (though only once), for the radiant presence (surely Christ) enthroned on the Tree of Life in the midst of Eden, and consciously weaves together throughout his *Hymns on Paradise* a series of parallels that sets in apposition Eden, Sinai, the tabernacle or temple, the Christian Church at worship, the Christian him- or herself, and overtones of the eschaton.[71] Here we might also recall the "seraphim of radiance *standing before* [*qāymîn qdām*]" the Presence in the *SAD*, terms that Aphrahat duplicates in *Demonstration* 18.4, regarding Sinai, and then, a paragraph later, applies to his proto-monks, the "sons of the covenant."[72]

The same terminology for the divine Presence, and the same interiorizing, can be found in Isaac of Nineveh, as well as other contemporaries and predecessors of the *SAD*.[73] Permit me, however, to quote from an East Syrian monk who wrote a couple of generations after both Isaac and our apocalypse in order to il-

theology of the Temple and Zion, see Tryggve N. D. Mettinger, *The Dethronement of Sabaoth: Studies in the Shem and Kabod Theologies* (Lund: CWK Gleerup, 1982), esp. 19–37 and 80–123.

70. For *škîntâ,* see *Demonstrations* 4.7, col. 152:1–2; 18.4, 828:8 (both describing Moses' vision of the Glory on Sinai); and 19:4, 857:6–7 (King Uzziah's presumptuous usurpation of the High Priest's function, entering behind the veil to see the Glory—see 2 Chron 26:16ff.). In all three cases, thus, the term answers to the Hebrew *kavod.* For the *'îqārâ* and *zîwâ* within the sage, which the angels serve and from which they veil their faces, see 14.35, 664:2–6; and compare the functionally identical description of the angels' service and veiling before the *škîntâ* and *zîwâ* revealed to Moses on Sinai in 18.4, 828:6–14. On *'îqārâ* as the Aramaic term that normally translates *kavod* in the Targumim, though usually in (perhaps) the older Palestinian Targumin, in construct with *škîntâ,* see D. Muñoz-Leon, *Gloria de la Shekina en los Targumim del Penteteuco* (Madrid:1977), esp. his summary in 487–94.

71. See the chart Sebastian Brock supplies in the introduction to his translation, *Hymns on Paradise* (Crestwood, NY: St. Vladimir's Seminary Press, 1998), 53, and his analysis of the *Hymns,* esp. 39–74. For Ephrem's use of *škîntâ,* see *Hymns* 2.11 (Brock, 89; Syr. in *CSCO* 174: 7). On this and other technical terms for the divine Glory in these poems, see Nicolas Séd, "Les *Hymnes de Paradis* et les traditions juives," *Le Muséon* (1968): 455–501, here 482–92.

72. So compare *Demonstration* 10.4, 828:6–14, with 10.5, 829:11–13.

73. For Isaac's use of *škîntâ,* see the texts cited and analyzed in Alfeyev, *The Spiritual World of Isaac the Syrian,* 45, 165, 167–68, and 170–71.

lustrate the continuity of these traditions and language. In his fifteenth epistle, John of Dalyatha encourages his monastic correspondent with the following:

> Man of God! Just how long are you going to console yourself with little obscurities [i.e., John's letters]? Become instead wholly a flame, and burn up everything around you in order to see the beauty hidden within you! And then make this prayer: ... "You who are hidden and concealed within me, reveal in me your hidden mystery; manifest to me your beauty that is within me. You who built me as a temple for you to dwell in, cause the cloud of your glory [*'aggen ... 'arpheleh šûbḥāk*] to dwell in me, so that the ministers [*mšamšānay*—recall *SAD,* chap. 29, "angels of glory ministering," *mšamšîn*] of your sanctuary may cry out, in love for you, "holy" [lit., "sanctify you," i.e., sing the thrice holy of Isa 6:3], as an utterance which burns as fire and spirit, in a sharp stirring [*zaw'â*—recall Isaac's terminology noted earlier] which is commingled [*(m)zwg*] with wonder and astonishment.[74]

This is nearly a complete summary of the *SAD*'s eschatological enthronement, together with echoes especially of Isa 6:3, and including even a suggestion of Sinai in the "cloud of glory," where the Syriac *'arpelâ* recalls the Hebrew *'araphel* of Exod 20:21.[75] What is significant, of course, is John's urging of this vision as an imminent possibility, available to his correspondent now, within the latter's heart. The reality he describes as an inner experience is fully in harmony with the *SAD*'s portrait of the outer world at the eschaton. The world is to become wholly a temple *then,* but even *now* the Christian—especially, as in these writers, the monk—may know that he or she is a temple, the "place" of the divine abiding, the revelation of the Glory.

My two additional examples come from the fourth century. Both Evagrius and the unknown author of the *Macarian Homilies* were Greek speakers, but, as noted above regarding the former, both were also quickly translated into Syriac

74. Letter 15.6 in *La collection des lettres de Jean de Dalyatha,* PO 39, 351:15–26. The English is in part my rendering, with the help of Beulay's French, and, beginning with the prayer, from S. Brock, *The Syriac Fathers on Prayer and the Spiritual Life* (Kalamazoo: Cistercian Publications, 1987), 362.

75. See thus the *SAD*'s use of *'arpelê,* above and n. 57, and cf. the *scholion* on Dionysius Areopagita's famous account of Moses' ascent into the darkness (*gnophos*) of Sinai in *Mystical Theology* 1.3. Taking up *gnophos* as rendering *'arapel* in the Hebrew of Exod 20:21, the anonymous scholiast remarks: "The Hebrew says that *'araphel* is the name of the firmament into which Moses went, for [the Jews] speak of seven firmaments, which they also call heavens"; PG 4: 421C. This apparent acquaintance with Jewish traditions of mystical ascent is at the least intriguing, particularly given the false *merkabah* vision that Antichrist represents in the *SAD,* together with Ananisho's—and Palladius'—obvious concerns with the same temptations, respectively, a century after and before the *Corpus Dionysiacum.* Dionysius was also translated very quickly into Syriac. For his influence on John and others, see Beulay, *La lumière sans forme,* 158–80.

where their subsequent influence was continuous, vast, and incontestable. In his thirty-ninth epistle, preserved for us exclusively in Syriac, Evagrius combines Sinai and Zion traditions regarding the "place" of divine manifestation, here the intellect of the Christian:

If then, by the grace of God, the intellect both turns away from these [i.e., the passions] and puts off the old man, then it will see its own constitution at the time of prayer like a sapphire or the color of heaven, which recalls as well what the Scripture names "the place of God" seen by the elders on Mount Sinai [Exod 24:10, LXX]. It calls this "place" and the vision "the peace" [cf. Ps 75:3] by which one sees in oneself that peace which surpasses every intellect and which guards our heart. For another heaven is imprinted on a pure heart, the vision of which is both light and the spiritual place.[76]

In an important, if unfortunately neglected article, Nicholas Séd remarked that, "Without knowing the technical Aramaic term, *škîntâ,* Evagrius follows the uninterrupted line of the traditional interpretation [of the Jewish *targumim*]: Salem, Jerusalem, vision of the peace, abiding of the Presence."[77]

Less the specific note of the Exodus theophany, but including virtually everything else I have touched on in my account of the *SAD*'s climactic theophany—from temple, priestly vestments and Glory to angels and the eternal feast—there is the following from the *Makarian Homilies,* the twenty-ninth in the still-untranslated first collection of the homilies, where I have ventured to highlight the elements that recall our discussion so far:

[O]ur Lord himself . . . said to *those who have* taken on themselves such *faith and zeal*: "*We shall come,* I and my Father, and *make our abode* with him"; and again, "he who loves me will be loved by my Father, and *I shall manifest myself* to him" [John 14:21 and 23]. Thus, just *as he is seated on his own throne,* so *he will* also *take up his rest in our hearts.* As it is written in Ezekiel that *God is seated while borne up by the* intelligible and divine and spiritual *living creatures* [i.e., the *hayyot* or cherubim], who are full of

76. Epistle 39, in the collection assembled by W. Frankenberg, *Evagrius Ponticus* (Berlin, 1912), 593, translating from Frankenberg's Greek retroversion. For other echoes of the "place" and Exod 24:10, see the "Chapters" supplementary to the *Kephalaia Gnostica:* 2 (Frankenberg, 425), 4 (427), 21 (441), and 25 (449). See relatedly C. Stewart, "Imageless Prayer and the Theological Vision of Evagrius Ponticus," *JECS* 9.2 (2001): 173–204, for a sensitive exploration of Evagrius's exegetical and theological use of "the place of God," though regrettably without any attention to the phrase's resonances in extra-canonical traditions, let alone its importance in Jewish rabbinical and Christian monastic literature, and see in contrast the article by Nicholas Séd cited below and n. 77.

77. Nicolas Séd, "La shekinta et ses amis araméens," *COr* XX (Geneva:1988): 233–42, here 242.

eyes throughout all their members in front and in back [cf. Ezek 1:18]; *so, too, the soul,* which has been *made worthy by* faith, and with much prayer, and by *zeal in all the commandments receives within herself the Great King, Christ,* and, *becoming his intelligible temple and throne, becomes* all light and all eye and *all heaven* and unspeakable beauty through *the divine power which mingles itself with her* substance and, by means of this fellowship, *turns her into heaven* and divine beauty.

Therefore blessed is that soul which has adopted such zeal for Christ that, from this very moment and while still in the flesh, *she attains to those heavenly good things,* whose body is made worthy of *becoming a temple and dwelling place* [*naos kai katoikētērion*] *of the Heavenly King.* [It is] as the Apostle says: "*Your bodies are the temples of the Holy Spirit that is in you*" [1 Cor 6:19]; and again, while exhorting his faithful listeners to strive zealously to be made worthy of this great rank through faith, he says: "Glorify God in your bodies!" [1 Cor. 6:20]. *Such a soul,* like the worthy bride of a worthy bridegroom, rejoicing together with the Lord in the house of its body through the mystical fellowship of the Spirit, *rejoices without ceasing,* as was said by the prophet: "In the way that a bridegroom rejoices with a bride, so does the Lord rejoice with you" [Isa 62:5].

[*T*]*he soul* which has been made worthy, through faith and virtue, to receive the Master and King who built her in the house of her body, and to become his pure and holy bride through the ineffable and mystical fellowship of the Spirit, *possesses there,* hidden away, all "*treasures of wisdom and knowledge*" [cf. Col 2:3] stored up *in the house of her body. There,* treasured up, are *the heavenly and shining robes* of the Spirit. There, filling everything, is the fragrance of the Holy Spirit. There *the festivals of the holy angels and powers* are always being celebrated, because *the Master and King, Christ, dwells within.* Simply put, such a soul is always being *filled with every* kind of *spiritual joy and heavenly delight.* She has the [company of] the heavenly Bridegroom dwelling in the house of her body [and] uninterruptedly present with it. Truly blessed is that soul which has been *made worthy here-below of such great good things*![78]

Note the imagery of throne and temple which reverberates throughout this long passage, the citations of Ezek 1, 1 Cor 6:19–20, Col 2:3, and John 14:21 and 23, together with the references to the vestments, treasures, fragrance, and festivals of the spiritual "house" (*oikos*) in paragraph three, which I take as an expression of the temple theme broached especially through the citation from

78. Homily 29.2.1–6, in Heinz Berthold, ed., *Makarios/Symeon. Reden und Briefe: Die Sammlung I des Vaticanus Graecus 694 (B), GCS* (Berlin: Akademie-Verlag, 1973), Vol.1: 262:25 to 264:19. On Macarius's handling of Ezekiel's chariot elsewhere in his oeuvre, and his suggestive affinities with Jewish *merkabah* mysticism, see again Golitzin, "A Witness to Christianity as Transfiguration," 136–41.

1 Corinthians in paragraph two. Now recall the *SAD*'s preoccupation in its opening thirteen chapters with Solomon's temple, the latter's sacred implements, including the incense altar and, especially, the priestly robes, together with the attention it pays to Solomon's wonderful throne and, in the closing theophany of the apocalypse, the double mention of the "Holy Cherub" and "throne of righteousness" (chapters 29 and 38).[79] While the picture Macarius gives us is of an entirely internalized temple and cult, it is surely not difficult to see a certain kinship between him and the *SAD*. That resemblance should direct us toward certain conclusions.

Theophany within and the Narrative Thread of the Temple: Toward a Provisional Reconstruction of the Monastic Setting and Intentions of the *SAD*

Allow me to return to the questions raised in the introduction to this essay, the curious absences which our apocalypse displays: its lack of interest in theodicy and its failure to refer to "current events." It is time to try to pick up the threads that we touched on above in order to see if we can weave them into a coherent shape. The imagery around the temple provides us with an essential pattern and our starting point. Regarding Daniel's story in the opening thirteen chapters, Henze observes that the "one theme that runs through the entire narrative framework . . . and connects the individual episodes together is the motif of the temple implements, and of the throne of Solomon."[80] The same may be said to apply to the end of the *SAD* as well, with the cherubim throne established on Zion and, as just noted, mentioned twice. True, there is no temple building at the end, but then, given the dependence on the book of Revelation which Henze has established, we may surely ascribe this absence to the simple fact that "there is no temple" in the New Jerusalem" because "its temple is the Lord God Almighty and the Lamb," just as there is no need for the exterior light of a *menorah* because "the glory of God is its light, and its lamp is the Lamb" (Rev 21:22–23).[81] The priestly robes, though unmentioned at the end of our

79. *SAD,* 29 and 38; Syr., 54 (line 10) and 61 (line 20); Eng., 103 (line 1) and 115 (line 1).

80. Henze, *SAD,* 24.

81. Cited by Henze, *SAD,* 117, n. 266. On the overall dependence of the apocalypse on Revelation, see Henze's remarks in 16–17 and 30.

apocalypse, do show up in the Revelation's robes of white which vest both the righteous (e.g., 7:9 and 14) and the heavenly host (cf. 19:14), while the fragrance of incense appears in both Rev 8:3–5, and in the "sweet-smelling blossoms" of the trees that "will sprout on Mount Zion."[82] Again, then, nearly everything that we find externalized in these apocalypses, the one dependent on the other, we have also found internalized in the citations from John of Dalyatha, Evagrius, and Macarius.

In between the reminiscences of Solomon's temple and the eschatological "temple" of the New Jerusalem, the *SAD* lists the woes of the last days, spectacular and catastrophic on a cosmic scale, interspersing them with the three warnings directed to its readers, with the sorrows culminating in a demonic counterfeit of the true divine visitation of the endtimes, a false *merkabah* vision of the type that prior monastic literature also warns against. I do not think it then so strange that this apocalypse should be missing a section specifically devoted to theodicy, nor that it avoids mention of actual current events, at least if we assume a monastic author. Like the writers of the ancient apocalypses, such as the author(s) of Daniel, our writer is also concerned lest the chaos outside his doors trouble or even overthrow the faith of his readers. The difference between him and the ancients lies in the nature of his readership. Our author's target audience is monastic, and the nature of the monks' calling is less simply to stand in attendance of the eschaton than it is, first and foremost, to seek to embody it, to become themselves, here and now, the "place" of the divine Presence, living temples, each one thus a revelation of Immanuel. To become such, however, requires sobriety and concentration, attention to the turnings, betrayals, and darknesses of the "inner man," to the "daily death" to all the world's ephemera which is the hallmark of the Christian ascetic. The very worst thing that can happen to a monk's sober pursuit of his vocation is to fall victim and give himself over to the alarms and agitations of the perishing world. This is exactly the danger that I understand the author of the *SAD* wants to confront, and to counter.

Let us therefore imagine a monk who is a leading figure in his monastery, perhaps even its abbot. He lives amid the chaos of the first half of the seventh century. Alarms and rumors of alarms are all around him, horrors seemingly without end or precedent: sieges of cities, famine and pestilence, the destructive

82. *SAD*, 32, 106; Syr., 56.

sweep of armies back and forth across the countryside, mass slaughters, floods of refugees bearing tales of misery and of more woes to come, and—should our monk have lived in the 630s and 640s—the overwhelmingly victorious tide of an alien faith, Islam, that in his eyes might well have appeared as a demonic distortion of his own Christianity. What if, as we know was in fact the case (e.g., the Pseudo-Methodius), other people around him are busy "discerning the times," predicting the end of things and, much worse, what if their preoccupation with prophecies and calculations, for which latter the book of Daniel was and remains a privileged source, is disturbing the brethren, provoking and unsettling them, creating dissatisfaction with the mundane and increasingly—to all appearances—irrelevant attention to their daily routine: the round of chores, the services in the monastery church, the nightly prayer in their cells, and the inevitable, subtle, and always difficult struggle with their own passions? What can our monk do in the face of these Daniel-spouters, would-be purveyors of visions and portents, times and signs, who are troubling the recollection of his own and other monasteries?

I think that the answer he comes up with is the *SAD.* He is, as it were, fighting fire with fire.[83] Thus, we find him drawing up a story, based on ancient legends, of what the holy prophet did and saw *after* what is recorded in the canonical book. Our author knows the holy books very well, indeed, just as he appears to have known a great deal of the extra-canonical literature. So well does he know these materials that he is able to reproduce a tone and quality which possess a genuinely antique, "Jewish" ring.[84] He also knows the literature of his vocation, the fathers of monasticism both Syrian and Greek, and he is fully capable of marshalling these different resources to his purpose, which is nothing more nor less than to recall his readers to the pursuit of their calling. Perhaps the melting earth, the terrestrial and celestial catastrophes, the cosmic upheaval and terror he describes in his apocalypse's "woes" are also meant to remind

83. I have elsewhere argued somewhat similarly for perhaps the most famous and influential pseudepigraphon ever to come out of Syria, the *Corpus Dionysiacum,* i.e., that "Pseudo-Dionysius" intended his work primarily to counter and correct unhealthy (in his view) preoccupation with other pseudepigrapha floating in the monastic ambient. See A. Golitzin, "Dionysius Areopagita: A Christian Mysticism?" *Pro Ecclesia* 12 (2003): 161–212.

84. Henze, *SAD,* 17, on the apocalypse's "close resemblance . . . in message, language, and genre to the Jewish 'historical' apocalypses of the Second Temple period." On Christian ability to compose "Jewish" works, see Kraft, "The Pseudepigrapha in Christianity," *Tracing the Threads,* 74.

its readers that the real thing, unlike the present difficulties which surround them, will be nothing so small as the collapse and rise of human empires. And perhaps, too, there is a suggestion that, even if the present sorrows do portend "the end of ends," the proper response is not to grow anxious, nor to indulge in speculation, nor, worse still, actively to seek out portents and visions. To do so is to open the door to Antichrist and his demons. Rather, throughout earthly sorrows, what matters is fidelity to "the covenant," to carry on the inner work of transformation, and so to begin to "resemble the Kingdom" from within. If by patient, humble labor, and by favor of God's grace, this does occur, then come what may, at "the end of ends" the faithful monks will be revealed as already blazing inside with divine fire, already "equals to the angels" and "sons of the eschaton." Only through faithfulness to their vows and all that the latter signify will they "enter through the fiery walls" of the City to come, and "the fire will turn to dew under their feet." The inside must come fully to match the eschatological outside. If that happens, then the Day of the Lord will not be for judgment, but will instead only reveal what the righteous already are.

These notes are constants in Christian ascetical literature. Nearly four hundred years after the *SAD,* a Greek monk in far-off Constantinople reproduces them exactly. There will be no judgment imposed from outside, writes St. Symeon the New Theologian, no weighing up of good deeds and bad. The revelation of God will, very simply, reveal what already is:

The revelation of his divinity becomes in fact a judgment for those to whom it is revealed. No flesh could have endured the glory of his divinity as manifested naked of its joining and expressible union in the God-man.... For the divinity, which is to say the grace of the all-Holy Spirit, has never appeared to anyone who was without faith; and, if it were to appear by some paradox among men, it would show itself as fearful and dreadful, as not illumining but burning, not as giving life but as punishing dreadfully... [he then goes on to cite the example of Paul as, still an unbeliever, blinded by the "unapproachable light of divinity" on the Damascus Road].

From this lesson [i.e., the story of Paul's conversion] we therefore learn that grace, on the one hand, is unapproachable and invisible to those who are still possessed by unbelief and the passions, and, on the other hand, is seen and revealed to those who with faith and in fear and trembling do the commandments and give evidence of a worthy repentance. This same grace of itself incontestably brings the future judgment to pass in them. Rather, indeed, it becomes itself the Day of Divine Judgment by which he who is purified is continually illumined, sees himself as he is in truth and in every detail ... he is as well judged and examined by the divine fire and, thus enriched by the water of his tears, his whole body is moistened and he is baptized entire, little by little, by the divine fire and Spirit, and becomes wholly immaculate, a son of the light and of the day.

The Day of the Lord will never come upon them because they are already in it forever and continuously. The Day of the Lord ... is not going to be revealed suddenly to those who are ever illumined by the divine light, but [rather comes unexpectedly] for those in the darkness of the passions ... for them it will be fearful, and they will experience it as unbearable fire.[85]

Eight hundred years before St. Symeon, and over four hundred before our apocalypse, another anonymous Syrian Christian ascetic put the matter more succinctly:

When the two have been made one, and the inside made like the outside, and the outside like the inside, and when what is above is like what is below ... then we shall enter the Kingdom.[86]

By way of a concluding observation, it strikes me that whoever first compiled the collection of materials in which the *SAD* was included had to have known what he was doing. That our apocalypse comes nearly at the end of a manuscript that devotes over two thirds of its space to the works of John of Dalyatha is surely both deliberate and appropriate. As we saw above, the latter's message is centered on the transformed human being as temple of the divine Glory, and on the accessibility of that Glory even in this life. I think it fitting,

85. *Ethical Discourse 10*. Greek text in *St. Syméon le nouveau théologien: traités théologiques et éthiques*, ed. J. Darrouzès, SC 129 (Paris:1967), 264–68, lines 82–140. ET: *St. Symeon the New Theologian on the Mystical Life: The Ethical Discourses*, vol. 1: *The Church and the Last Things*, trans. A. Golitzin (Crestwood, N.Y., 1995), 145–47. Note Symeon's play on the simultaneity of fire and water in the second paragraph, and recall the discussion above and nn. 22–25.

86. I have lightly paraphrased and shortened *logion* 22 of *The Gospel of Thomas*, ET: T. O. Lambdin, in J. M. Robinson, ed., *The Nag Hammadi Library*, Third Revised Edition, J. M. Robinson, ed. (San Francisco, 1990), 22. The complete version extends the idea of transformation: "Jesus said to them, 'When you make the two one, and when you make the inside like the outside, and the outside like the inside, and the above like the below, and when you make the male and the female one and the same, so that the male not be male nor the female female; and when you fashion eyes in place of an eye, and a hand in place of a hand, and a foot in place of a foot, and a likeness in place of a likeness; then you will enter [the kingdom].'" On this particular apocryphon as based on a mysticism of light and acquired likeness to the divine form similar (and perhaps, ancestral) to the *SAD* and the related monastic literature discussed in this essay, see again DeConick, *Seek to See Him*, 99–125 and 148–71.

indeed, that his writings should be succeeded by a work whose whole concern amounts, in sum, to the eschatological vindication of John's not atypical understanding of the monk's vocation. The compiler seems to have thought that the *SAD* belonged in a collection of monastic literature, and I choose to read his decision as another confirmation of the thesis which this essay has sought to advance.

Michael J. Hollerich

5. A SYRIAC LIFE OF ATHANASIUS OF ALEXANDRIA

In 1978 Arthur Vööbus published a brief description of a Syriac life of Athanasius of Alexandria, which he had discovered in the manuscript collection formerly of the Mar Hananya Monastery in Tur ʻAbdin.[1] This *Vita Athanasii syriaca* (VAS) was bound in a large codex (now MS Dam. Patr. 12/17) with a mass of other biographies, encomia, and histories of ecclesiastical figures. Although the codex lacked a colophon, Vööbus believed he could date the Estrangelo script to the twelfth century. It was written on parchment in three-column format. The Athanasian vita bore the full title, "The History of the Holy and Great Athanasius, Patriarch of Alexandria, by the venerable Amphilochius, bishop of Iconium." Also at Mar Hananya he found a second version of the work in Serta script in a similar though smaller collection of saints' lives (now MS Mardin Orth. 269). In Jerusalem at the Monastery of St. Mark he found a third version in Arabic (MS 620). In 1988 several fragmentary pages of a previously unidentified Syriac manuscript now at Harvard were recognized as belonging to the VAS. Like Dam. Patr. 12/17, the Harvard manuscript (Harv. syr. 34) too was written in three columns in Estrangelo and dated to about the twelfth century.[2]

1. A. Vööbus, "Entdeckung einer unbekannten Biographie des Athanasius von Alexandrien," *Byzantinische Zeitschrift* 71 (1978): 36–40.

2. Cf. Moshe H. Goshen-Gottstein, *Syriac Manuscripts in the Harvard College Library Catalogue* (Missoula, Mont.: Scholars Press, 1979), 50. My thanks to Prof. Sebastian Brock for sending me a transcription of the Harvard fragments, whose relation to Vööbus's Syriac vita had not been recognized, although

Examination of the VAS will show that its contents are largely derivative. It is therefore of limited value as a source for the biography of Athanasius. Nevertheless, it is worth studying as evidence for the reputation and the influence of Athanasius in the Syrian Orient. Syriac-speaking Christians cared enough about Athanasius to translate several of his works into their own language.[3] As the defender of the faith against the Arian heresy, he exercised a genuinely ecumenical appeal among separated Christians who still agreed on the authority of Nicaea, however much they debated Ephesus or Chalcedon. The Nestorian historian Barḥadbešabba ʿArbaia (late sixth century) devoted a chapter to Athanasius in his collection of biographies of church fathers and heretics.[4] Athanasius's resistance to imperially sponsored heresy may have been attractive to Monophysites engaged in the same kind of resistance to the pro-Chalcedonian views of Byzantine emperors. Severus of Antioch, for example, delivered an encomium on Athanasius in 516 which survives in Syriac translation. In the address Severus insists that opposing Arius also meant opposing two natures in Christ after the incarnation.[5] In short, there is good evidence for an Athanasian "trajectory" in Syriac Christianity. This article is intended to contribute towards its reconstruction. The first part examines the literary character of the text itself, in order to determine date, authorship, language of composition, and the purposes for which it was written. The second part defines the relationship between the VAS and other sources on Athanasius.[6]

Dr. Philip Amidon had suggested their ultimate provenance was Theodoret's *Church History* (letter from Brock, October 5, 1988). They were part of a collection of about 134 manuscripts purchased from Rendel Harris in 1905 (letter from Elizabeth Farley, Acting Curator of Manuscripts, Houghton Library, Harvard University, September 22, 1992). The collation of the Damascus, Mardin, and Harvard manuscripts, represented here by the sigla D, M, and H, is the work of Prof. Brock.

3. On Syriac translations of Athanasius's works, see A. Baumstark, *Geschichte der syrischen Literatur* (Bonn: A. Marcus and E. Webers Verlag, 1922; repr., Berlin: Walter de Gruyter, 1968), 81–82; I. Ortiz de Urbina, *Patrologia syriaca,* 2 ed. (Rome: Pontificium Institutum Studiorum Orientalium, 1965): 235–36; R. W. Thomson, "A Syriac Corpus of Athanasiana," *Studia Patristica* 3 (1961): 142–45; Thomson, "The Text of the Syriac Athanasian Corpus," in J. N. Birdsall and R. W. Thomson, eds., *Biblical and Patristic Studies for R. P. Casey* (Freiburg, 1964), 250–64. See the editions and translations of R. W. Thomson in *Athanasiana Syriaca* I–IV, CSCO 257–58, 272–73, 324–25, 386–87 (Louvain, 1965–77).

4. *L'Histoire de Barḥadbešabba ʿArbaia* 9, ed. F. Nau, PO 23 (1932), 223–34.

5. But note that the homily was delivered two years before the accession of Justin led to the ascendancy of pro-Chalcedonian views at court. Text and translation in PO 25:7–27. Cf. PO 25:24 for the statement of dogmatic affinity between Athanasius and the Monophysites.

6. See preliminary assessment of this text in M. Hollerich, "The Sources of Ps.-Amphilochius's *Vita Athanasii Syriaca* (MS. Mard. Orth. 269)," in René Lavenant, ed., *Quintum Symposium Syriacum 1988,* Orientalia christiana analecta 236 (Roma: Pontificium Institutum Studiorum Orientalium, 1990), 273–83.

Analysis

According to its title, the author of the VAS was Amphilochius, bishop of Iconium and a cousin of Gregory of Nazianzus. However, no such work by Amphilochius is mentioned in antiquity.[7] Furthermore, the VAS is clearly dependent on sections of Theodoret's *Church History,* which was finished in 449 or 450. Since Amphilochius was born between 340 and 345 and is last mentioned as an attendee at the Synod of Constantinople in 394, it is scarcely possible that he was the author.[8] Perhaps he was recommended to the actual author on the strength of his bold proclamation of Nicene orthodoxy before the emperor Theodosius.[9] A vita and an encomium on Basil of Caesarea that circulated in Syriac versions were also written in Amphilochius's name.[10]

Though not by Amphilochius, the VAS may nevertheless be quite ancient. Dependence on the fifth-century church historians Socrates and Theodoret establishes a *terminus ante quem* in the 440s. The *terminus post quem* cannot be determined.

There are two reasons to believe that the language of composition is Syriac instead of Greek. First, the main sources for the vita are the church histories of Theodoret and Socrates, sections of which survive in Syriac translation.[11] Sozomen, on the other hand, does not appear to have been used, perhaps because his church history was apparently not translated into Syriac. This suggests, though it does not prove, that the epitomizer was restricted to sources already available in his own language. Second, the biblical citations are from the Peshitta. The following is a list of citations arranged by paragraph number in the order in which they appear in the text:[12]

1 Col 3:17; Ps 9:10
3 2 Tim 4:2 (reference)

7. M. Geerard, *Clavis patrum graecorum* (Brepols: Turnhout, 1974) 2: 230–42 (nos. 3230–54).

8. J. Quasten, *Patrology,* 4 vols. (Westminster, Md.: Christian Classics, 1983–86), 3:296–97.

9. Theodoret, *Historia ecclesiastica* [hereafter, *HE*] 5.16; L. Parmentier and F. Scheidweiler, eds., Theodoret, *Kirchengeschichte,* 2nd ed., GCS 44 (Berlin: Akademie Verlag, 1954).

10. *Clavis patrum graecorum* 2:241f. (nos. 3252, 3253).

11. Baumstark, 107. A Syriac version of Socrates existed by the early seventh century; see *Sokrates Kirchengeschichte,* ed. Günther Christian Hansen, GCS, N.F. 1 (Berlin: Akademie Verlag, 1995), xxxi–xxxiii. Cf. use of Vat. syr. 145 below, in discussion of VAS 51–66 and Theod., *HE* 2.16.

12. My thanks to Prof. Brock for help in identifying the citations.

25	Jer 6:15 (= Jer 8:12)
26	Isa 28:15 (free)
27	2 Sam 16:1–4 (reference)
31	Acts 1:18 (reference)
58–59	Dan. 3 (reference)
67	Jer 2:13
70	Matt 13:5–6 (free)
71	Mark 13:20
74	2 Kings 6:18 (reference)
79	Matt 5:10, 10:22 (also 24:13 = Mark 13:13); Acts 14:22; 2 Tim 3:12; Rom 5:3–4; Heb 11:37–38; Matt 7:26–27 (free)
82	2 Cor 4:17, 11:26–28 (freely, with influence from 2 Cor 6:5); Matt 5:14, 5:13
83	1 Tim 4:16; 2 Tim. 3:13 (free)
84	Matt 5:12
85	James 1:12
86	Luke 22:28–29

In all but one case these quotations and allusions seem to reflect the text of the Peshitta. For example, VAS 1 quotes Col 3:17 with the addition of "Christ" to "in the name of the Lord Jesus," a Peshitta reading which is otherwise quite unusual: *kull meddem d-sāʿrîn ʾa(n)tûn b-melltâ w-babādâ ba-šmeh d-māran yešûʿ mšîhâ hwaytun ʿābdîn.* Only Codex Sinaiticus and a few other codices add *Christou* to *en onomati kyriou Iêsou.*[13] The only exception to conformity to the Peshitta is an anomalous citation in VAS 79 that echoes minor features of the Greek text of Acts 14:22.[14] The great majority of the biblical citations come from the epitomizer himself and not from his sources. The Peshitta must therefore have been the version with which he was familiar. Even a biblical citation found in one of his sources, a letter of Athanasius preserved by Theodoret, reflects the Syriac idiom of the Peshitta rather than the Septuagint, which suggests that the sources too were in Syriac translation.[15]

13. Cf. Kurt Aland, Barbara Aland, et al., eds., *Novum Testamentum Graece,* 27th ed. (Stuttgart: Deutsche Bibelgesellschaft, 1993), 529.

14. Both VAS 79 and the Greek use the first person rather than the third person plural in the indirect discourse of Acts 14:22, as well as the plural noun "persecutions" (*ʾûlṣānê = thlipseis*) rather than the singular found in the Peshitta.

15. Jer 2:13 as cited in VAS 69, dependent on Theod., *HE* 2.23.2.

The choice of particular texts for citation may offer an indication of the purpose of the VAS. These are predominantly hortatory passages emphasizing discipleship and fidelity under persecution, an aspect of Athanasius's career which especially impressed the epitomizer. The passages at the end of the text appear to have been chosen on the basis of key words such as *rdap, saybar,* and *'ûlṣānê.*[16] It is plausible that the original setting of the epitome was therefore sometime in the sixth century during one of the various repressive campaigns waged against dissenters from the Council of Chalcedon. And yet there is no definite evidence of anti-Chalcedonian sentiments. The VAS lacks any distinctive doctrinal tendency other than an unsophisticated endorsement of the Council of Nicaea and the *homoousion.*[17] Nor is there any hostility to western, hence pro-Chalcedonian, Christians. Bishops Julius (337–52) and Liberius (352–66) of Rome are treated with great respect, though this is probably a reflection of their standing in the sources used by the epitomizer.[18] But an anti-imperial bias would help make sense of oddities such as the detailed exchange between Bishop Liberius of Rome and the Emperor Constantius. This lengthy episode occupies space disproportionate to its relevance to Athanasius' story (VAS 51–66), but its prominence becomes more comprehensible if the author had contemporary motives for comparing a Roman emperor with Nebuchadnezzar.[19] The author's own statement of purpose is consistent with the hypothesis of an anti-imperial bias:

This history I am beginning to write has nothing that is new. But [because] when it is mixed in the various histories of the church, which are very finely and loftily writ-

16. VAS 79: Matt. 5:10, 10:22; Acts 14:22; 2 Tim. 3:12; Rom. 5:3–4; Heb. 11:37–38. VAS 82: 2 Cor. 4:17. VAS 84: Matt. 5:12. VAS 85: James 1:12.

17. VAS 68: "All these fights and battles occurred because of the truth that the Son is consubstantial with the Father" (*meṭṭul hy d-'îtaw(hy) brâ bar-'îtût d-'abbâ*).

18. See VAS 38–39, 50–66. Note that the epitomizer does not flinch from repeating Socrates's strong statement of the authority of the bishop of Rome. According to Socrates, a church canon forbade the churches to pass canons contrary to the judgment of the bishop of Rome (Soc., *HE* 2.17.7; cf. 2.8.4). The VAS personalizes this by saying that Julius did not even permit them to hold a council without his command (VAS 39).

19. VAS 59. Cf. Theod., *HE* 2.16.15. Theodoret claims to have obtained his account of this exchange from anonymous predecessors who were contemporary with Athanasius (*HE* 2.15.10). The source is actually Athanasius's summary of Liberius's address to the imperial eunuch Eusebius on an official trip to Rome (*Hist. Arian.* 36). Athanasius reports as a separate incident a subsequent interrogation of Liberius by Constantius, after Liberius was brought forcibly to Constantinople. He celebrates Liberius's *parrhesia* before the emperor, but says that Constantius made no reply (ibid., 39–40, PG 25.740A–B). Theodoret rewrote the material by conflating the two interviews and composing Constantius's part in the dialogue. Sozomen contains a condensed account of this material (*HE* 4.11.3–10).

ten for those who are devoted to learning, it may appear, as it were, poor and common to some, since they are unable to comprehend so much material in their minds, accordingly, I have preferred to isolate a little from the whole, and to write the narrative on its own, so that the virtue of the holy Athanasius, patriarch of Alexandria, might be manifest and clear to simple people, and his marvelous struggle on behalf of the saving faith [*ʾagôneh tmîhâ d-ʿal haymānûtâ prûqāytâ*], and the continual assistance of our Lord on his behalf.[20]

The purpose of the epitome is therefore to popularize Athanasius's *ʾagônâ* on behalf of orthodoxy for the benefit of readers too uneducated to study the story for themselves. The author found that story spread throughout the pages of "the histories of the church," by which he must mean the works of Socrates and Theodoret. He made it his task to compose a continuous narrative based on their numerous but scattered references to Athanasius, and, to a much lesser degree, on documents they preserved.

Certainly his desire to edify outweighed his historical interest. Even though abundant historical information lay to hand, the epitomizer ignored most of it. Despite the rich documentation in his sources, only two documents are actually cited, and one of those, Athanasius's *Letter to the Africans,* is only used to provide a biblical quotation.[21] The other document mentioned is a paraphrase of Athanasius's letter to the emperor Jovian.[22] The VAS gives no precise dates. Exact time intervals are limited to the following data: Athanasius' accession as bishop of Alexandria came five months after Bishop Alexander's death (VAS 6; cf. Theod., *HE* 1.26.1). His exile in Trier lasted two years and four months according to Theod., *HE* 2.1; the VAS omits the months in its narrative (VAS 35), but adds them in a summary at the end (80). Athanasius's forty-six-year tenure as bishop is mentioned twice (78, 80), as is a six-year stay with a virgin in Alexandria (81) and a reference to his six years of peace after the fifth and last exile (82). Geographical references are scanty and sometimes garbled. Athanasius's exile to Trier is described as the city of Tiberius (*Tybryws mdî(n)tâ*), a misreading of *Triberis,*[23] the Greek name for Latin Treveri. He mistaken-

20. VAS 1.

21. VAS 67; cf. Theod., *HE* 2.23.2.

22. VAS 77; cf. Theod., *HE* 4.3.2–3. Despite the fragmentary condition of this part of the VAS and the highly periphrastic character of the citation, the letter appears to have nothing to do with the spurious *Letter to the Emperor Jovian,* edited by R. W. Thompson, *Athanasiana Syriaca* III, CSCO 324 (Louvain, 1972), 150.

23. Cf. Soc., *HE* 2.2 (PG 67: 188C), and Theod., *HE* 1.31.5 (GCS 44: 88.20), 2.1 (GCS 44: 94.4).

ly identifies Arsenius, the Meletian bishop of Hypsele in upper Egypt, whom Athanasius was accused at Tyre of having mutilated, as "bishop of Mitylene" (VAS 14), probably based on a misreading of Socrates' text.[24] The number of eastern and western bishops at the Council of Serdica is reversed.[25] The location of the site of the eastern council of Seleucia in 359 (while a western counterpart was meeting at Ariminum) is placed in Syria rather than Isauria. This may be due to the epitomizer's confusion of Seleucia in Isauria with Germanicia in Syria, which Socrates mentions just a few lines later.[26] Many of the names that are found in the author's sources disappear in the epitome, presumably because they were judged marginal to the story line. To cite one example, the VAS omits the names of the four bishops who accused Athanasius of threatening to withhold the shipment of grain from Egypt, though they were readily available in Socrates's account.[27]

The author's real interest is revealed in his marked taste for the colorful and the dramatic. He prefers dialogue to narration, and occasionally substitutes direct discourse for indirect discourse in the source material.[28] Picturesque and even lurid details abound, such as the dramatic debunking at the Council of Tyre of charges of rape and murder (VAS 14–22). The choice of stories reflects a well-developed Athanasian mystique, which endowed him with the qualities of a prophet and a populist folk hero of biblical proportions. Martin Tetz has drawn attention to the way later tradition invested Athanasius with this prophetic and biblical aura. Two episodes that Tetz singles out for study also show up in the VAS: Athanasius's escape up the Nile from Alexandria after being banned by Julian and his refuge during his third exile in the home of a consecrated virgin in Alexandria.[29] In Tetz's analysis these stories show Athanasius as a man inspired with prophecy and wisdom, so that he can foretell the shortness of Julian's reign, and like Elisha of old (cf. 2 Kings 6:8–23) can cleverly evade his would-be captors. He relies on his wise insight, *ho de sophêi gnomêi chrêsamenos,*

24. *d-'rsnyws 'episqôpâ d-mytwlyny = Arseniou tinos episkopou tês melitianôn thrêskeias* (Soc., *HE* 1.27.18 [GCS, N. F. 1: 78.12–13]).

25. VAS 41. Cf. Soc., *HE* 2.20.5.

26. Cf. VAS 67 and Soc., *HE* 2.37.7. Whether this and the previous errors are due to the carelessness of the epitomizer or of unknown copyists cannot be determined.

27. VAS 26; cf. Soc., *HE* 1.35.2.

28. E.g., VAS 29. Cf. Soc., *HE* 1.38.4.

29. VAS 72.75, 81; cf. Martin Tetz, "Zur Biographie des Athanasius von Alexandrien," *Zeitschrift für Kirchengeschichte* 90 (1979): 158–92, esp. 164–73.

to use a phrase from Socrates, which seems to stand behind a fragmentary sentence in the VAS.[30] The saint's life and also his writings thus actually become a form of hermeneutics, an interpretation of scripture.[31]

This is an approach that can be extended to other pericopes from the hagiographical tradition inspired by Athanasius's life, such as the story of how he first came to the attention of Bishop Alexander of Alexandria. Narrative convention made this anecdote a nearly universal choice for opening the story.[32] According to its standard form, Alexander singles Athanasius out when he is still a boy, after seeing him pose as a bishop during a children's game on the feast day of the martyred bishop Peter of Alexandria. Alexander subsequently takes charge of his education and eventually sponsors his ordination to the diaconate. This portrayal of their relationship may owe something to a biblical model such as the prophet Samuel's apprenticeship with the priest Eli.[33] The VAS concludes its version of the story with a comparison not to Samuel but to the patriarch Joseph. The allusion is a brief but rhetorical question asking why the symbolic meaning of Athanasius's clerical role-playing should be any less impressive as a predictor of his future destiny than the dreams of Joseph (VAS 6). The comparison, which is unique to the Syriac vita, seems at first sight to be rather gratuitous. Perhaps it springs from the author's awareness of Joseph's special popularity in Egypt. Its point appears to be that Athanasius's eminence among his youthful peers is comparable to Joseph's status among his brothers, and that Athanasius too will be the compassionate and resourceful benefactor of his people.[34] Besides Joseph, the VAS compares Athanasius to Moses, Job, and Paul (VAS 82, 84).

30. VAS 73 says that Athanasius "… used wise [ ] …" (*'etḥaššaḥ* [ ] *ḥakkîmtâ*), a phrase that seems modeled after Socrates (*HE* 3.14.2 [GCS, N. F. 1: 208.24]), and for which *bzebyônâ* is probably to be supplied for the lacuna.

31. Tetz, "Zur Biographie des Athanasius," 183ff.

32. Earliest attestation in Rufinus, *HE* 10.15 (GCS 2, pt. 2: 980.21–982.7); also cf. Soc., *HE* 1.15.1; VAG I.2; VAG II.1; VAG III.1; VAS 2-3,6. It retained its popularity in other Syriac sources besides the VAS: Bar. Arb., *Hist.* 9 (PO 23: 224.7–225.4) and Sev. Ant., *Hom.* 91 (PO 25: 10.5–12.1).

33. Cf. 1 Sam. 1–3. This biblical antecedent is actually more relevant to the story Severus ibn al-Muqaffa tells about how Athanasius's mother came to present him to Alexander (cf. 1 Sam 1:24–28). According to that story Athanasius resists his pagan mother's attempts to arrange a suitable marriage for him. His precocious asceticism recalls how Hannah, pregnant with Samuel, promised to dedicate her son as a nazirite (1 Sam 1:22). However, Severus's version inverts the mother's attitude for the sake of highlighting the son's willing choice (cf. *Hist. Patr. Alex.* [PO 1, pt. 4: 407f.], as quoted in Tetz, 168). Tetz sets more store by this version than the one in Rufinus, which he regards as "biographically worthless." (M. Tetz, "Athanasius von Alexandrien," *Theologische Realenzyklopädie* 4: 333–49, at 334.)

34. Tetz noted the utility of the comparison with Joseph but did not know that it occurred in the

The chief value of the VAS may be in adding further documentation to the religious and literary vitality which Tetz has identified in the tradition of the *Vita Athanasii*.[35]

The following is a summary of the narrative in the VAS:

2–3	Athanasius comes to the attention of Bishop Alexander while playing as a bishop in a children's game.
4–5	Council of Nicaea.
6	Death of Alexander, accession of Athanasius.
7–10	Reconciliation of excommunicated bishops to Nicaea.
11	First charges of party of Eusebius of Nicomedia against Athanasius: confiscation of imperial tribute of linen garments and treasonous gold payment to a usurper.
12	Acquittal before the emperor.
12–14	Charges raised by Ischyras and Arsenius, in conjunction with the Eusebians.
15–24	Synod of Tyre called by Constantine to deal with charges; two exposed as false: a rape charge made by an Alexandrian virgin and the charge of mutilation (for magical purposes) and murder of Arsenius; seizure of Athanasius and his escape to the capital; deposition of Athanasius in his absence by the Eusebians.
25	Transfer of synod to Jerusalem, consecration of new church, reception of Arius into communion.
26	Eusebians also go to Constantinople to lobby the emperor, charge made that Athanasius threatened to withhold grain shipment.
27	Athanasius exiled to Gaul.
28–31	Emperor's audience with Arius; Bishop Alexander of Constantinople fasts in protest; Arius's death in the capital just as he was being hailed in triumph.
33–34	Death of Constantine, succession by his three sons; Eusebians in custody of his will—their cooptation of Constantius.
35	After two years Constantine II allows Athanasius to leave Trier and go home.

VAS ("Zur Biographie des Athanasius," 172). Severus of Antioch compared Athanasius's first exile to Trier with Joseph's imprisonment by Potiphar because of the wife's calumny (*Hom.* 91 [PO 25: 16.11–15]).

35. Tetz himself pointed to the need for such an evaluation of the Syriac vita: ibid., 173.

36 Return of Athanasius to Alexandria in triumph; Eusebians hold Synod of Antioch, pass a new creed, condemn Athanasius's unsanctioned return to his see, appeal to Julius of Rome; charges laid before Constantius. Imposition of a new bishop by Eusebians, under aegis of a Roman commander with 5,000 men.

37 Athanasius's dramatic escape from besieged church during liturgy.

38 Athanasius's flight to Rome; his enemies burn a church in Alexandria.

39 Return of Athanasius from second exile, under authorization of Julius of Rome.

40 New accusation that Athanasius had confiscated the grain subsidy established by Constantine for the poor; his flight to the Emperor Constans in the west.

41–42 Constans's letter of support sent to Constantius; Council of Serdica convened, with eastern bishops withdrawing to Philippopolis in Thrace in protest over failure of bishops at Serdica to condemn Athanasius; easterners draft a creed subverting the *homoousion.*

43 Constans and Constantius clash over latter's refusal to allow Athanasius to enter Alexandria; Constantius sends three letters to Athanasius.

44–45 Athanasius leaves Rome with Julius's endorsement; his successful negotiations with Constantius and entry to Alexandria. Apparent reference to death of Gregory, the Arian bishop of Alexandria.

46–49 Death of Constans, and Constantius's alienation from Athanasius, who flees Alexandria again. Atrocities in the city at hands of Roman troops sent to install George the Arian as bishop.

50 Councils of Sirmium, where three symbols were formulated; and of Milan, where attempts by easterners to secure a condemnation of Athanasius were resisted by westerners led by Liberius, Bishop of Rome.

51–66 Liberius's interview with Constantius; his banishment to Beroea in Thrace.

67 Councils of Ariminum and of Seleucia, where a new creed was formulated. A successor council at Constantinople also formulated a creed, the tenth such anti-Nicene synod, according to Athanasius.

68 [Short statement of theological issue at stake in struggle over the *homoousion.*]

69 Death of Constantius and accession of Julian; banished bishops allowed to return to their sees.

70 Return of Athanasius from exile. Julian's reversion to paganism; his permission to Jews to rebuild their temple.

71 Julian's entry to Antioch, en route to war with Persia, and subjection to ridicule for his beard; Christian saints pray for his death.

72 Julian's condemnation of Athanasius to death; his prophecy of Julian's demise.

73–76 Athanasius's escape by riverboat from Alexandria. Headed at first for the Thebaid, he returns instead to the city, saved from pursuers by his evasive strategem; concealment in city until death of Julian.

77 Jovian's succession to Julian after latter's death in Persia; Jovian's permission given to exiled bishops to return; Athanasius's letter to Jovian congratulating him on his adherence to Nicaea; death of Jovian.

78 Athanasius's death after forty-six years in the episcopate.

81 Appended report of a six-year stay of Athanasius with a virgin in Alexandria, plus a four-month period in a tomb of his fathers.

This is a highly simplified account of Athanasius's turbulent career, which spanned almost a half century of complex ecclesiastical politics and theological development. The episodes which receive the greatest attention are the Council of Tyre and its sequel in Jerusalem in the summer of 335 (15–25), and the dialogue between Constantius and Liberius of Rome (51–66). We have already proposed explanations for their disproportionate positions. Otherwise the story line consists of Athanasius's early career before Tyre, followed by the pattern of exile and return during the years between 335, when Constantine banished him to Gaul, and 363, when Julian's death allowed him to return to Alexandria. References to two other periods of concealment are appended at the end of the VAS but no attempt is made to integrate them in the chronology of Athanasius's life.

The major anomalies in the arrangement are the erroneous dating of the Council of Serdica during Athanasius's third exile rather than during his second, and the omission of the fifth exile under the Arianizing emperor Valens in 366. According to the VAS there were two returns from exile during the reign of

Constantius, one before and one after Serdica (39, 44–45), a construction which the Syriac *Index to the Festal Letters* shows is certainly incorrect.[36] The source of the confusion is the epitomizer's reliance on a contaminated chronology in the *Church History* of Socrates, who conflated two separate episodes and mistakenly dated Serdica to 347, hence after the return from the second exile in 346.[37] The omission of the exile under Valens is more puzzling, since it is found in Socrates's history (*HE* 4.13.4) and was therefore readily available to the compiler. Instead of placing it in its proper place after the exile under Julian, he referred to it indirectly in his allusion to a four-month concealment in an ancestral tomb at an unspecified time during Athanasius's career. This is certainly the brief period of hiding to which Socrates refers, because he too mentions four months of hiding in an ancestral tomb.[38] The VAS also says of this concealment in a tomb that it has been alluded to previously (cf. 81). However, no such reference is found in the text in its present form. Whether an earlier form of the text may have had such an episode, is uncertain.

The episode with which it is paired, Athanasius's six year stay with a consecrated virgin in Alexandria, is impossible to situate in its present form in any of the five exiles.[39] The third exile between 356 and 362 is the most plausible setting for this story, which is found in fuller form in Sozomen's *Church History* and in Palladius's *Lausiac History*.[40] The six-year length must be rejected, since Athanasius himself speaks of time in the desert during Constantius's reign.[41] If the story has a historical foundation, it may have originated in an episode al-

36. *Fest. Index* 15. *Histoire "acéphale" et index syriaque des lettres festales d'Athanase d'Alexandrie,* A. Martin and M. Albert, eds., SC 317 (Paris, 1985), 240–43; cf. p. 289, n. 42.

37. Soc., *HE* 2.11, 20. See discussion in next section.

38. According to the Alexandrian chronicle known as the *Historia acephala,* Athanasius's place of hiding was a villa along the "new river," probably the canal that cut across the city; cf. *Hist. aceph.* 5.4–6, 162–64; on the "new river," ibid., 206–7, n. 137. The *Index to the Festal Letters* for the year 365 speaks of a garden along the "new river" (*Fest. Index* 37, SC 317:268; cf. n. 94).

39. See Tetz's analysis, "Zur Biographie des Athanasius," 170–73.

40. Sozomen, *Historia ecclesiastica* [hereafter, *HE*] 5.6, Sozomenus, *Kirchengeschichte,* ed. J. Bidez and G. C. Hansen, GCS (Berlin, 1960); Palladius, *Historia Lausiaca* 63, ed. C. Butler, *The Lausiac History of Palladius,* 2 parts, Texts and Studies 6 (Cambridge, 1898–1904), 2:158–60. For the pericope in Syriac recensions of the *Lausiac History,* see René Draguet, *Les formes syriaques de la matière de l'Histoire lausiaque,* CSCO 399 (Louvain, 1978), 339–42. The story was sufficiently interesting to circulate independently: it is the seventy-eighth (154v–156r) in a collection of 177 stories listed in E. Sachau, ed., *Verzeichnis der syrischen Handschriften der Königlichen Bibliothek zu Berlin,* 2 vols., Die Handschriften-Verzeichnisse der Königlichen Bibliothek zu Berlin, Bd. 23 (Berlin, 1899), MS 175 (Sachau 329).

41. *Apol. ad Const.* 27.2, 32.1, 32.2, as cited in Tetz, 171.

luded to in the *Index to the Festal Letters* for the year 360, which says that a virgin named Eudemonis was tortured by the *dux* Artemius while searching for Athanasius in her house and small cell.[42]

The *Vita Athanasii syriaca* and Other Sources for the Life of St. Athanasius

There is no contemporary life of Athanasius.[43] The main sources for his life are therefore the fund of information in his own works and two brief but invaluable summaries probably based on the archives of the church of Alexandria. The first of these has been known as the *Historia acephala* ever since its discovery by Scipio Maffei in 1738. It describes the length and the circumstances of Athanasius's third, fourth, and fifth exiles, thus from 346 to his death in 373. Because it ignores the first eighteen years of Athanasius's episcopacy, Maffei presumed it was incomplete, hence the name *acephala.* For various reasons it is now recognized that the work was probably never intended to cover events before 346.[44] The other summary is an index to a collection of Athanasius's Easter pastoral letters, extant only in a Syriac translation. Though it is even terser than the *Historia,* it has the advantage of covering Athanasius's entire episcopacy.[45]

42. *Fest. Index* 32 (SC 317: 261). The editor notes that according to the *Acta Petri* (PG 16: 462C) a virgin occupied a small cell (*asceteriolum*) in the cemetery of St. Mark east of the city (297, n. 79).

43. Fundamental issues of dating and chronology are dealt with in Timothy D. Barnes, *Athanasius and Constantius* (Cambridge, Mass.: Harvard University Press, 1993), esp. xi–xii (chronology of Athanasius's career and writing), 1–9 (on the sources for Athanasius's life), and 200–204 (valuable critique of Socrates's erroneous chronology in book 2 of his *Church History*). See also Annick Martin, *Athanase d'Alexandrie et l'église d'Egypte au IVe siècle (328–373),* Collection de l'Ecole française de Rome 216 (Ecole française de Rome, 1996). For other studies see Quasten, *Patrology* 3: 20–22; F. Halkin, *Bibliographia hagiographica graeca,* 3rd ed., Subsidia Hagiographica 89 (Bruxelles, 1957), 68–69; C. Kannengiesser, "The Athanasian Decade 1974–84: A Bibliographical Report," *Theological Studies* 46 (1985): 524–35; the articles of Martin Tetz cited above; G. C. Stead, "Athanasius," *Encyclopedia of the Early Christian Church,* ed. A. Di Berardino, 2 vols. (New York: Oxford University Press, 1992), 93–95; Rudolf Lorenz, *Der zehnte Osterbrief des Athanasius von Alexandrien: Text, Übersetzung, Erläuterungen* (Berlin: Walter de Gruyter, 1986). Still valuable is the work of E. Schwartz, reprinted in his *Gesammelte Schriften* under the titles "Zur Geschichte des Athanasius," vol. 3 (Berlin, 1959), and "Zur Kirchengeschichte des vierten Jahrhunderts," vol. 4 (Berlin, 1960), 129–213.

44. A. Martin adduces the circumstances of its origin in a dossier sent from the church of Alexandria to the church of Carthage, as well as the fact that Sozomen, who knew the Greek original, only uses it for his recounting of the last three exiles of Athanasius's career, relying instead on Socrates's erroneous chronology of the first two exiles. Cf. *Histoire "acéphale,"* 21–23, 25–27.

45. Both the Syriac *Index to the Festal Letters* and the *Historia acephala* are available with introduc-

Besides these sources the only other nearly contemporary witness is an encomium by Gregory of Nazianzus, delivered in Constantinople in 379 or 380.[46] Its scant historical value was noted long ago by Athanasius's Maurist editor, Bernard Montfaucon, who commented wryly that after reading it we are scarcely better informed than when we began.[47] In addition we have the notices about Athanasius and accompanying documentation assembled in Rufinus's addition to Eusebius's *Church History* and in the later Greek church historians, principally Socrates, Sozomen, and Theodoret; three Greek hagiographical lives from the Byzantine period; the chapter on Athanasius in Barḥadbešabba's *History*; fragments of a eulogy and a vita in Coptic; and the tenth-century Arabic life of Severus ibn al-Muqaffa in his *History of the Patriarchs of Alexandria.*[48]

Among this disparate mass of material, the VAS is very largely dependent on two sources, the histories of Socrates and Theodoret. An especially good demonstration of this is Liberius's dialogue with Constantius as reported in Theodoret, *HE* 2.16, a portion of Theodoret's book for which we have a Syriac translation extant in a Vatican MS. The following excerpt from the Syriac translation corresponds to the parallel passage in the VAS (51–53) quite closely. It contains Constantius's opening statement, Liberius's answer, and Constantius's rejoinder:[49]

---

tions and commentary in the SC edition of Martin and Albert noted above. See the lengthy review by T. D. Barnes in the *Journal of Theological Studies,* n.s. 37 (1986): 576–89. See also the review of Rudolf Lorenz, "Autour de l'*Histoire acéphale* et de sa dernière édition," *REA* 34 (1988): 267–73, and his critique of Albert's "La 10e lettre festale d'Athanase d'Alexandrie," *Parole de l'Orient* 6/7 (1975/76): 69–90, in *Der zehnte Festbrief des Athanasius von Alexandrien,* 1, 45 n. 5. My thanks to Charles Kannengiesser for bringing Lorenz's work to my attention.

46. *Or.* XXI, "In laudem magni Athanasii." (PG 35: 1081–128.) Also available in *Grégoire de Nazianze: Discours 20–23,* ed. Justin Mossay, SC 270 (Paris, 1980), 110–92.

47. "Verum ille [sc. Gregory] ut scite atque naviter oratoris munus explevit, ita jejune et tenuiter res, acta, tempora tetigit, ut ejus *Enkomioi* perlecto haud multum doctiores abeamus, imo vero incertiores in plerisque quam dudum fuimus, ob minus accuratam certarum rerum memoriam." Reprinted in PG 25: liv.

48. Rufinus, *Historia ecclesiastica,* ed. T. Mommsen, in *Eusebius' Werke,* vol. 2, parts 1–2, GCS 9, parts 1–2 (Leipzig: J. C. Hinrichs, 1909); Greek lives are in PG 25: clxxxv–ccxlvi, cited here as VAG I (PG 25: clxxxv–ccxi), VAG II (PG 25: ccxi–ccxxiii), and VAG III (PG 25: ccxxiii–ccxlvi); *L'Histoire de Barḥadbešabba 'Arbaia* 9, ed. F. Nau, PO 23 (1932): 223–34; the Coptic texts have been edited by Tito Orlandi, *Testi Copti. 1) Encomio di Atanasio. 2) Vita di Atanasio,* Testi et Documenti per lo Studio dell'Antichità 21 (Milano: Istituto Editoriale Cisalpino, 1968); *History of the Patriarchs of the Coptic Church of Alexandria,* ed., trans., and annotated by B. Evetts, PO 1, part 4 (1904): 403–23. Brief fragments of an Arabic vita have been found in the monastery of St. Macarius in Wadi Natroun by Fr. Matta al-Maskin. Judging from an English translation made by Joseph Amar, it appears to be wholly legendary and unconnected with extant sources on Athanasius. I would like to thank Charles Kannengiesser for providing me with this information and with Joseph Amar's translation.

49. Vat. syr. 145 (ff. 65v–68v), cited by permission of the Pontifical Oriental Institute (November 4,

ܩܘܣܛܢܛܝܢܘܣ ܡܠܟܐ ܐܡܪ: ܡܛܠ ܕܐܝܬܝܟ ܟܪܣܛܝܢܐ ܘܐܦܝܣܩܘܦܐ ܕܡ
ܕܫܘܐ ܐܢܬ ܕܬܗܘܐ ܠܡܕܝܢܬܐ ܕܡܠܟܘܬܢ، ܘܗܘ ܫܕܪܢ، ܘܐܦܝܣܢܟ
ܠܡܦܪܫ ܒܫܘܬܦܘܬܐ ܕܥܡ ܡܥܩܡܘܬܗ ܠܐ ܡܬܡܠܠܢܝܬܐ ܕܪܫܝܥܐ ܐܬܢܣܝܘܣ ܗܕܐ
ܓܝܪ ܕܝܢ ܐܪܥܐ ܟܠܗ̇ ܕܬܪܝܨܐ ܗ̇ܝ، ܘܒܕܝܢܐ ܕܣܘܢܗܕܘܣ ܒܗܕܐ ܗܘܬ ܦܪܝܫܐ
ܕܫܘܬܦܘܬܐ ܕܥܕܬܐ.

ܠܝܒܪܝܘܣ ܐܦܝܣܩܘܦܐ ܐܡܪ: ܕܡ̈ܠܟܐ ܕ̈ܝܢܘܗܝ ܕܥܕܬܐ ܒܚܬܝܬܘܬܐ ܣܓܝܐܬܐ
ܘܙܕܩ ܕܢܗܘܘܢ. ܘܡܛܠܗܢ ܐܢ ܫܦܝܪ ܠܗܝܡܢܘܬܟ ܕܦܩܘܕ ܕܢܬܟܢܫ ܕܝܢܐ ܦܩܘܕ܀
ܘܐܢ ܢܬܚܙܐ ܕܫܘܐ ܠܡܬܚܝܒܘܬܐ ܗܘ ܗܝܕܝܢ ܕܝܢܗ ܐܝܟ ܢܡ̈ܘܣܐ ܥܕܬܢܝܐ ܢܬܦܣܩ ܓܝܪ ܕܝܢܐ
ܥܠܘܗܝ. ܠܐ ܓܝܪ ܡܫܟܚܐ ܠܢ ܕܢܚܝܒ ܠܓܒܪܐ ܕܠܐ ܒܕܝܢ ܫܡܥܢܝܗܝ، ܠܕܝܢܗ.
ܩܘܣܛܢܛܝܘܣ ܡܠܟܐ ܐܡܪ: ܐܪܥܐ ܟܠܗ̇ ܚܝܒܬܗ ܘܓܙܪܬ ܬܫܢܝܩܐ ܥܠ
ܪܫܝܥܘܬܗ. ܘܡܢ ܫܘܪܝܐ ܡܒܙܚ ܗܘܐ ܒܗܠܝܢ ܥܠܬܐ.

The VAS version of this reads:[50]

(51) ܗܝܕܝܢ ܩܘܣܛܢܛܝܘܣ ܡܠܟܐ ܐܡܪ ܠܠܝܒܪܝܘܣ: ܣܝܢ ܡܛܠ ܕܐܝܬܝܟ
ܦܛܪܝܪܟܐ ܕܪܗܘܡܝ ܣܒܬܐ ܡܦܝܣܝܢ ܠܟ ܕܬܦܪܘܫ ܒܫܘܬܦܘܬܐ ܗ̇ܝ ܠܐ
ܢܡܘܣܝܬܐ ܕܪܫܝܥܘܬܗ ܕܐܬܢܣܝܘܣ. ܗܐ ܓܝܪ ܡܦܠܚܘܬ ܗܝܡܢܘܬܗ ܠܟܠܢܫ
ܝܕܝܥܐ. ܘܒܕܝܢܐ ܕܣܘܢܗܕܘܣ ܦܪܝܫ ܐܝܬܘܗܝ، ܠܫܘܬܦܘܬܐ ܕܥܕܬܐ܀

1992), which kindly provided a photocopy of the relevant folios. The MS consists of excerpts from the church histories of Socrates and Theodoret; cf. Baumstark, 107 n. 1, and *Sokrates Kirchengeschichte,* ed. Hansen, p. xxxi. In the translation here and in the English translation of the VAS in the following note, the italicized words are verbally identical or nearly identical in the two Syriac texts:

"*The Emperor Constantius said, 'Because you are* a Christian and a bishop who was deemed worthy of our capital city, *we have* sent and *urged you to renounce communion with* the unutterable perversity of *the impious Athanasius. For* the whole world has decided that this is right *and by the judgment of the synod* he was made *separate from communion with the church.'*

"Bishop *Liberius said, 'O Emperor, it is right that the judgments of the church be made with great precision. And therefore if it seems good to your faith, command that* a court should be convened. *And if it should seem that he deserves condemnation, then let the judgment on him be passed according to the ecclesiastical canons. For it is not possible for us to condemn a man until we have heard his case.'*

"*The Emperor* Constantius *said, 'The whole world has condemned him and has decreed* punishment *for his impiety. And from the beginning, he has made sport of these occasions.'"*

50. "(51) Then *the Emperor Constantius* said to Liberius, *'Because you are* the patriarch of the elder Rome, *we urge you to renounce* illegal *communion with the impiety of Athanasius. For* behold, the perversity of his belief is known to everyone, *and by the judgment of the synod* he is *separate from communion with the church.'*

"(52) *Liberius said, 'It is right. O Emperor, that the judgments of the church be made with great precision. And therefore if it should seem good to your faith, command that* there should be an inquiry. *And if it should seem that he deserves condemnation, then let the judgment on him be passed according to the ecclesiastical canons. For it is not possible for us to condemn a man until we have heard his case.'*

"(53) *The emperor said, 'The whole world has condemned him and has decreed* judgment *upon his impiety. And behold, from the beginning he has made sport of these occasions.'"*

(52) ܠܝܒܪܝܘܣ ܐܡܪ ܕܝ̈ܢܝܗ ܕܥܕܬܐ ܐܘ ܡܠܟܐ ܒܫܘܝܘܬܐ ܦܣܩܐܬܐ
ܘܥܡ ܕܢܗܘܘܢ، ܘܡܕܒܠܗܢ ܐܢ ܡܬܚܫܒܐ ܠܗܝܡܢܘܬܢ ܦܘܩܕ ܕܢܗܘܐ ܒܫܝܢܐ.
ܘܐܢ ܢܬܦܣܐ ܕܥܒܕܐ ܠܫܠܡܘܬܐ ܗܝܕܝܢ ܐܝܟ ܢ̈ܡܘܣܐ ܕܥܕ̈ܬܐ ܢܦܘܩ ܠܒܪ
ܕܝܢܐ ܕܟܠܗܘܢ، ܠܐ ܡܫܟܚܐ ܕܢܣܒ ܠܓܒܪܐ ܕܠܐ ܒܕܝܠ ܡܚܝܒܝܢܗ، ܠܕܝܢܗ܀
(53) ܡܠܟܐ ܐܡܪ: ܐܪܥܐ ܟܠܗ̇ ܫܡܥܬܗ ܘܦܣܩܬ ܕܝܢܐ ܥܠ ܦܘܫܥܗ. ܘܗܘܐ ܡܢ
ܫܘܪܝܐ ܡܫܛܥܐ ܒܗܘܢ ܒܙܒ̈ܢܐ܀

The close parallels between these two passages suggest that the epitomizer may have had this Syriac version of Theodoret before him as he wrote. The author's dependency on the Syriac Theodoret may be further demonstrated by minor anomalies in his text. In the passage just quoted, Constantius says that Athanasius had from the beginning dismissed the judgment of what Constantius claims was the whole world. The literal meaning of the Greek is "from the beginning he mocks the occasion (*ex archês ton kairon diapaizei*)."[51] Both the VAS and Vat. syr. 145 translate this expression literally, despite the strangeness of the Syriac idiom: *men šûrāyâ mešṭaʿâ b-hôn b-zabnê.*[52] In another place Constantius asks Liberius to enter into communion with the other churches that have condemned Athanasius. The Vatican Syriac version of Theodoret (*HE* 2.16.23) has him say, in scrupulous fidelity to Theodoret, "communion with the churches," whereas the VAS makes Constantius ask Liberius to enter into communion with *him*: "For I want you to enter into communion with us" (VAS 63), a divergence from Theodoret that perhaps originated in a confusion of *d-ʿam* with *d-ʿamman.* In a passage immediately following this one, the Vatican Syriac version of Theodoret may help explain another discrepancy between Theodoret's Greek and the VAS. According to the Harvard (H) fragments of the VAS Liberius tells Constantius that he has already bade farewell to the church (H: *l-ʿêdtâ*) in Rome. H's reading of "church" may be a correction of the more difficult reading *l-ʾîdâ* ("hand") found in both the Damascus (D) and Mardin (M) manuscripts of the VAS. According to the Greek text of Theodoret, Liberius says he has bade farewell to the brethren (*tois adelphois*) in Rome, which Vat. Syr. 145 accurately rendered as *l-ʾaḥê. L-ʾîdâ* may have originated as a misreading of *l-ʾaḥê,* which H then corrected to the more comprehensible *l-ʿêdtâ.*

The writer must have worked with both Socrates's and Theodoret's histories

51. Theod., *HE* 2.16.3 (GCS 44: 132.2–3).

52. Cf. VAS 53 and Vat. syr. 145 (f. 65v), which are nearly identical here. The same awkward idiom is found in the Latin translation of Cassiodorus, which has *tempus illudit* (Theod., *HE* 2.16.3 [GCS 44: 132]).

in front of him, or a collection of excerpts such as Vat. syr. 145, moving from one to the other to weave his synopsis of Athanasius's life. Of the two sources, Socrates seems to have provided the primary structure, but Theodoret is also used extensively. Between the two of them, all of the episodes listed in the previous section are accounted for, save for the story of his six-year refuge with an Alexandrian virgin (VAS 81), to which we have already referred. Though found in Sozomen's *Church History* (*HE* 5.6), it is first attested in Palladius's *Lausiac History* (chap. 63).[53] Given the apparent lack of a Syriac version of Sozomen and the absence of any other material peculiar to his history, it seems most plausible to conclude that Palladius, whose work circulated in Syriac, was the source for the epitomizer, though perhaps as reported in oral, rather than written, form.[54]

The VAS's reliance on Socrates led to its confused account of the Council of Serdica and the third exile under Constantius, to which we referred above and which we will examine here more closely. Socrates's chronology erred in placing the Council of Serdica during the consulship of Rufinus and Eusebius, that is, in 347, whereas the council actually met in 343.[55] The misdating skewed his account of Athanasius's exiles, since he was led to place the return from his second exile (*HE* 2.15.6) and departure on his third exile (*HE* 2.17.3) *before* the council. The same sequence is found in the VAS which places the return from the second exile (VAS 39) and the departure for the third exile (VAS 40) just prior to Serdica (VAS 41). But Athanasius's second exile did not end until 346, following the death of Gregory in 345, the Arian incumbent in the Alexandrian see.[56] The VAS also follows Socrates's garbled narrative in *HE* 2.11 and 2.14, which conflated two distinct episodes in Athanasius's career, his flight from the church of Theonas in Alexandria in 339, right before the coming of the

53. Also found in the Greek lives; see below.

54. On Syriac versions of the *Lausiac History*, see Draguet's edition, *Les formes syriaques de la matière de l'Histoire lausiaque*, CSCO 389–90, 398–99 (Louvain, 1978).

55. Soc., *HE* 2.20.4. Cf. the consular list in App. IV, *Histoire "acéphale" et Index syriaque*, 314. According to the *Index of the Festal Letters*, the council met in 343 (*Fest. Index* 15 [SC 317: 243]), though some modern scholars argue that the correct date is 342. See bibliography in the apparatus in Hansen, ed., *Sokrates Kirchengeschichte*, 117, and the discussion of Martin and Albert, *Histoire "acéphale" et index syriaque*, 289 n. 42, where the accuracy of the Index's dating is defended. Barnes accepts 343 (*Athanasius and Constantius*, 71).

56. For the date of Gregory's death, see Martin, *Histoire "acéphale,"* 171 n. 3. Barnes describes Socrates's account of a second return from exile before Serdica as "sheer fantasy" (*Athanasius and Constantius*, 201).

Arian bishop Gregory, and his flight from the same church in 356, when the *dux* Syrianus invaded the building during a violent campaign to install another Arian adherent, George, as bishop of Alexandria.[57] Despite the chronological difficulties created by his dependence on Socrates, the epitomizer seems to have placed the removal of Gregory from Alexandria *after* the council of Serdica, which happens to be the correct historical sequence. A fragmentary passage in VAS 45 alludes to Gregory at the time of Athanasius's return to the city sometime after Serdica, in contradiction to Socrates's account, which says that the Arians replaced Gregory with George because of his unpopularity (Soc., *HE* 2.14). The explanation for the deviation is the epitomizer's shift to Theodoret at just this point, for Theodoret, unlike Socrates, correctly placed Gregory's death (lynched by the mob) prior to Athanasius's return from his second exile (Theod., *HE* 2.12). Theodoret was also the source for other elements of the VAS narrative: the comparison in VAS 27 of Constantine's deception at the hands of his Arian bishops with the deception practiced on King David by Ziba, the servant of Mephibosheth;[58] the discrediting at the Council of Tyre of the rape charge against Athanasius;[59] and the statement that Julian the Apostate had ordered Athanasius's execution, not merely his banishment.[60]

Having established the dependency of the VAS on Socrates and Theodoret, I turn now to the Greek hagiographical tradition as preserved in the three Byzantine lives reprinted in Migne.[61] They show a great deal of overlap with one another and must represent a vulgate version of the life of Athanasius. Most of the material in the VAS is also found here, except for the dialogue of Liberius and Constantius and some of the biblical allusions. So great is the duplication that in the absence of the fifth-century church histories one might suppose that the Syriac life was derived from them. Nevertheless, the demon-

57. See *Fest. Index* 11 for 339 (SC 317: 237–39); ibid., 28–29 (SC 317: 257) for 356 and 357; also *Hist. aceph.* 1.10–2.2 (SC 317: 142.66–146.13). Athanasius himself describes the first episode in *Hist. Ar.* (PG 25: 705B) and the second in *Apol. de fug.* 24 (PG 25: 673C–676B) and *Apol. ad Const.* 25 (PG 25: 625B–628A). See Barnes, *Athanasius and Constantius,* 46–50 and 118–19, for these episodes. Confusion of the names of Gregory and George may have led to Socrates's conflation of the two episodes.

58. Theod., *HE* 1.33. For the story of the servant of Mephibosheth, crippled son of Jonathan, see 2 Sam. 8:1–13, 16:1–4, 19:24–30.

59. VAS 16–19. Cf. Theod., *HE* 1.30.3–6.

60. VAS 72. Cf. Theod., *HE* 3.9.2.

61. Brief discussion of the dependence of the Greek lives on earlier historical sources in Friedhelm Winkelmann, "Zur Überlieferung der Vita Athanasii praemetaphrastica (BHG Nr. 185)," *Sacris Erudiri* 31 (1989–90): 455–63, esp. references to earlier work of Beck and Scheidweiler at 455 nn. 2–5.

strable dependence of the VAS on Socrates and Theodoret makes otiose the hypothesis of a mediation through Byzantine hagiography. Furthermore, the VAS avoids a clumsy chronological error common to all the Greek lives, which place some of the events at Tyre after Constantine's death. As a result the accusations of rape and mutilation are adjudicated in Constantius' reign rather than Constantine's.[62]

The sequence in the Greek lives is as follows: convocation of the council by Constantine in the thirtieth year of his reign; examination and refutation of charges such as the seizure of the linen vestments, the sacrilege in the church of the priest Ischyras, and the financial support of a would-be rebel; raising of the charge that Athanasius had threatened to withhold the shipment of grain to the capital, which led to his exile in Gaul; Constantine's death; resurgence of the Eusebian party under Constantius; recall of Athanasius from exile by Constantine's son Constantine II; renewed campaign by the Eusebians, who presented Constantius with the charges about Arsenius's severed hand and the rape of the Alexandrian woman.[63] This contradicts the sequence of events in Socrates (*HE* 1.28–32) and Theodoret (*HE* 1.30), and in the VAS (14–27, 33) as well, which all recognize that the rape and mutilation charges were adjudicated at Tyre during Constantine's lifetime.[64] Finally, had the Syriac epitomizer worked from the Greek lives, he would not have needed to put the stories of Athanasius's concealment in an ancestral grave and of his refuge with an Alexandrian virgin in an appendix. The Greek lives set both stories in a narrative context, the second during the reign of Constantius and the first during the reign of Valens.[65]

Despite the evidence that the VAS drew directly from Socrates and Theodoret, it is nevertheless worthy of note that the Syriac vita shares two bib-

62. It appears that Severus's homily on Athanasius also displaces part of the Council of Tyre to the reign of Constantius; cf. his account of the exposé of Arsenius at Tyre, *Hom.* 91 (PO 25: 20.3–21.5).

63. See VAG I.9–14. The "anger of Constantius" is alluded to at the close of this section (VAG I.14 [PG 25: cxcviii]). The sequence is the same in VAG II.3–7 and VAG III.3–8.

64. Barnes notes (*Athanasius and Constantius,* 200) that the displacement of the Council of Tyre after the death of Constantine is one of the errors in Rufinus's account (*HE* 10.17) that Socrates discovered belatedly, after having depended on Rufinus in the first two books of his own history, leading him to rewrite books 1 and 2 and to make greater use of Athanasius's writings and of other materials (see Soc., *HE* 2.1.1–5). The traditions that eventually fed into the Greek lives also had their chronology contaminated by this error.

65. Concealment in an ancestral tomb: VAG I.28 (PG 25: ccx), VAG II.14 (PG 25: ccxxii), and VAG III.17 (PG 25: ccxl).

lical allusions with the Greek hagiographical tradition that do not seem to occur elsewhere. The first is a passing reference to Isa 28:15 found in VAG, 1.9, which recounts the Eusebians' accusation that Athanasius had threatened to withhold the shipment of grain. Quoting Isaiah, the text refers to Athanasius's accusers as those *hoi, kata ton pammegan Ēsaian, kuousi ponon, kai tiktousin anomian, hoi pseudōs ethento tên elpida, kai tôi pseudei, eipon, skepasthêsometha.*[66] In exactly this context VAS 26 quotes the same words of Isaiah: *ʾa(y)k d-ʾemar nbiyâ sāmw b-daggālûtâ reʿyānhûn, wa-b-ʿûlâ ʾesattar(w)* ("As the prophet said, 'They made their resolutions in deceit, and took shelter in wrongdoing'"), a free citation of the Peshitta of Isa 28:15: *meṭṭul d-sāmn b-daggālûtâ tûklānan, wa-b-šûqrâ ʾesattarn* ("because we placed our hope in a lie, and in falsehood we were sheltered"). The other biblical allusion is a comparison of Athanasius with Elisha in the account in VAS 74–75 of Athanasius's evasion of a riverboat pursuit on the Nile, also found in VAG 1.26 and VAG III.15. The VAS is unique in (mistakenly) identifying Elisha's enemies as Edomites.[67] It represents an ornamental elaboration of the type that, according to Tetz, was designed to show him as a prophetic figure.[68] The occurrence of these allusions in the same places in both the VAS and the Greek lives is unlikely to be coincidental. And yet, a literary dependency is hard to reconcile with the evidence we have presented for a direct and unmediated connection between the VAS and Socrates and Theodoret.

With one or two exceptions, no linkage can be made between the VAS and the other Athanasian biographical accounts mentioned above. The possibility cannot be ruled out that the epitomizer knew the *Historia acephala,* although this seems unlikely. The *Historia acephala* treated Athanasius's episcopate as a period of forty years in its calculation of the exact time spent in exile and on his episcopal throne, thus making the last period of six years an irrelevant appendage. The reason has been debated. The most recent editor argues that 368, rather than 373, was chosen in order to give a round figure of forty for figuring the exact totals of years, months, and days spent in exile and in office.[69] The VAS makes the same distinction between the forty year oscillation of exile and

66. PG 25: cxcii.

67. PG 25: ccviii–ccix; PG 25: ccxliii. Cf. 2 Kings 6:18.

68. Tetz, "Zur Biographie des Athanasius," 166.

69. Martin, *Histoire "acéphale,"* 24. Lorenz's review of the Martin edition of the *Historia acephala* cites Schwartz's judgment that the forty-year period reflects the fact that it was first composed on the fortieth anniversary of Athanasius's episcopate, and later expanded ("Autour de l'Histoire Acéphale," 271).

office and the final six years of peace.[70] This is a slender thread on which to base a connection. As for the *Index to the Festal Letters,* despite its existence in Syriac, there is no evidence that the epitomizer was familiar with it.

The short Athanasian biography in Barḥadbešabba's *History* is a more interesting case. The two accounts share much material, as the following summary demonstrates. The pertinent sections of the VAS are given in parentheses.

Introduction (1).

Youthful discovery of Athanasius by Bishop Alexander (2–3).

Death of Alexander and accession of Athanasius (6).

Reconciliation of Theognis of Nicaea, Eusebius of Caesarea, and seven other excommunicates (7–10).

Their accusations before Constantine of confiscation of cloth and treasonous gift of gold (11).

Acquittal of Athanasius before Constantine (12).

Further accusations of murder, adultery, and sacrilege against the sacrament and the scriptures (12–14).

Council [of Tyre]: disproof of charges concerning the Alexandrian woman and Arsenius (15–24).

Disposition of charges made by Ischyras at another council [Jerusalem], at which bishops depose Athanasius (25).

Athanasius exiled after accusation about grain shipment (26–27).

"George the Arian" (sic) sent to Alexandria by Athanasius; enemies (36); his atrocities (49).

Return of Athanasius with permission of Bishop Julius of Rome (39).

Constantius, under pressure from Constans, acquiesces in Athanasius's return; sends him three letters (43).

Fresh accusations laid before Constantius: Athanasius confiscated the poor relief (40).

Constantius orders his death (48).

[Second] flight of Athanasius; his return, again with help from Julius and Constans (40-41).

Death of Constans, further accusations [unspecified] by Arians; Constantius again orders Athanasius's death; his [third] flight (46–48).

70. VAS 82. The datum is also found in VAG II.14 (PG 25: ccxxiii).

Athanasius secretly succoured for six years by a virgin in Alexandria (81).
Death of Constantius and return of Athanasius (69).
Julian's order to destroy Athanasius; his word about the passing cloud (72).
[Fourth] flight, via the riverboat ruse (73–74).
Return to Alexandria and concealment for four months in ancestral tomb (75, 81).
Emperor [Jovian] assures Athanasius of his safety (77).
Justification of Athanasius's flights by reference to Athanasius's *Apololgia de fuga* as cited in Soc., *HE* 3.8.
The impotence of Valens in face of Athanasius' popularity in his city.
Death of Athanasius after forty-six-year reign (78).

The parallels are close but far from complete. There are also numerous differences. Barḥadbešabba uses many personal names that do not occur in the VAS. He quotes Julius's letter to the Alexandrians and cites Rufinus by name as the source of the story about Athanasius's childhood.[71] He includes the detail, unique to his account so far as can be determined, that the woman at Tyre accused Athanasius of impregnating her.[72] The story about the sojourn with the Alexandrian virgin is set during the reign of Constantius.[73] The biblical exempla that he uses to justify Athanasius's flights come from Socrates's citation of Athanasius's *Apology for His Flight.* He is not much interested in the events following the death of Constantine. Such differences therefore make it unlikely that Barḥadbešabba knew the VAS.

It seems more probable that his version originated in the same way as the VAS, as a synopsis of material available in the fifth century ecclesiastical histories. The pericope of the six-year sojourn with the Alexandrian virgin shows up here too, though set in the reign of Constantius. As we have noted, the story is not found in Socrates and Theodoret. Its earliest attestations are Palladius and Sozomen, neither of whom is mentioned by the modern editor as a source for Barḥadbešabba's history.[74] This raises the intriguing possibility that it had

71. Letter to Julius: PO 23: 231.3–12, taken from Soc., *HE* 2.23. Rufinus's anecdote (PO 23; 224.7–225.5) comes via Soc., *HE* 1.15.

72. PO 23: 227.13.

73. PO 23: 232.9–11.

74. F. Nau, *La second partie de l'Histoire de Barḥadbešabba 'Arbaia,* PO 9 (1913), 500.

already found its way into a standard rendition of Athanasius's life, perhaps at an oral stage of transmission. The version in Barḥadbešabba would thus be a parallel witness to the VAS of the evolution of an Athanasian saga. Severus's homily, already cited, might also have grown out of such a standard account which would have been familiar to his listeners, making all the more effective his rhetorical contrast between the *'agûnâ* of the Christian athlete and those of pagan Olympic athletes.[75] All three texts may therefore constitute variations on a theme. The hypothesis of a standard oral version could also explain anomalies such as the parallel biblical citations in both the Syriac and the Greek lives, which might have crept into the tradition at some earlier stage in the formation of the saga. Scribal transcription would have been the work of those with the education to use written sources to fill out the narrative. The VAS is thus seen to be embedded in a larger tradition of Athanasian biography, which was fertile and versatile enough to cross linguistic, geographical, and confessional lines, being found in Byzantine, Monophysite (Severus of Antioch), and Nestorian (Barḥadbešabba) sources. The tradition's broad and diversified attestation may serve as a reminder of those deeper unities which, despite confessional strife, still linked the separated Christian churches of the Middle East.

75. Cf. the heading of the homily (PO 25: 7.3), the comparison near the end (PO 25: 25.6–26.12), and elsewhere (PO 25: 16.1, 17.1, 18.9, 19.6, etc.).

Sebastian P. Brock

6. RADICAL RENUNCIATION

The Ideal of msarrqûtâ

Msarrqûtâ is the beginning of the way
of exit from within the world,
it is the head of the road of crucifixion
and of the apostolic way of life.
As if from fetters the mind
is liberated from every care
and the bonds of all its thoughts
are severed and cast from it entirely;
it has cast the world away from its limbs
and has gone out to the wilderness with our Lord
as it takes upon its shoulders the toil
of voluntary afflictions.
By these two things is the athlete
accompanied for the beginning of the battle—
msarrqûtâ and a life of sojourning (*ʿedyāyûtâ*)—
for freedom of life in the wild.[1]

Although this passage from one of the *Sermones* attributed to Ephrem cannot possibly be by the saint himself,[2] it usefully serves to introduce right at the

1. E. Beck, *Des heiligen Ephrem des Syrers Sermones,* CSCO 334, Scr. Syri 148 (Louvain: Secrétariat du CorpusSCO, 1973), IV.i.21–36.

2. This is indicated by a number of features, such as the adjectival form *ṣebyānāyâ,* which is not attested until the late fifth century (once in Narsai) and only becomes common in the sixth century.

outset some of the main features of *msarrqûtâ.* But before drawing out these features, we need to face the problem of how best to render the term in English. Dictionaries and modern translations offer a variety of possibilities, such as "privation," "voluntary poverty," "renunciation," "voluntary renunciation of worldly goods," "self-deprivation," "emptying of self," "nonpossession," "nonpossessiveness," etc. Since (as will be seen) the term has somewhat different connotations in different sources, it will be best for the present purpose simply to use the transcription, so as not to prejudge these connotations.

The noun formation is based on the pa^{c}el of *s-r-q,* which normally has the sense of "to empty," and in fact it is perfectly clear that is based on the occurrence of the verb in a particular passage, Phil 2:7, *heauton ekenōsen,* or as the Peshitta translates it, *napšeh sarreq.* It so happens that *msarrqûtâ* is not attested in either Aphrahat or Ephrem, and appears for the first time in Syriac in the *Liber Graduum.* However, both Aphrahat and Ephrem do have passages employing different derivatives of the same root which happen to be of direct relevance.[3] Aphrahat employs the pa^{c}el of the verb with the reflexive on two occasions, neither of which has Christ as subject (as in Phil 2:7, whose phraseology Aphrahat must certainly have had in mind):

There is the person who fasts from anger and subdues his inclination (*yaṣreh*), so that he is not defeated; and there is the person who fasts from possessions in order to empty himself (*da-nsarreq napšeh*) for his ministry (*pûlḥāneh*). (Demonstration 3.1)

And

In the case of the person who empties himself (*d-napšeh nsarreq*), struggle befits him, because he is not calling to mind anything behind him and turning back to it. (Demonstration 7.20)[4]

Ephrem employs a noun derived from the pa^{c}el:

The law is divided up for us into three forms for it accords honor, consecration (*qûdšâ*) and virginity—(involving, respectively) possessions, renunciation (*sûrrāqâ*) and perfection (*gmîrûtâ*).[5]

3. Both also use the verb in a negative sense as well, "be emptied of, deprived of."

4. Cited from J.Parisot, PS 1 (Paris: Firmin-Didot, 1894).

5. E. Beck, *Des heiligen Ephraem des Syrers Hymnen contra Haereses,* CSCO 169, Scriptores Syri 77 (Louvain: Imprimerie Orientaliste, 1957), 45.10.

Two points in particular should be noted here. Firstly, both Aphrahat (Dem. 3) and Ephrem associate the "emptying" with "possessions."[6] They will certainly have had in mind three Gospel passages: Matt 19:21, where Jesus says to the rich young man, "Go and sell your possessions (*qenyānāk* C P; "all you have" S) and give to the poor ... "; Luke 12:33, "Sell your possessions (*qenyānkon* P; "everything you have" S C) and give alms"; and Luke 14:33, "Everyone of you who does not abandon all his possessions (*qenyāneh* S C P) cannot be my disciple." Ephrem in fact provides a second link with Matt 19:21, since he places *sûrrāqâ* midstage between possessions and perfection: this accords exactly with the Old Syriac (S C) reading where Jesus prefaces his instruction with "If you wish to become (*d-tehwê*) perfect" (Greek, P and Syriac Diatessaron apud Ephrem, C.Diat. XI.16, "to be").

Secondly, the wording of the second quotation from Aphrahat clearly reflects another utterance of Jesus concerning discipleship: Luke 9:62, "no one who puts his hand to the plough and looks behind him is fit for the kingdom of God."

How did the term *sûrrāqâ* (and later, *msarrqûtâ*), derived from Phil 2:7 *napsheh sarreq,* come to be associated with the giving up of possessions in the context of discipleship? The missing link would seem to be provided by mention of "the death on the cross" in Phil 2:8 and another of Jesus' sayings concerning discipleship, to be found earlier in Luke 14, at verse 27, "he who does not take up his cross and come after me cannot be a disciple of mine" (the parallel in Matt 10:38 is slightly different, with "is not worthy of me"). Discipleship thus demands "self-emptying." To see how this is developed in the Syriac tradition one needs to turn to the *Liber Graduum (Book of Steps),* probably from the late fourth century.[7]

It is in the *Book of Steps* that the derivative *msarrqûtâ* is first attested in Syriac, and it occurs four times.[8] Before turning to these, it is worth noticing a passage where the unknown author specifically uses the phrase *sarreq napšeh* of a disciple of Christ. At 6.1 (= col. 141, line 10) he states that the Paraclete is sent to "the person who has humbled himself from all that exists on earth ... and has emptied himself (*sarreq napšeh*) of all that he possesses." It will be noticed

6. For Ephrem's further association of *sûrrāqâ* with *qûdšâ,* see below.

7. Cited from M. Kmosko, PS 3 (Paris: Firmin-Didot, 1926).

8. The author also uses *sûrrāqâ* in much the same sense at 9.19 and 20.6.

that the author in fact reflects Philippians twice over, since "humbled himself" echoes 2:8. A considerable number of other passages in the *Book of Steps* link other derivatives of the verb *s-r-q* with the "emptying," or stripping away, of possessions: 27.4 (= col. 776, line 9), "as our Lord said (Matt 19:21), 'Come after me, being stripped (*kad msarrqîn*) of what is visible.'"[9]

The very first occurrence of the abstract *msarrqûtâ,* while clearly reflecting Phil. 2, likewise links the term with Christ's "greater commandments" (as the author designates them), concerning radical discipleship, to be found in the various Gospel passages already cited above: thus (1.2 (= col. 16, line 9):

Let us abandon everything (Luke 14:33) and go in the humility and *msarrqûtâ* of our Lord, which consists in the great commandments.

Significantly, the author subsequently (3.5) combines Luke 14:33 with mention of the cross in Matt 10:38, and inserts into Christ's words "and imitates me." Elsewhere it emerges that this motivation to imitate Christ arises when people "gaze on their Lord in heaven, as though in a mirror in their minds" (16.12).

Later passages point to three important further associations of *msarrqûtâ,* namely *qaddîšûtâ* (lit. "holiness," but here in the technical sense of marital continence), *meskînûtâ,* or poverty, and *'îḥidāyûtâ,* or singleness (again in the technical sense).[10] At 21.9 the author presents the Evil One as having said to Adam and Eve: "Acquire possessions and enjoy them ... throw away from yourselves asceticism (*'anwāyûtâ*), *msarrqûtâ,* and 'holiness,' and likewise humility ... "; and at 29.12 he speaks of fasting "in poverty, in *msarrqûtâ,* and in singleness (*'îḥidāyûtâ*)."

In connection with the first passage it is interesting to note the specific contrast with Christ who (21.11) "emptied himself also of what Adam desired, wanting to become a god, with earthly wealth." The idea that Adam wanted to become a god is already found in Ephrem.[11] Mention of "earthly wealth" (*'ûtrâ*) contrasts with yet another key passage in the Pauline corpus, 2 Corinthians 8:9, where Christ, "being rich, became poor" (*etmaskan kad 'îtaw(hy) 'attîrâ*). At the

9. Cp 3.6, "stripped (*kad msarrqîn*) and not possessing anything."

10. For these terms, see especially S. H. Griffith, "Asceticism in the Church of Syria: The Hermeneutics of Early Syrian Monasticism," in Vincent L. Wimbush and Richard Valantasis, eds., *Asceticism* (New York: Oxford University Press, 1995), 220–48.

11. E.g., Carmina Nisibena 69:12. "The Most High knew that Adam had wanted to become a god, / so He sent His Son who put him on in order to grant him his desire."

very beginning of chapter 21 the author tells his flock, if you want to come alive after the death caused by the Tree of Knowledge that slew our father Adam, and also us, "empty yourself (*estarraq*) and keep away from Satan and his teaching" (identified as "the world" and concern for it).[12]

The association at 21.9 of *msarrqûtâ* with *qaddîšûtâ* in its technical sense is illustrated at 9.19, where the author says that if God had told the Old Testament patriarchs "be emptied (*estarraq(w)*) of your wives and abandon your possessions, they would have done so."[13] At 7.2 these two ascetic ideals are further linked with "taking up the cross."

A fourth occurrence of the abstract *msarrqûtâ* is to be found at 12.1, where it emerges that there are two different levels, visible and hidden:

> since we believe that there is a hidden *msarrqûtâ* of the heart that abandons the earth and is raised up to heaven, let us be emptied (or stripped; *nestarraq*) in body too of our possessions and our inheritance, and then we will be keeping the commandments of him who gives life to all.

These two levels of "self-emptying," of the body and of the heart, are also mentioned elsewhere:

> The great, acceptable and perfect will of our Lord is this: that all human beings should keep their bodies in virginity, and that their hearts should be emptied out (*nestarrqûn*) of all hateful thoughts of sin, and (so) become sanctified, and that they should imitate our Lord and take up his cross and go after him and become perfected in his love which loves all and which gives peace to all. [The author goes on to quote Matt 10:37 and 19:29.][14]

An important element in this statement concerns the "becoming perfect in his love which loves all." What this implies is made explicit in 20.14:

> A person will not grow and become perfect unless he makes himself poor, is emptied of self (*mestarraq*), is made holy, and humbles himself, according to the likeness which our Lord showed us, loving his enemies and those who would kill him, praying for them in love.[15]

12. Compare 3.15 "emptied of the world" (*msarraq men 'almâ*); almost exactly the same phrase features in the *Macarian Homilies* (cited in n. 38); it is found in later Syriac writers, e.g., Isaac of Antioch (Paul Bedjan, ed., *Homiliae S. Isaaci Syri Antiocheni* [Leipzig: Harrassowitz, 1903], 534), and Philoxenus (see n.27).

13. A similar phrase recurs at 28.11, *netqaddaš men 'a(n)tteh.* In a similar way the passage cited above from Ephrem, *Hymnus contra Haereses* 45.10, places *surrâqâ* in parallelism with *qûdšâ.*

14. 30.25; compare also 10.8, "In the case of anyone whose heart is emptied of the earth and of his possessions, his body will also be emptied of it."

15. Similar passages will be found in 3.12 and 25.7.

In the *Book of Steps, msarrqûtâ* (together with related phrases) is an ideal only for the "mature," or "perfect" (*gmîrê*), who seek to do Christ's "perfect will" (15.11, 30.25) and carry out the "great commandments"; it is not something to which the *kî'ne,* or "upright" are able to aspire.

It is interesting that the most detailed fourth-century witness to the ideal of *msarrqûtâ* was evidently living in the Persian Empire.[16] The various links between the *Book of Steps* and the *Macarian Homilies,*[17] however, indicate that the ascetic mentality of the *Book of Steps* was also known in Roman Syria, and it is in a Syriac writer associated with Apamea that the abstract *msarrqûtâ* next appears. John of Apamea, or John the Ihidaya (conventionally, but not very satisfactorily, translated "the Solitary"), could be said to pick up from where the *Book of Steps* left off, for he is primarily concerned with what the *Book of Steps* called *msarrqûtâ* of the heart: as he emphasizes on several occasions, *msarrqûtâ* of possessions is but the first step on the road to perfection. In the *Dialogue on the Soul,* in answer to Eusebius's question "What is the beginning of the mode of life (*dûbbārâ*) of the inner person?" John replies, "*msarrqûtâ* of the love of money," to which he adds immediately that "it is absolutely necessary to go on and to empty oneself (*d-nestarraq*) of the passion of vainglory."[18] Likewise, in the Letters "*msarrqûtâ* from possessions is not perfection, but only the firstfruits (*rîšîtâ*) of the mode of life of faith."[19] Evidently there were some who thought that getting rid of one's possessions was a quick way to perfection:

> What shall be say about the many people who suppose that they have attained perfection with *msarrqûtâ* from possessions? Just as alongside fasting from foodstuffs, another kind of fasting, from evil, is appropriate, so alongside *msarrqûtâ* from bodily possessions, *msarrqûtâ* from the possession of evil passions is required.[20]

It is probably significant that John sometimes speaks of *msarrqûtâ* of "the love of money" (*reḥmat kespâ,* the Peshitta's rendering of *philarguria* in 1 Tim

16. The evidence for this lies in the reference to the river Zab (30.14).

17. These have been well brought out by Columba Stewart, *"Working the Earth of the Heart": The Messalian Controversy in History, Texts, and Language to AD 431* (Oxford: Clarendon, 1991). See n. 11 for a further phraseological link.

18. S. Dedering, *Johannes von Lycopolis, Ein Dialog über die Seele und die Affekte des Menschen* (Leipzig: Harrassowitz, 1936), 6.

19. L. G. Rignell, *Briefe von Johannes dem Einsiedler* (Lund: A-B. Ph. Lindstedts Univ., Bokhandel, 1941), 56, line 3; compare 64, line 18, "*msarrqûtâ* from possessions is (just) the beginning of the mode of life of the inner person."

20. *Briefe,* p. 64, line 11ff.

6:10), for it would seem that for him, *msarrqûtâ* of possessions primarily involved nonpossessiveness, rather than nonpossession. This, at least, would seem to be implied by his statement that "the self-emptying of the passion of bad thoughts" can only take place after one has begun on *msarrqûtâ* from possessions."[21] In the same passage John goes on to describe the next stage on the spiritual journey: "and unless one is emptied of the passions of hateful stirrings, one will not acquire purity of soul—which is the beginning of the mode of life (*dûbbārâ*) of the New Person"; here it is clear that "the mode of life of the New Person" is an advanced stage of "the mode of life of the inner person." In the *Dialogue on the Soul* the same progression is described in slightly different terms:

> From *msarrqûtâ* of the love of money there begins the mode of life of the inner person, and this moves on to luminosity of soul (*šapyût napšâ*), and from there onwards a person begins on the mode of life of the New Life, with the continual growth of (spiritual) knowledge.[22]

Later in the *Dialogue on the Soul* John distinguishes three different levels of *msarrqûtâ,* following his well-known tripartite division of the level of the body (*pagrānûtâ*), the level of the soul (*napšānûtâ*) and the level of the spirit (*rûḥānûtâ*):

> Bodily *msarrqûtâ* is the abandonment of possessions, *msarrqûtâ* on the level of the soul (*napšānîtâ*) is the stripping off of the passions, while *msarrqûtâ* on the level of the spirit (*rûḥānîtâ*) is the removal of all suppositions (*masbrānwātâ*).[23]

He goes on to explain that here on earth we are emptied of possessions and we are also able to be emptied of the passions, but *msarrqûtâ* from suppositions belongs to the life after the resurrection.

In another work, John provides the starting point for a development of the theme of *msarrqûtâ* along different lines when he states that the interior self-emptying involves the various senses: "sight, hearing, and the rest of the senses, which act as fetters."[24] John does not himself use the term "freedom" or "liberation" in this connection, but the idea that *msarrqûtâ* brings "freedom" is one

21. *Briefe,* p. 56, line 13.

22. *Ein Dialog über die Seele,* 8.

23. I.e. only then will it be a matter of reality, as opposed to hope and supposition. *Ein Dialog über die Seele,* 85.

24. L.G. Rignell, *Drei Traktate von Johannes dem Einsiedler (Johannes von Apameia),* Lunds Universitets Årsskrift, N.F. Avd.1, Bd 54, 4 (Lund: CWK Gleerup, 1960), 4.

that appears in several later writings (including the *mêmrâ* falsely attributed to Ephrem, quoted at the outset). Thus the title of a poem by one of the various poets named Isaac actually identifies *msarrqûtâ* as "true freedom,"[25] but it is Isaac of Nineveh who gives particular attention to this aspect. Before turning to Isaac and other seventh-century authors, however, some attention should be paid to what Philoxenus has to say on the subject in his *Discourses.*

Ironically, in the one discourse that is actually entitled "On *msarrqûtâ,*" Philoxenus in fact only rarely uses the term, and it is mostly in other discourses that he employs it.[26] Since Philoxenus takes over the "two-tier" pattern of the *Book of Steps*'s "upright" and "perfect" (or "mature"), though altering the term "upright" to "just," it is not surprising that he should follow the *Book of Steps* in his teaching about *msarrqûtâ.* Thus he states that Christ "handed down (the ideal of) perfection to his disciples in those commandments which he gave them concerning *msarrqûtâ,*" and that this applies to anyone who strives after perfection.[27] A little further on (240) he urges: "Let us therefore accept the yoke of *msarrqûtâ,* just as our Saviour has commanded us." Again, like the *Book of Steps,* he speaks of *msarrqûtâ* both "from possessions" and "from the world" (14, 16). On the other hand he reflects John of Apamea when he distinguishes between *msarrqûtâ* of body and that of the soul (16), and he follows him too when he states that the latter presupposes the former:

> Once a person has stripped off the world in this manner and has become someone completely emptied (*msarrqâ gmîrâ*) of all that is visible, then he will begin to strip off the evil passions (269).

Although at one point (273) Philoxenus says that "perfection is to be found in *msarrqûtâ* from possessions," he evidently means that *msarrqûtâ* is simply a sine qua non, for elsewhere he emphasizes that "when someone is emptied of all that he has, this person does not yet commence on the road of (Christ's) teaching, seeing that *msarrqûtâ* is the end of the road of righteousness which is performed in this world," whereas "Take up your cross and follow me" is the beginning of the way

25. Bedjan, *Homiliae S. Isaaci Syri Antiocheni,* p. 135.

26. This is a homily that, in an abbreviated form, was also transmitted under the name of Gregory of Nyssa; the true author was identified by M. Parmentier, "Pseudo-Gregory of Nyssa's Homily on Poverty," *Aram* 5 (1993): 401–26.

27. E. A. W. Budge, ed., *The Discourses of Philoxenus* (London: Asher & Co., 1894), 1:236 (Syriac text; the page numbers of the Syriac are also given in the English translation in volume 2).

of the spiritual mode of life (349).[28] *Msarrqûtâ* (from possessions) is elsewhere described as "the gate" from this world to "the other (or next) world of the spirit" (344). A little earlier in the same discourse Philoxenus uses the analogy of birth: there are three kinds of birth, he says (342): from the womb into the created world; from slavery to freedom—that is, from being an ordinary human being to becoming a child of God "which happens through grace at baptism"; and "when a person is born in his will, out of the bodily mode of life into the spiritual, the womb that gives birth to him in this way being *msarrqûtâ* from everything."

A two-stage model of the spiritual life, found in the *Book of Steps* and Philoxenus, also features in an anonymous East Syriac commentary on the *Asceticon* of Abba Isaiah. In this the author distinguishes between the two kinds of *msarrqûtâ,* from possessions, and from evil thoughts; the former he associates with "bodily mode of life" (*dûbbārâ pagrānāyâ*), whereas the latter belongs to "the mode of life of the cross, which is the mode of life of the mind."[29] Another seventh-century East Syriac commentator on Abba Isaiah's *Asceticon,* Dadisho Qatraya, subdivides interior *msarrqûtâ* into that which is "from possessions," that which is "from the senses," and that which is "from the passions." It is only the combination of all three that constitutes "complete *msarrqûtâ.*"[30]

The poem cited at the beginning of this chapter spoke of *msarrqûtâ* as "liberating" the mind from its fetters and bonds. This is an emphasis that Isaac of Nineveh gives on several occasions. The Fathers of old, he tells us (537), "put on *msarrqûtâ* as armor, since it liberates from many struggles,"[31] and elsewhere he states that *msarrqûtâ* "releases our stirrings from bonds" (439).[32] Isaac curiously reflects the thought of another *mêmrâ* wrongly attributed to Ephrem when he speaks of someone "being raised above the world by his *msarrqûtâ*" (539): in this poem *msarrqûtâ* flies up to heaven, and the author urges: "On the wings of *msarrqûtâ* let us fly off and meet (the saints)."[33]

In Isaac's writings *msarrqûtâ* goes hand in hand with *šelyâ,* or the solitary's

28. Compare 423, where *msarrqûtâ* is said to constitute "the end of the road of the world"; similarly 292–93, 340.

29. René Draguet, ed., *Commentaire anonyme du Livre d'Abba Isaie (fragments),* CSCO 336, Scriptores Syri 150 (Louvain: Secrétariat du CorpusSCO, 1973), 41.

30. René Draguet, ed., *Commentaire du Livre d'Abba Isaie par Dadisho Qatraya (VIIe siecle),* CSCO 326, Scr. Syri 144 (Louvain: Secrétariat du CorpusSCO, 1972), 9.

31. Paul Bedjan, ed., *Mar Isaacus Ninivita de Perfectione Religiosa* (Leipzig: Harrassowitz , 1909), 537.

32. Compare also 56, 67.

33. Beck, *Sermones,* 4.2, lines 28, 53.

life of stillness. One of the temptations for those who had adopted this exalted, but difficult, way of life was to perform acts of charity. The temptation is posed dramatically in a question to an elder: Should I chose what disturbs my stillness (*šelyûtâ*) in order to "give rest" to my neighbor, or should I neglect this in order to persevere in stillness and *msarrqûtâ,* just being concerned with minutiae concerning my own soul, not allowing myself to fall into many worries and concerns about others? The reply is that works of charity are for lay people and for those solitaries who are deficient in their ministry (*pûlḥānâ*) of stillness: true solitaries should not abandon the ministry of heavenly matters, which resembles that of the angels (147). Similar advice is given in another passage (56):

If you have already set yourself the goal of *msarrqûtâ* and, by the grace of God, you have been freed from care and become above the world in your *msarrqûtâ,* take care lest, out of love for the poor, you are attracted to fall into concern from possessions and material things on the pretext of performing charitable acts.

From another passage in Isaac, it is clearly a question of priorities (440):

Love of God comes from converse with him; the converse of prayer comes through stillness; stillness comes with *msarrqûtâ*; *msarrqûtâ* comes through perseverance; perseverance comes through disgust at the lusts, and disgust as the desires comes through fear of Gehenna.

Furthermore, the role of the solitary should be seen as performing a ministry on a cosmic, and not individual, level: "Oppression (in society) is eradicated by means of (a solitary's) compassion and *msarrqûtâ*" (63).

Alongside the emphasis given to the "greater commandments" as the rationale for *msarrqûtâ,* the *Book of Steps* had also spoken of it as being part of the imitation of Christ himself. It is this latter perspective that is found in several writers of the East Syriac monastic tradition of the seventh and eighth centuries. Thus Sahdona speaks of the monk who "places before himself the *msarrqûtâ* of Christ whom he loves and rejoices in converse with him."[34] A little further on, Sahdona combines both perspectives (33):

He (Christ) taught that everyone who was willing to be *msarrqâ,* should be emptied of everything, like himself, seeing that he, being in the likeness of him who had sent

34. *Martyrius (Sahdona). Oeuvres spirituelles,* ed. A. de Halleux, CSCO 200, Scr. Syri 86 (Louvain: Secrétariat du CorpusSCO, 1960), 1:32.

him, who is rich in everything, had become emptied (*estarraq*), the one who "had emptied himself" (*sarreq napšeh*) and become poor of his own will for our sakes, so that through his poverty he might enrich us.... This is the glorious combination of the solitary's mode of life: *msarrqûtâ* ... with perfect love.

Another East Syriac writer who brings out the aspect of the imitation of Christ is the anonymous commentator on Abba Isaiah's *Asceticon*:

Blessed is the solitary who has subdued his body with ascetic labors and slain sin, whose heart has been purified and he has arrived at perfection, seeing that he has travelled in the footsteps of our Lord and imitated his *msarrqûtâ* and humiliation, his gentleness and his compassion, and has suffered and been afflicted like him. Such a person our Lord has held worthy of his love, and of the sight of his glory—here in pledge, in the revelation of light, and there perfectly, in the Kingdom of heaven, just as the holy apostle said, "If we suffer with him, we shall also be glorified with him" (Rom. 8:17).[35]

Isaac of Nineveh's writings were translated into Greek at the Palestinian Monastery of Mar Saba in the late eighth or early ninth century, and this provides a convenient way of discovering what was considered to be the Greek equivalent of *msarrqûtâ.* Although in one passage it is rendered by *ptōcheia,*[36] in the vast majority of cases the translator employs *aktēmosunē,* "nonpossession, nonpossessiveness." The choice was felicitous in many ways, for this happens to have been the term used already in the early third century by Clement of Alexandria in connection with the disciples' question to Jesus concerning riches.[37] That *aktēmosunē,* and the related form *aktēmōn,* were already considered counterparts to *msarrqûtâ* and *msarrqâ* in the fourth century is suggested by the passages where these terms occur in the *Macarian Homilies.*[38]

The Greek counterpart to *msarrqûtâ* brings us to a final significant point. The Greek term, though used of the various Gospel injunctions about leaving behind possessions, has no obvious link with the Greek wording of Philippians 2:7, Christ's own "self-emptying." It is the deliberate desire to link the passage

35. Draguet, *Commentaire anonyme,* 55.

36. Bedjan, *Mar Isaacus Ninivita,* 56 = N. Theotokou, *Tou hosiou patros hēmōn Isaak ... ta heurêthenta askêtika,* ed. I. Spetsieris (1895, repr., Thessaloniki: B. Rhegopoulos, 1977), 100.

37. *Quis dives salvetur,* 20.

38. *Makarios/Symeon. Reden und Briefe. Die Sammlung I,* ed. H. Berthold, GCS (Berlin: Akademie Verlag, 1973), 1:28, 108, 120, 162. At 2:190, however, the author uses *kenoō: kenōn heauton apo tou kosmou toutou.*

in Philippians with the "greater commandments" of the Gospels that led to the adoption of the term *msarrqûtâ* in connection with the latter: to follow these "greater commandments" is not just to carry out Christ's bidding, it is also—and more importantly—an *imitatio Christi* in a very profound sense.[39]

39. Conversely, Christ is seen as having told his disciples to do, *mutatis mutandis,* what he had himself already done at the *kenosis/msarrqûtâ* of the incarnation. Other examples of early Syriac tradition adopting a particular choice of wording in order to bring out connections perceived between two different biblical passages can be found in my "Passover, Annunciation and Epiclesis: Some Remarks on the Term *aggen* in the Syriac Versions of Luke 1:35," *Novum Testamentum* 24 (1982): 222–33, and "The Gates/Bars of Sheol Revisited," in W. Petersen, J. S. Vos and H. J. de Jonge, eds., *Sayings of Jesus Canonical and Non-canonical,* Supplements to Novum Testamentum 89 (Leiden: Brill, 1997), 7–24.

Susan Ashbrook Harvey

7. HOUSEKEEPING

An Ascetic Theme in Late Antiquity

One of the motifs especially dear to early Christian writers was that of the house as a metaphor for the human person, or of the body as a temple or sanctuary. Biblical allusions from both the Hebrew Bible and New Testament underlay this imagery. In Late Antiquity, however, this complex of building metaphors gained an additional set of images with the development of housekeeping as an image for ascetic discipline. In particular, the tasks and methods of cleaning house proved to be effective tropes for the practice of long-term asceticism, as a means for maintaining the self-identity of the Christian devotee whose vocational life was conducted with permanent commitment. Where the imagery of house *building* was suggestive for the task of constructing and establishing a given religious identity, house*keeping* provided a rhetoric that stressed continual attention to the state of the self. It signaled the need for constant, diligent, at times unpleasant drudgery as a necessary component of ongoing ascetic vocation; it counteracted any tendency to romanticize the ascetic life. Above all, it addressed pragmatically the fact that sustained asceticism (such as that of the monastic or recluse), as opposed to short-term practice (such as Lent or specific penances might warrant), could lead to lethargy, psychological dullness, or complacency.

At the same time, the occurrence of housekeeping images in a Christian literature produced predominantly by and for male subjects is striking. Its appearance may alert us to interesting social consequences in the emergence of the single-sex household as various forms of the ascetic life and monasticism rose into view over the course of the fourth century. For the most part, housekeeping as a cleaning enterprise had been obscured in earlier literature of the ancient Mediterranean—occluded from the historian's gaze by its relegation to the domain of "female" activity. Its presence in late antique ascetic discourse across a diversity of social locations indicates a genuine change in social organization. That change makes evident a further set of considerations that ought to command the attention of the religious historian of the ancient world. One is an apparent shift—in some literature, at least—away from a rhetoric concerned with the cultic conditions of purity and pollution, and a turn instead towards a stress on moral psychology through the ordering (cleaning) of the passions. Another is a subtext within monastic literature that indicates a prevalent concern with how the practice of asceticism affected basic cultural assumptions of health and illness. Clearly, then, imagistic play with the tasks, methods, effects, and results of housekeeping allowed a rhetorical space in which ascetic advocates and practitioners could negotiate the difficult terrain of a shifting social, religious, and cultural landscape.

Sources for the Imagery

An eclectic array of biblical texts lay behind the image. In the Book of Proverbs, for example, Wisdom builds her house strongly with seven pillars (Prov 9:1), while Folly would tear it down (Prov 14:1). Proverbs contrasts the house of the harlot, prepared for seduction, with that of the good wife who runs her household with efficiency, wisdom, and kindness (Prov 7:6–23, 31:10–31). Indeed, biblical writers seem to assume a direct identification between the temple or sanctuary prepared as a place fit for the Lord's dwelling, and the human person as the microcosm thereof. The elaborate preparations described in Exodus, chapter 40, for the erection, anointing, and adornment of the tabernacle, and then for the washing, vesting, and anointing of its priests, find their parallel in passages that treat the preparation of the person who would be cleansed and purified for God (Ps 51:2), just as much as they resemble Levitical injunctions for cleansing the property of an infected house (Lev 14:33–54). Human and divine persons, it would seem, should seek to share the same dwellings, whether built by hands, by morals, or by personal intention; therefore, dwelling places of all varieties require appropriate construction, preparation, and adornment.

Yet the Psalms admonish, "Unless the Lord builds the house, those who build it labor in vain" (Ps 127:1). The faithful believer was thus one whose own hands worked as instruments for the Lord's purpose, whether as designer, construction engineer, or household servant. New Testament writers take up the house image as one that serves to identify the human person in relation to the divine. In their usage houses both conceal and reveal their contents, with unequivocal moral consequences. In Matthew, Jesus castigates the scribes and Pharisees as hypocrites who are "like whitewashed tombs, which outwardly appear beautiful, but within they are full of dead men's bones and all uncleanness" (Matt 23:27). By contrast, the Gospel of John plays on the image of Jesus as the one who replaces and fulfills the Jerusalem temple with the "temple (*naos*) of his body" (John 2:13–22);[1] and Jesus instructs his disciples, "If a man loves me, he will keep my word, and my father will love him, and we will come to him and make our home (*monê*) with him" (John 14:23).[2]

These occasional threads of house imagery are brought together in the New Testament letters with particular clarity and weight. Paul speaks in several places of the human body as God's "building" (*oikodomê*), but especially as God's "temple" (*naos*)—a holy place in which the Holy Spirit should dwell, and which ought accordingly to be kept clean of defilement and worthy of its purpose (1 Cor. 3:9, 16–7; 1 Cor. 6:19–20; 2 Cor. 6:16–7.1).[3] With echoes of the Psalmist's admonition, Paul uses house building to describe a human-divine partnership in the construction of the believing community: "According to the commission of God given to me, like a skilled master builder I laid a foundation, and another man is building upon it. Let each man take care how he builds upon it. For no other foundation can any one lay than that which is laid, which is Jesus Christ" (1 Cor 3:10–15). Subsequently, 2 Timothy reminds the faithful that any great house has both precious vessels of gold and silver and ignoble ones of wood and clay; the exhortation here is to make oneself "a vessel (*skeuos*) for noble use, consecrated and useful to the master of the house, ready for any good work" (2 Tim 2:20–1). In a famous passage from 1 Peter, the faithful commu-

1. The disciples perceive that Jesus speaks not of the Jerusalem Temple, but "*peri tou naou tou sômatos autou*" (John 2:22).

2. *Monên par' autô(i) poiêsometha* (John 14:23).

3. Compare 2 Cor. 5:1–8, where Paul speaks of the body as an "earthly tent," in contrast with the "building (*oikodomên*) from God, a house not made with hands (*oikian acheiropoiêton*)" that awaits the faithful believer in heaven.

nity is urged to come to Christ "the living stone" (*lithos*) and "be built into a spiritual house" (*oikos pneumatikos*), with Christ "the stone which the builders rejected" now become the very cornerstone of the building (1 Pet 2:4–8, quoting from Ps 118:22).

Biblical texts present a diverse base of house imagery. Houses, their construction, preparation for habitation, and adornment could serve as a flexible motif in discussions about the human person in relation to God. The motif was found serviceable for Jewish writers as well as Christian ones. Philo of Alexandria, for example, found it useful for correlating with Platonic imagery of God as the demiurge or craftsman of the universe (e.g., *Cherubim* 127–28). He found it further useful to urge consideration of the human self as a building in which the rational mind of the person dwelt, and which the divine Logos would enter and scrutinize to determine its true condition (*Worse Is Wont to Attack Better,* 22–24; *On the Unchangeableness of God,* 134–35; *Questions on Genesis,* 4.62). Like Paul, but at greater length, Philo pursued the image of the virtuously devoted human soul as a fit dwelling for God. The challenge was to render oneself worthy of such an inhabitant:

> Seeing then that our souls are a region open to his invisible entrance, let us make that place as beautiful as we may, to be a lodging fit for God. Else he will pass silently into some other home, where he judges that the builder's hands have wrought something worthier. When we think to entertain kings, we brighten and adorn our own houses. We despise no embellishment, but use all such freely and ungrudgingly, and make it our aim that their lodging shall have every delight and the honor withal that is their due. What house shall be prepared for God the King of kings, the Lord of all?[4]

In this passage, Philo goes on to consider what building materials and types of ornamentation would prove most appropriate to the divine dwelling place. Elsewhere, again not unlike Paul, Philo plays with the notion of the soul as the altar of God, a space that must be treated and kept just as the physical altar in the temple, urging that one should seek to become "an animate shrine of the Father."[5] At one point Philo takes the imagery one step further, to include not

4. Philo, *Cherubim* 98–9, trans. F. H. Colson and G. H. Whitaker, in *Philo,* Loeb Classical Library (New York: G. P. Putnam's Sons, 1929), 2:68–69.

5. Philo, *Questions and Answers on Exodus* 2.51, in *Philo: Supplement* II, trans. Ralph Marcus, Loeb Classical Library (Cambridge, Mass.: Harvard University Press, 1970), 97–99. See also *Special Laws* I, 269–72, 287–88.

only construction, preparation, and ornamentation, but—apparently—basic maintenance, too.

> But God is said to inhabit a house not in the sense of dwelling in a particular place, for he contains all things and is contained by none, but in the sense that his special providence watches over and cares for that spot. For every master of a house must needs have the care of that house laid on him as a charge. Verily let everyone on whom the goodness of God's love has fallen as rain, pray that he may have for his tenant the All-ruler who shall exalt this petty edifice, the mind, high above the earth and join it to the ends of heaven.[6]

As we should expect with this background, Origen, too, will pursue the imagery of the human person as a house, but especially as a tabernacle or sanctuary for God. In his *Homily 9 on Exodus,* Origen considers how one might go about constructing God's proper dwelling in the human body, and in the Christian community. Prompted by the detailed instructions from Exodus on the building and adornment of the tabernacle, Origen applies the imagery to present both the life of virtue and the ritual practices of the Christian. His exposition is influenced by Paul, who used the Hellenistic philosophical trope of clothing the person with virtues as with garments.[7] In Origen's presentation, then, the virtues in their diversity are fitting adornments for the sanctuary's ornamentation, when that sanctuary is the collective body of the believing community or when it is the body of the individual believer. Moreover, the virtues are fit clothing for the "inner man" who would serve as "high priest" for an interior liturgy modeled on that conducted by the church itself. In the interior tabernacle of the believer, sacrifice, prayer, incense offerings, and all the ritual actions prescribed in Exodus—and, by implication, enacted in the liturgical life of the historical church—find their counterparts in the proper disposition of soul, the practice of contemplation, and the virtuous conduct of the faithful individual.[8]

Elsewhere, however, in his *Homily 27 on Numbers,* Origen makes a passing allusion to a different aspect of houses as dwelling places. Discussing the need for vigilant discipline of one's soul, Origen reminds his readers that unsalted

6. Phil, *On Sobriety,* 63–64; *Philo,* trans. Colson and Whitaker, 3:476–77.

7. E.g., Col. 3:12–17.

8. Origen, *Homily 9 on Exodus,* "On the Tabernacle," in *Origen: Homilies on Genesis and Exodus,* trans. Ronald E. Heine, Fathers of the Church 71 (Washington, D.C.: The Catholic University of America Press, 1982), 334–45.

meat, no matter its quality, will rot.[9] The comment is not overtly linked to the construction or adornment of houses. Instead, it points to the less glamorous, and generally less visible, dimension of living in houses: without basic housekeeping, not only of the building but also of its rooms, its furnishings, its décor, and indeed of the daily necessities of those who dwell in it (i.e., food and drink), no house will remain a healthy place in which to live. Housekeeping—as opposed to house building or decorating—seems rarely to have been included in the imagistic play on houses found in biblical texts or early commentators like Philo or Origen. Yet Origen often foreshadows themes that become important in late antique ascetic writings, and so, too, in the brief instance from *Homily 27 on Numbers.* From the fourth century on, Christian ascetic writers often find housekeeping a useful image for their purposes. The usage is striking for its deliberate distinction from the earlier imagery of constructing, preparing, and adorning a building. It presents basic maintenance as a continuing and necessary concern; it does not always elicit the glorious context of royal or temple imagery; its focus is often hygienic. For the remainder of this paper, I would like to examine instances of the housekeeping motif as it occurs in late antique ascetical literature. My purpose is to ask how house*keeping*—as opposed to house *building*—contributed to late antique ascetical discourse as a discourse of sustained self-maintenance.

Housework, Hidden Work

Historians have sometimes complained that we know less about ancient housekeeping than we might wish. The reasons for the lacuna in evidence are to be expected: in the highly gendered division of labor seen throughout the ancient Mediterranean, men built the houses, while women cleaned them. With the vast majority of our surviving literature authored by men, the absence of any serious treatment of house cleaning is no surprise. Like the account of the "good wife" given in Proverbs 31:10–31, Greek and Roman authors discussed the responsibilities and activities of housewives in terms of what men would have seen of the household economy. The supervision of slaves, servants, and

9. Origen, *Homily 27 on Numbers,* in *Origen: Selected Works,* trans. Rowan Greer (New York: Paulist Press, 1979), 263.

children; the buying and selling of household goods and food; the production of meals; the production and upkeep of clothing, linens, utensils, tools; the appropriate appearance of the house—all of these find their mention in Greek and Roman treatments of a wife's duties.[10] What are missing are the descriptions of household spaces and uses, and of how things were done: details on cooking, weaving, embroidery, and especially on the challenges of housework in a premodern culture are rarely to be found.[11]

We can sometimes learn more from medical and scientific literature. In Pliny's *Natural History,* for example, we may find instructions on which plants are effective pesticides for storing clothing, or which plants provide healthful fumigants;[12] we may learn that soaking books in citrus oil would protect them from moths; frequent fumigations with myrrh would help wine to store better in jars and cellars.[13] Aromatics in general were widely used in ancient Mediterranean cultures to ward off insects, rodents, and snakes; they were also used as cleaning agents for objects, places, and persons.[14] Natural histories, botanical lists, and discussions of *materia medica* all provide interesting sidelights on the products used in the care and maintenance of the household.

But a better sense of the mundane picture emerges with early Christian writings, where descriptions of domestic housekeeping duties become part of a commonly heard rhetoric exhorting the Christian to abandon traditional family life for the life of celibate devotion to God. Christian authors take an interest in the details of domesticity because of their own agenda to redefine the nature and composition of the household. Jerome's description of the herculean labors confronting the harried housewife and mother when her husband arrives

10. For an excellent overview of Greek and Latin literature on the subject, see Susan Treggiari, *Roman Marriage: Justi Conjuges from the Time of Cicero to the Time of Ulpian* (New York: Oxford University Press, 1991), 185–228. For the notion that basic housecleaning may have been fairly simple because the ancient household was simpler than the modern one, see Lionel Casson, *Everyday Life in Ancient Rome* (Baltimore: Johns Hopkins University Press, 1998), 32-33.

11. Gillian Clark, *Women in Late Antiquity: Pagan and Christian Lifestyles* (New York: Oxford University Press, 1993), 94–118, gives a trenchant view of the evidence and its problems. There is much help in understanding the basic mechanics of daily household routines in Eunice Dauterman Maguire, Henry Maguire, and Maggie J. Duncan-Flowers, *Art and Holy Powers in the Early Christian House* (Urbana, Ill.: University of Illinois Press, 1989).

12. E.g., Pliny, *Natural History* 12.7 (on citron to store and protect clothing), 12.40 (on the stobrus tree for purposes of fumigation); 12.45 (on styrax as a fumigant).

13. Pliny, *Natural History* 13.27, 14.27.

14. Béatrice Caseau, *Euodia: The Use and Meaning of Fragrances in the Ancient World and Their Christianization (100–900 AD)* (Ann Arbor: University Microfilms, 1994).

home with unexpected dinner guests is both comical and hair-raising.[15] It also provides some useful details: for company the vigilant wife would wish to have couches smoothed, floors swept, a table properly laid, and the food ready—to say nothing of well-behaved, orderly servants and quiet, tidy children.

John Chrysostom, in turn, bluntly condemns clergy or monks who have serving women—even if they are consecrated virgins—living in their households. He insists there is no good reason for the women to be there. There is nothing so difficult in the basic requirements of housework that men cannot perform such tasks better than women, he reasons. Since men are physically stronger than women, it cannot be hard for them to oversee clothing storage, setting the table, making the bed, looking after linen and carpets, keeping the fire, or washing feet.[16] Similar concerns clearly lie behind the early fifth-century Syriac Rabbula canons when they forbid the consecrated virgins known as the Daughters of the Covenant from serving the priests, deacons, or Sons of the Covenant.[17] Most pointedly, these canons admonish that the male clergy "shall not compel the Daughters of the Covenant to weave garments for them by force." [18] It seems not to have been uncommon for those men who had taken vows of celibacy to seek, nonetheless, to continue to follow established social customs in the care and keeping of a household: if they did not take wives, they at least seem to have attempted traditional household maintenance, with women in service.

Indeed, the emergence of the ascetic, single-sex household—and later its organized communal form, the monastery—appears to have brought a sea change in the (male) awareness of and attunement to the nature of mundane housework. We may sense the shift when Ephrem Syrus (d. 373) portrays God as an effective housekeeper, likening God's work in the defeat of heretics to that of the housekeeper who makes a broom of thorny twigs, sweeps up loose debris, binds it together in a tidy bundle, and throws it away.[19] Ephrem's representation

15. Jerome, *Against Helvidius,* 20.

16. Chrysostom, "Instruction and Refutation Directed against Those Men Cohabiting with Virgins," sec. 9, in *Jerome, Chrysostom and Friends: Essays and Translations,* trans. Elizabeth A. Clark (New York: Edwin Mellen Press, 1979), 164–208, at 191–92.

17. "The Rules of Rabbula for the Clergy and the Qeiama," in Arthur Vööbus, ed. and trans., *Syriac and Arabic Documents Regarding Legislation Relative to Syrian Asceticism* (Stockholm: Estonian School of Theology in Exile, 1960), 34–50, esp. Canons 3 and 4.

18. "Rules of Rabbula for the Clergy and the Qeiama," Canon 3; Vööbus, *Syriac and Arabic Documents,* 38.

19. Ephrem, *Hymns against Julian* 2.11-12, in *Ephrem the Syrian, Hymns,* trans. Kathleen McVey (New York: Paulist Press, 1989), 237–38.

in this instance is sometimes cited as an example of feminine imagery for the divine, which Ephrem, like other Syriac writers, did not hesitate to employ.[20] But perhaps this is not an instance of feminine imagery so much as the marker of a societal shift in the gendered roles of the household. In his second *mêmrâ* (verse homily), "On Admonition," Ephrem includes a section on the human person as a temple of God. Calling on the community of faithful to become builders who will turn their minds into temples fit for God, he presents the care and maintenance of the person—God's house—in terms that mirror the tending and cleaning of the church building:

> For your mind to become a temple
> Do not leave filth in it.
> Do not leave in the house of God
> Anything hateful for God.
> Let the house of God be adorned
> With whatever is proper for God.
> But if there is passion there
> Harlotry will dwell there.
> But if there is anger there
> Smoke will rise up there.
> Expel wrath from there
> And envy whose smell is abhorrent,
> Bring in and set charity there,
> A censer full of fragrance.
> Sweep and cast out dung from there,
> Hateful company and habits.
> Scatter in it good deeds
> Like flowers and like blossoms,
> And instead of rose or lilies,
> Adorn it with prayers.[21]

20. E.g., Ephrem, *Hymns on Nativity* 21.5 (Divinity wove herself a garment in Mary's womb). See also McVey, *Ephrem,* 10–11, n. 28. Ephrem also sometimes describes Christ in feminine terms, as breastfeeding creation, as in *Hymns on Nativity* 4.149–53. Syriac writers before the year 400 regularly employed feminine imagery for the Holy Spirit, grammatically a feminine term in Syriac. See Susan Ashbrook Harvey, "Feminine Imagery for the Divine: The Holy Spirit, the Odes of Solomon, and Early Syriac Tradition," *St. Vladimir's Theological Quarterly* 37 (1993): 111–39.

21. Ephrem, *Mimra* 2. 93-123, here at 105–23 (my trans.); Edmund Beck, ed., *Des Heiligen Ephraem des Syrers Sermones* I, CSCO 305, Scr. Syr. 130 (Louvain: Secrétariat du CorpusSCO, 1970), 12–49, at 14. German trans. in CSCO 306, 131.

In this passage, Ephrem describes cleaning the house of the self as a threefold process. Every bit of dirt—or whatever is "hateful to God"—must be cleared out; "dirt" includes material refuse, unpleasant sensations, and bad moral condition. The house must then be cleansed and disinfected by fumigation, one of the most common cleaning methods of the pan-Mediterranean ancient world. Finally, it should be adorned with whatever is "proper to God," including sweet-smelling scents and right religious behavior. This threefold sequence is the most often cited cleaning routine in late antique texts.

The earlier motif of house building continues to be commonly used by late antique writers, with its various related themes.[22] But the motif now appears along with remarks on basic maintenance tasks. Aphrahat the "Persian Sage" (fl. 340s), for example, speaks not only of the house of the soul as one that must be properly built, protected, and purified, but further, as a place that must be swept clean if it is to be fit for Christ.[23] Other housekeeping tasks receive occasional use as images instructive for the ascetic practitioner: laundry; the eradication and prevention of lice, vermin, and other pests; food preservation.

Laundering appears to have been appealing as an ascetic image because it combined notions of cleansing and of hard labor in the process. Consider the advice offered to aspiring monks by John Climacus (579–649). If a person wants to overcome vices, he writes,

> He ought to go live in a monastery, as if it were a fuller's shop of salvation.... He will be spiritually stretched and beaten by insults, injuries and rebuffs of the brothers. He may even be physically beaten, trampled on, and kicked, so that he may wash out the filth still lying in the sentient part of his soul. There is an old saying that reproof is the washtub for the soul's passions, and you ought to believe it, for people in the world who load indignities onto someone and then boast about it to others like to say, "I gave him a good scrubbing."[24]

In John's hands, the image carries clear associations of violence, as well as concern about filth. Cleanliness can be effected in this passage only by bru-

22. E.g., Aphrahat, *Demontration* 1.2–4; Gregory of Nyssa, *On Pilgrimages*; *Apophthegmata Patrum*: John the Dwarf, 16; Poemen, 130; Syncletica, 12; Benedicta Ward, trans., *Sayings of the Desert Fathers,* rev. ed. (Kalamazoo: Cistercian Publications, 1984), 88–89, 185, 233; John Climacus, *Ladder of Divine Ascent,* Step 15, Step 27, trans. Colm Luibheid and Norman Russell (New York: Paulist Press, 1982), 173, 262, 263; Augustine, *Confessions,* 2:2, 5:6.

23. Aphrahat, *Dem.* 4.10.

24. John Climacus, *Ladder of Divine Ascent,* Step 8; trans., Luibheid and Russell, 149–50.

tal treatment that includes pounding, kicking, trampling, pulling. In the fifth-century *Life of St. Syncletica,* one of the legendary Desert Mothers of Egypt, the image of laundering as inherently harsh is used to distinguish between ascetics of weaker and stronger dispositions. Asked by a group of women disciples to comment on voluntary poverty as an ascetic practice, the holy woman urges moderation even in this most basic ascetic activity. Laundering, she points out, can cleanse a garment or destroy it by the very same process, depending on the condition of the cloth undergoing the treatment. So, too, the effect of strict voluntary poverty on monastic women with differing degrees of experience or spiritual prowess:

For just as heavy clothing is washed and bleached by treading and vigorous wringing, so also the strong soul is strengthened to a greater degree through voluntary poverty. But those with a weaker disposition have the opposite experience to the first women. Indeed, when they are rubbed a little, they disintegrate like torn garments, not lasting through the wash with their virtue. And, although the fuller may be the same, the outcome for the clothes is different; some are torn and perished while another is bleached and renewed.[25]

Yet the great Byzantine writer Symeon the New Theologian (942–1022), himself influenced by John Climacus, used the image less abrasively to expound on the role of tears and penitential weeping in the cultivation of compunction as a monastic virtue. Just as clothing cannot be cleaned without water, he writes, so, too, the stains of the soul cannot be washed without tears.[26] Symeon plays out the metaphor with descriptions of washing, scouring, rubbing, fire (to burn out the worst of the passions), flooding, moistening, and refreshing. The work is hard, but without the harshness of the earlier John Climacus or Syncletica passages.

Interestingly, the passage from the *Life of Syncletica* attributes the harshness of laundering as much to the ingredients (especially bleach) as to the method

25. Pseudo-Athanasius, *The Life and Activity of the Holy and Blessed Teacher Syncletica,* sec. 30, trans. Bonge, p. 25. Only three women are identified by name in the collection of the *Apophthegmata Patrum*: Sarah, Syncletica, and Theodora. See the remarks of Benedicta Ward, "The Apophthegmata Matrum," *Studia Patristica* 16.2, ed. E. A. Livingstone, TU 129 (Berlin: Akademie Verlag, 1985), 63–66.

26. Symeon the New Theologian, *Catechetical Discourses,* 4.10, in C. J. deCatanzaro, trans., *Symeon the New Theologian: The Discourses* (New York: Paulist Press, 1980), 81–82. Compare 8.4, where he likens the monk without love to a person in filthy clothes who tries to sneak into the company of "bright-robed" saints at the Messianic Banquet.

of pounding, rubbing, and trampling. The Syncletica *vita* is a curious text that claims a distinctly female-gendered voice. The teachings are represented as instructions of Syncletica to the nuns of her convent, and a deliberately gendered rhetoric attends a number of the chapters—as in the case of the analogy to laundry, where the presenter apparently intends to engage "female" experience.[27]

But the *Life of Syncletica* is also a highly imagistic text in general. Elaborate metaphors and similes accompany the ascetic instructions. The text carries a strong emphasis on physicality, bodily experience, and above all, sensory awareness. The laundering passage must be considered in this light. House imagery is laced throughout this text, including images of house building, house tending, house design, house guarding, and the kinds of activities that go on in households (of which the doing of laundry is one example).[28] The saint instructs her disciples in self-discipline and control of the passions by discussing the dangers of inadequately constructed roofs, windows, walls, or building foundations (secs. 13, 46, 79); the danger of damage from black smoke from outside if house windows are not kept closed (sec. 25); the annoyances of smoke inhalation when trying to light fires (sec. 60); the foul smell and stain-producing qualities of garbage (sec. 63); the training of household servants (sec. 77).

In addition to the laundry passage, one other account of cleaning receives an extended discussion—that of controlling lice and other household pests. The passage is an admonition to severe vigilance in the control of one's passions. The imagery combines strict ascetic personal practices with analogies to housecleaning. The ascetic cuts her hair, Syncletica teaches, to signify the cutting off of worldly passions and desires. But a more diligent attention is needed: the virtuous ascetic must further remove any lice which can now be seen to have been rooting in the head—the various vices that afflict the ascetic even when withdrawn from the temptations of marriage and family life in a civic context. Just as hair provides a cover under which lice and such devouring insects can thrive, so, too, worldly affairs conceal the dangerous passions that eat away at a person's soul. The ascetic must keep watch over the condition of her soul as over a strictly clean house, one in which the smallest bug would immediately be noticed and destroyed.

27. See especially Elizabeth A. Clark, "Ideology, History, and the Construction of 'Woman' in Late Antique Christianity," *JECS* 2 (1994): 155–84.

28. E.g., *Life of Syncletica,* sections 9, 13, 25, 26, 30, 46, 60, 66, 77, 79, 80, 92, 93.

> We must, then, keep cleaning our "house" [the soul] continually and be on the lookout lest any of the soul-devouring "beasties" slip past us into the store rooms of the soul. And we must fumigate our places with the holy incense of prayer. For just as the stronger fumigants drive out the venomous creatures, so prayer with fasting chases out foul patterns of thought.[29]

The imagery in this passage relies on common cultural and social practices of the ancient Mediterranean: the use of fumigants as pesticides and cleaning agents; the hygienic concern that negligence in cleaning breeds lice and other harmful vermin; the apotropaic as well as therapeutic use of aromatics; the view that cleanliness depends upon continual attention and vigilance. Like the passage on laundry, this one assumes a significance of bodily awareness as well as bodily activity. Sensory engagement and material conditions are highlighted as means by which the ascetic might examine and order various components of the self. The passage also assumes that the audience will recognize and participate in a moral discourse that is constructed and maintained through particular sensory associations; smells, especially, serve to mark cleanliness or filth, health, or disease, and the process of restoring good hygiene. In the *Life of Syncletica,* smells and textures are especially highlighted as carrying moral, epistemological, and even cosmological meaning. From this perspective, the imagery of housekeeping includes the active participation of the body as a qualitatively significant domain in the practice of the ascetic life—not simply as something to be disciplined or renounced, but further, as something that contributes important knowledge about a person's (or one's own) moral condition.

Housework, Holy Work

John Climacus's use of laundering as a metaphor with violent connotations links the passage to another theme in his *Ladder of Divine Ascent*: that the ascetic must first destroy the self in order to construct a new one.

> Violence and unending pain are the lot of those who aim to ascend to heaven with the body, and this especially at the early stages of the enterprise, when our pleasure-loving disposition and our unfeeling hearts must travel through overwhelming grief toward the love of God and holiness. It is hard, truly hard.[30]

29. *Life of Syncletica,* 80, trans. Bonge, pp. 50–51.
30. John Climacus, *Ladder of Divine Ascent,* Step 1, trans. Luibheid and Russell, 75.

The theme is a classic one in eastern Christian monastic literature. Hence the saying of Abba Alonius, "If I had not destroyed myself completely, I should not have been able to rebuild and shape myself again."[31] The intention of John Climacus, as other writers in this genre, is to lead the monk through the stages of the ascetic life in order to arrive at the brilliant tranquility of pure prayer. His occasional use of house imagery serves that purpose. Apart from laundry, John is concerned with the materials utilized in house construction (step 15), and with the house as a building that can be tightly closed up (step 27). Yet the physical conditions of the dwellings occupied by his monks concerned him in practical terms, a reminder that the violence included in the laundry metaphor was not superfluous to the author's purpose. At one point, he is shocked when a monk chooses to battle an assault of evil thoughts by engaging in "intense prayer against the enemy" in the monastery latrine. Criticizing him for choosing this most inappropriate place, John is chastened to hear the monk's reply, "I chose an unclean place in which to pray to be cleansed from filth, that I might drive out unclean thoughts."[32]

The location (both social and moral) of the latrine in this episode allows John to link images of cultic pollution and purity with the moral effort to control (cleanse) and order the passions.[33] Yet the latrine does more. Like the image of laundering as an activity of visceral assault, the image of a latrine as a place of prayer serves to evoke—deliberately—an immediate sense of disgust in the audience. As William Miller has pointed out, disgust is a response that invariably carries intense moral weight.[34] An author's intentional evocation of disgust presumes the capacity of the image to elicit sensory and physical asso-

31. E.g., *Sayings of the Desert Fathers,* Alonius 2, Ward, 35.

32. John Climacus, *Ladder of Divine Ascent,* Step 15, trans. Luiheid and Russell, 185.

33. In late antique Christian literature, the latrine is a place where persons of extraordinary evil or moral depravity meet a wretched death. Notably, one has the examples of the archheretics Arius (Theodoret of Cyrrhus, *History of the Monks of Syria* 1.9) and Nestorius (Theodore Nissen, Supplementary Tales to John Moschus's *Spiritual Meadow,* 220, trans. John Wortley [Kalamazoo: Cistercian Publications, 1992], 197–98); and, in the sixth century Syriac *Cave of Treasures,* the death of King Herod of Judea (trans. Wallis Budge, 218–19). Christian writers here draw on the classical literary tradition that assigned physically horrifying deaths to morally depraved leaders. See Jacques Schamp, "La Morts en Fleurs: Considérations sur la maladie 'pédiculaire' de Scylla," *L'Antiquité Classique* 60 (1991): 139–70. In her early seventh-century hagiography, St. Radegunde was held renowned for her ascetic practice of voluntarily cleaning her convent, with particular devotion to cleaning the latrine; Venantius Fortunatus, *Life of Saint Radegunde,* 1, in Joan Petersen, trans., *Handmaids of the Lord: Holy Women in Late Antiquity and the Early Middle Ages* (Kalamazoo: Cistercian Publications, 1992), at 391.

34. William Ian Miller, *The Anatomy of Disgust* (Cambridge, Mass.: Harvard University Press, 1997).

ciations that unnerve the audience and, at the same moment, construct clear boundaries of order and meaning. When John wants to stress the harshness and rigor that must attend the monk's every moment, his evocation of disgust is meant to arouse an overwhelming compulsion in his audience to be vigilant in their self-regard. Images of filth (the latrine) and violent cleaning (laundry) serve his agenda well.

Yet John is not unconcerned with the physical reality behind his images. In step 5, he describes with palpable horror the asceticism pursued by the extreme penitents in a monastic community known as "the Prison."[35] The grim severity of their various mortifications seems to him sufficient admonition to jolt any complacent monk into attentive self-examination. What shook John's own equilibrium when he visited the community, however, were the basic living conditions of these penitents: "There was no rest for them in beds, no clean and laundered clothing. They were bedraggled, dirty and verminous.... What a dreadful place they lived in! It was dark, stinking, filthy, and squalid."[36] While John does not flinch to employ such rhetoric when describing the disciplining of the self, he shudders at the enactment of such discipline in practical terms. The physical and bodily counterpart to the moral imagery of ordering the passions was not itself a dimension of experience easily accepted in late antique culture. This was so, even—as in the case of an ascetic author like John Climacus—in a context where such consequences seemed dictated by circumstance.

There is a notable tension in the ascetic literature of late antiquity. This literature advocated practices that would seriously challenge bodily norms—fasting, vigils, abstinence from bathing, living in the wilderness, in caves, or in tombs. Yet there is evident cultural discomfort with the sensory qualities of the resulting physical conditions, even for those who celebrated such a state. Smells were often identified as particularly disconcerting: the bad breath of the one who fasted; the odors of unwashed flesh; the stench of corpses in tombs; the smells of food left to rot before a monk would eat, or palm leaves left too long in their soaking water, so that the rancidity would contribute to the ascetic's discipline. All are identified across a wide variety of texts as problematic both for the ascetics themselves and for the laity who encountered them.[37]

35. John Climacus, *Ladder of Divine Ascent,* Step 5.

36. John Climacus, *Ladder of Divine Ascent,* Step 5, trans. Luibheid and Russell, 125, 127.

37. The poor hygiene ubiquitous to the ancient Christian ascetic life led to constant problems with

The ancient Mediterranean world, despite its diverse cultures, shared a sensibility that identified sweet smells with goodness, beauty, and divinity, while bad smells signaled decay, corruption, and mortality.[38] In the Christian view, mortality itself was the result of sin and therefore invariably more a moral than a physical condition.[39] Mortality was tantamount always, and only, to the stench of sin. So fundamental was this view to the Christian mind that the olfactory dimensions of ascetic practice were commonly described as the most disconcerting: the "odor of sanctity" was often an ambiguous experience. At one and the same time, stench indicated the enormity of humanity's sinful condition as well as—in the diligent ascetic—the rigorous discipline undertaken to correct that state. Hagiographical and monastic literature that emphasizes illness, wounds, sores, mud and muck, vermin, rodents, and demon possession generally is also rife with references to incense piety, blessed oil, heavenly scents, and perfumed divine apparitions. Olfactory imagery and symbolism most often worked with contrasting extremes. Foremost was that between the richly sweet fragrances of liturgical worship (incense, myron, perfumed candle wax, and lamp oils) and the grim odors generated by and encountered with the saint's chosen practices.

The counterpoint between liturgical and mortal smells was accomplished with an almost singular dexterity by housekeeping imagery. The *Spiritual Homilies* of Pseudo-Macarius offer an especially rich example. These homilies abound with imagery of the human person as the dwelling place of God—a house, a sanctuary, a palace. These are not usages that cite the process or materials of house building. They assume construction to have been finished. Instead, they engage a recurrent narrative of a disjointed relationship between the owner of the house, God (or Christ, or the Holy Spirit), and the house itself, the monk. The house belongs to its owner, and in its right state is worthy of its owner.[40]

---

festering sores, infections, and gangrene. See Evelyne Patlagean, *Pauvreté économique ed pauvreté sociale à Byzance 4e–7e siècles* (Paris: La Haye, 1977), 74–112. For the cultural dilemmas posed by sanctity and stench in late antiquity, see Susan Ashbrook Harvey, "On Holy Stench: When the Odor of Sanctity Sickens," Studia patristica 35, ed. M. F. Wiles and E. J. Yarnold (Leuven: Peeters, 2001), 90–101; Harvey, *Scenting Salvation: Ancient Christianity and the Olfactory Imagination* (Berkeley: University of California Press, 2006), chap. 5, "Sanctity and Stench."

38. Important basic works are C. Classen, D. Howes, and A. Synnott, *Aroma: A Cultural History of Smell* (New York: Routledge, 1994); M. Detienne, *Gardens of Adonis: Spices in Greek Mythology* (Princeton: Princeton University Press, 1994); S. Lilja, *The Treatment of Odours in the Poetry of Antiquity,* Commentationes Humanarum Litterarum 49 (Helsinki, 1972).

39. Harvey, *Scenting Salvation*; B. Caseau, *Euodia.*

40. Pseudo-Macarius, *Homilies,* 1.2, 1.7, 5.7, 10.4, 15.45.

But it is most often found to be in an unworthy condition: in disarray and disrepair; dilapidated, dirty, run down, filled with bad smells, with thick smoke, with moldering cadavers.[41] If the owner is to resume occupancy, the locked doors must be opened, the rooms repaired and cleaned.[42]

Pseudo-Macarius describes a vastness in the house of the human person: "There are found reception rooms, bedrooms, doors, antechambers, many offices and exits. There is found the office of justice and of injustice. There is death and there is life. There takes place upright business as well as the contrary."[43] As in its "earthly" counterpart, if this building is to be fit for a royal owner it must be cleaned, ordered, fumigated, disinfected, and beautified with fine perfume.[44] Servants must utilize the proper serving dishes, in their appropriate usage and in the correct sequence.[45] A variety of spices will fitly season the food.[46] Everything will be in order. The dwelling place will be inhabited, with glory and grandeur.

This imagistic narrative is played out over the course of the fifty *Spiritual Homilies.* But its summarized purpose can be seen in the very first homily of the collection, in an extended metaphor about salt as a preservative for meat. The passage begins by naming the apostles the salt of the earth, who have "seasoned and salted every believing soul by the salt of the Holy Spirit.... keeping them free from decay and from anything harmful, away from the fetid corruption they were in."[47] The significance of the image is brought out by the careful explication that follows:

> Indeed, it is just as flesh—if it is not salted, it will decay and give off a stench so that all bypassers will turn aside from the fetid odor. Worms crawl all over the putrid meat; there they feed, eat, and burrow. But when salt is poured over it, the worms feeding on that meat perish and the fetid odor ceases. It is indeed the nature of salt to kill worms and dispel fetid odors.
>
> In like manner every soul not seasoned with the Holy Spirit and made a participator of the heavenly salt, which is the power of God, grows corrupt and is filled with the stench and fetidness of bad thoughts so that the countenance of God turns away from the awful stench of vain and dark thoughts and from the disorderly affections that dwell in such a soul. The harmful and wicked worms, which are the spirits

41. Pseudo-Macarius, *Homilies,* 15. 33, 15.45, 16.12, 27.19, 28.1, 33.3, 43.7
42. Pseudo-Macarius, *Homilies,* 11. 15, 15.32–33, 15.45.
43. Pseudo-Macarius, *Homilies,* 15.32.
44. Pseudo-Macarius, *Homilies,* 15. 33, 15.45.
45. Pseudo-Macarius, *Homilies,* 15.5.
46. Pseudo-Macarius, *Homilies,* 16.9.
47. Pseudo-Macarius, *Homilies,* 1.5, citing Matt. 5:13.

> of wickedness and the powers of darkness, crawl up and down in such a soul. There they feed, burrowing deeply inside. They crawl all over and devour it and thoroughly corrupt it. "My wounds stink and are festering" (Ps 38:5).
>
> If indeed the soul takes refuge in God, believes and seeks the salt of life, which is the good and human-loving Spirit, then the heavenly salt comes and kills those ugly worms. The Spirit takes away the awful stench and cleanses the soul by the strength of his salt. Thus the soul is brought back to health and freed from its wounds by the true salt in order again to be useful and ordered to serve the Heavenly Lord.[48]

The passage is arresting for its meticulous attention to the process of decay. But if the stages of rancidity are recited with tiresome detail, the text is further striking because it is, in fact, a text about cleaning. Salt, the preservative par excellence of the ancient world, could be used to prevent such decay. Yet here salt is not used as a preservative but as a cleansing agent. As such, its capacities are indeed wondrous. It can halt the disintegration, destroy its instrumental means (worms), clean the festering wounds, disinfect, deodorize, and perfume. It can restore to health. In this passage salt can restore the right relationship between the household and its owner, between the self and the passions, body and soul, between the divine and the human. Elsewhere Pseudo-Macarius remarks, "And just as the house that has its master at home shows forth an abundance of orderliness, and beauty and harmony, so too is the person who has his Lord abiding in him. He is full of every beauty and uprightness. He has the Lord with his spiritual treasures inhabiting within and as his charioteer."[49] Such an ordered relation is what housekeeping makes possible, long after the building has been constructed and adorned.

Holy Habitation

The language of divine indwelling was commonplace in the theology of Late Antiquity. It was a frequent trope in any kind of discussion of the incarnation.[50] It was a common image for the experience of prayer in the ascetic whose

48. Pseudo-Macarius, *Homilies,* 1.5; compare 24.4, in Pseudo-Macarius, *The Fifty Spiritual Homilies and the Great Letter,* trans. George Maloney (New York: Paulist Press, 1992), 39–40.

49. Pseudo-Macarius, *Homilies,* 33.3, trans. Maloney, 202.

50. Although indwelling language became a hallmark of Antiochene Christology, its usage—positively as well as negatively—was much broader. See, e.g., Aloys Grillmeier, *Christ in Christian Tradition,* trans. John Bowden (Atlanta: John Knox, 1975), 1: 184, 299–301, 304–5, 312, 327, 359, 428–37, 417, 477, 492,

practice had rendered the self open to divine encounter.[51] The ubiquity of the concept surely contributed to the interest in and usefulness of an ascetic rhetoric of housekeeping—a rhetoric that set a focus not on construction but on maintenance, not on materials or ornamentation but on the methods of keeping the dwelling fit for habitation.

Most often, I have found housekeeping to be part of a complex of images that serves to strengthen commitment to the continual discipline of ascetic practice. That continual attention, the imagery asserts, is intrinsically valuable for the task of maintaining a clear sense of self—a healthy, clean, well-ordered self. Without proper cleaning, a building could not effectively serve its purpose. The housekeeping cited in these texts is not the light maintenance work of daily dusting and sweeping, but rather the hard drudgery of a thorough spring cleaning. It represents the periodic effort to take serious stock of one's condition: to take everything apart in the cleaning process in order to put it back together again with shining freshness. The ascetic self, engaged in a daily discipline, could yet acquire the build-up of unwanted sentiments or emotions or passions. A thorough, harsh cleaning scrubbed the ascetic back to a fit and proper dwelling for divine habitation.

One final text deserves attention in this chapter. Thus far I have emphasized texts where the cleaning imagery serves to highlight dirt, bugs, vermin, and stench. The cleaning methods described are often violent, as brutal in their impact as they are effective in their results. A different kind of housekeeping text appears in the first festal homily on the Nativity of Jacob of Serugh (d. 521). In this extended passage, the Virgin Mary is seen immediately following the annunciation of the Archangel Gabriel that she will conceive and bear a son. Her next task is to prepare herself to be a place fit for her Lord to dwell in—to make sure that her body really is a church, a sanctuary suitable as God's house. To do this, she must clean, thoroughly and carefully. She must rid herself of all dirt and refuse, she must cleanse and purify. Here is Jacob's description of the process.

> [Mary] gathered and removed all [inappropriate thoughts] from her mind.
> She sprinkled her pure temple with love before the Holy One.
> She swept her house with the holiness that was within her,

513–16, discussing Eusebius of Caesarea, Eustathius of Antioch, Eusebius of Emesa, Athanasius, Diodore of Tarsus, Theodore of Mopsuestia, Cyril of Alexandria, Theodoret, and Nestorius.

51. A most helpful discussion can be found in Columba Stewart, *Working the Earth of the Heart: the Messalian Controversy in History, Texts, and Language to AD 431* (Oxford: Clarendon, 1991), 203–23.

And she embellished its inner walls with all kinds (of acts) of reverence.
Again in it she set in order the good signets of perfection.
She replenished it with blossoms of all manners of modesty.
She leveled its land (Mark 1:3) with the choice implements of virginity.

Mary's actions of cleaning and preparation are not unlike the regulations prescribed in Syriac canons for the cleaning of a church sanctuary and of the liturgical objects that would be the necessary furnishings of the altar area.[52] The use of special cleaning implements, of water specially scented, of particular disposal methods for refuse and for the dirtied water afterwards, as well as careful instructions for the disposal of sacred vessels that had grown rancid from spoiled wine or holy oil—all such regulations, carefully enumerated in the various canon collections, seem to echo in the actions Jacob's homily ascribes to Mary. The initial chores complete, Mary then turns to the further preparatory requirements. Cleaned and ordered, Mary's body—soon to receive the incarnate Son—must next be outfitted and furnished as a sanctuary fit for divine occupation.

She hung up as ornaments, crowns of praises of watchful care.
She took up and laced together veils of chastity;
She spread out and stretched out spacious garments of watchfulness.
She poured out as oil good deeds in her lamp (Matt 25:1–13)
And her great flame has been inflamed in the temple of her body.
She burnt the fragrance of her prayers warmly
So that the pure fire of her faith should serve as incense.
She threw, as sweet spices, the sounds of praise into the fire of her love
And from her thanksgiving breathed the fragrance of choice incense.
Her words went out like guards from the royal court
So that the Royal Son might enter along with them by the door of the ear.
And while the house was made radiant by these things in a holy manner,
The Son of the King entered and dwelt in the shrine of virginity.
She answered to the watcher with great love, "Let your Lord come.
Behold, I am prepared so that according to his will he might dwell
within me."[53]

52. Arthur Vööbus, *The Synodicon in the West Syrian Tradition*, vol. 1, CSCO 367–68, Scriptores Syri. 161–62 (Louvain: Sécretariat de CorpusSCO, 1975), *Severus to Caesaria Hypatissa; Answers of Johannan to Sargis; Answers of Ja'qob to Johannan 'Estunara.* These texts date from roughly the same period as Jacob's *Homily.*

53. Jacob of Serugh, *Festal Homily* I, *On the Nativity* I, 387–412, trans. Thomas Kollamparampil, in *Jacob of Serugh: Select Festal Homilies* (Rome: CIIS, 1997), 41–93, at 59–60.

In Jacob's homily, Mary's undertaking of household decoration moves beyond the refurnishing stage, and into a series of acts of adornment that in fact mirrors the liturgy itself: the burning of incense, offering of hymns, carrying of candles, and proclamation of God's word, all to prepare the body—to sanctify it—for God's salvific action. The textual recounting of Mary's singular cleaning and preparation of her house for holy visitation becomes, in Jacob's rendering, an account of the purification and sanctification of the church in the divine liturgy celebrated by the church body as a whole. Cleaning, furnishing, adorning, beautifying: the sequence becomes both the unique moment of salvation effected at the incarnation and its repeated representation in the collective activity of the ecclesial community.

Jacob's text returns us from the notion of the body as a sanctuary to that of the body as a house in which the Lord would dwell. To be an appropriate home for the Lord—a palace, a temple—the building must be thoroughly, meticulously cleansed; it must moreover be fittingly furnished and decorated. The stale, harmful, and injurious odors of decay and neglect must be cleared away; the fumigations which clean must also disinfect; the space must be filled anew with scents and sensory elements that engage bodily awareness and experience, bringing the self to a new and glorious condition. In Jacob's passage, the imagery of housekeeping includes both the cultic imagery of pollution and purity and the moral psychology of purified and ordered passions. Jacob was an itinerant priest and bishop who knew well the problems of building maintenance in the changing landscape of late antique society. With this passage we are shown the curiously efficacious beauty of a literary trope that marked Christianity's emergence as an institutionalized religion in a time of continuity and change.

PART III

AFTER EPHREM THE SYRIAN

Robin Darling Young

8. THE INFLUENCE OF EVAGRIUS OF PONTUS

In about 460, a young Persian Christian named Aksenâyâ traveled north from his home province of Beth Garmai to become a student at the school of Edessa. Already committed to the monastic life, he undertook there a study of the works of Cyril of Alexandria. That study convinced him of the errors of the East Syrian theology with which he had probably been raised, and eventually led him to go further west, allying himself with the anti-Chalcedonian monasteries and hierarchies of northern and western Syria.

An eloquent symbol of his relocation was the new name that Aksenâyâ was given by his bishop, Peter the Fuller of Antioch: he became Philoxenos, now taking on a Greek name that incorporated and changed the meaning of his Syriac name. He was no longer "the stranger" but "the hospitable one," that is, "the lover of strangers," a kind of guestmaster.

Coincidentally or not, his change of name reflects Philoxenos's entire program for the reform of Syriac-speaking Christianity: to make the language and its theology more suitable for reflecting the more exact and technical theology of the Greek-speaking church to its west. Previously, the Syriac-speaking world had been more receptive to the theology associated with the region of Antioch—exemplified by the works of Diodore of Tarsus, Theodore of Mopsuestia, and Nestorius. Philoxenos wanted to introduce to the Syriac-speaking tradition the theology associated with the city of Alexandria.

In the matter of Christology, then, he was loyal to the works and vocabulary of Cyril of Alexandria, the standard of orthodoxy for those dissenting from the Chalcedonian formula. In the matter of the monastic life, Philoxenos was an admirer of the works of Evagrius of Pontus, a student of the Cappadocians who had become a student of the learned monks of Nitria and Scetis and had revived the ascetic thought of Clement and Origen to combine it with the practical instruction he had learned in Egypt.

Philoxenos seemed to think that the more ancient form of Syriac-language thought, associated with Ephrem and Philoxenos's own contemporary Jacob of Sarug, was inadequate to preserve the terminology needed to guard the orthodox faith against the distortions of a two-nature Christology. Equally, however, he appeared to think the monastic heritage of Syria required an infusion of Evagrian expertise in order to safeguard against some of the dangers of the ascetic life.

Thus Philoxenos became a medium for the introduction of Evagrian thought into Syria and the Syriac language. Yet he was not the only monk to have been impressed by Evagrius and some of the directions implied in Evagrius's thought but not taken by him. That these latter presented some dangers to themselves and their readers we can learn from reading Philoxenos's own works. But the chief interest of the present essay is to show what the similarities are between Philoxenos and Evagrius in the matter of one aspect of the monastic life, the imitation of Christ.

The essential connection between the thought of Philoxenos and that of Evagrius has, of course, been discussed for some sixty years, in a variety of monographs and articles. It took, however, that great scholar of oriental spirituality, Irenée Hausherr, to set the two authors together and to demonstrate Philoxenos's manifest dependence on the ascetical works of Evagrius for his own description of the spiritual life of the Christian—primarily that of the monk, with whose guidance Philoxenos was always and foremost concerned, even though he was a bishop who had responsibility for all kinds of Christians in his rural region.

Further work on the subject of the connection between these two has been done by Harb and Watt, as well as by Vööbus, but the dominant interpretations have been provided by De Halleux, in his *Philoxène,* and a subsequent article on Philoxenos's spirituality, and by Guillaumont's well-known discussion of the progress of Evagrius's thought among Greek- and Syriac-speaking Christians.[1]

Guillaumont's reconstruction of the absorption of Evagrian ideas by Syrian monasticism has been extremely influential, and has been largely accepted in European and American scholarship, with the exception of Guillaumont's admittedly hypothetical ascription of the "common" (S1) translations of Evagrius's *Praktikos* and *Kephalaia Gnostika* to Philoxenos.[2] The latter seems not to have been good enough at Greek to have undertaken such a delicate job as translating the apophthegms of Evagrius. According to Guillaumont's portrait, Evagrius was an Origenist, a "philosophe au desert" whose speculative cosmology and Christology were the joint springboard for an esoteric mysticism discovered only later to be heretical, and even "pantheistic." Guillaumont thought that this mysticism was consciously "filtered" of its "germs" by Philoxenos (and, for the Greeks, by Nilus of Ancyra) but faithfully transmitted in a frankly gnostic, pantheistic framework by the idiosyncratic Stephen Bar Sudaili.[3]

This view itself depends on an interpretation of Evagrius's thought as being primarily speculative or mystical, and probably the majority of scholars would still interpret Evagrius's thought in this way. Reading the unexpurgated (S2) version of the *Kephalaia Gnostika* as the key to Evagrius's work, they would probably hold that although Evagrius was outwardly orthodox in matters eschatological and Christological, he esoterically held a Christology in which Christ as Son of God yields to a monistic union of restored minds with a unified, non-Trinitarian godhead.

Such a portrait of Evagrius's thought has come to be disputed in recent

1. Andre de Halleux, *Philoxène de Mabbog. Sa vie, ses écrits, sa théologie* (Louvain: Imprimerie Orientalist, 1963), and Halleux, "Monophysitismus und Spiritualität nach dem Johanneskommentar des Philoxenus von Mabbug," *Théologie und Philosophie* 53 (1978): 353–66. For Philoxenos's use of Evagrius, see further Paul Harb, "L'attitude de Philoxene de Mabboug a l'egard de la spirituatlité savante d'Evagre le Pontique," Memorial G. Kouri-Sarkis (Louvain: Peters, 1969), and Harb, "Le role exercé par Philoxène de Mabbug sur l'évolution de la morale dans l'église syrienne," *Parole de l'Orient* 1 (1970): 21–48. Also Eugene Lemoine, "La spiritualite de Phloxene de Mabboug," *L'Orient Syrien* 3 (1958): 91–102, and Lemoine, "Physionomie d'un moine syrien: Philoxene de Mabboug," *L'Orient Syrien* 3 (1953): 91–102; Irenee Hausherr, "Spiritualite syrienne: Philoxene de Mabboug," *Orientalia christiana periodica* 23 (1957): 171–85, and Orientalia christiana analecta 183 (1969): 285–99, also Hausherr, "Contemplation et saintete. Une remarquable mise au point par Philoxène de Mabboug (+ 523)," *Revue d'Ascèse et de mystique* 14 (1933): 171–95. Finally, "Philoxenos of Mabbug," Part 2 of Roberta C. Chestnut, *Three Monophysite Christologies: Severus of Antioch, Philoxenus of Mabbug, and Jacob of Sarug* (Oxford: Oxford University Press, 1976).

2. See J. W. Watt, "Philoxenus and Evagrius," *Oriens Christianus* 64 (1980): 65–81.

3. See Antoine Guillaumont, *Les Kephalaia Gnostica* (Paris, 1962), and Guillaumont, with Claire Guillaumont, "Evagre," in *Dictionnaire de Spiritualité* 4: 1731–44.

years by a revisionist camp of Evagrian scholarship inspired and characterized by the work of Gabriel Bunge. But here it is well to avoid the discussion of eschatology and monism, and instead quickly review Evagrius's soteriology as it functioned across the spectrum of his works, before turning to Philoxenos's own promotion of it.

The Imitation of Christ According to Evagrius

The whole of the Christian life, in Evagrius's opinion, is to be an imitation of Christ and, of course, it begins at the level of the *praktikē,* the monastic labor. As he remarks in a contemplative work, the *Scholia on the Psalms,* "Homoiosis is that imitation through good actions. Where it is not to sinners, but to those succeeding in living the good life to be made like the Lord."[4]

If we turn to Evagrius's conception of life on the practical plane, we will notice that it is assumed to be an arena of constant combat between Christ and his followers, on one side, and Satan and his, on the other. At the outset of the Christian life, while the human is still, like Israel, "ascending from Egypt," Evagrius warned that there would be lengthy, armed hostilities. It was for those in this beginning stage that he wrote the *Praktikos* (*On Prayer*), many of his letters, and the paraneiseis to monks and virgins. On the first two of these works, where "likeness" is just taking root in the human being, there are scant references to Christ. But these are important.

The introductory letter attached to the *Praktikos* tells the recipient, Anatolius, of the christological significance of the monastic habit for those who are as yet "children in Christ." Various parts of the clothing signify characteristics of Christ—his charity, or his gentleness, or his death. The staff of the monk is the "tree of life," or Christ, upon which symbolism Evagrius expands in the *Kephalaia Gnostika.* Here and throughout his works, Evagrius will insists that the Christian must be "clothed in Christ," another way of indicating the deeper significance of the baptismal garment as "putting on Christ." At the outset, this is literal, as Christ's *tapeinosis* and *praotes* are mimicked by monastic

4. Evagrius, *In Psalmos 49* (50): 21. For a discussion of the fragmentary *Scholia on the Psalms* by Evagrius, see Marie-Joseph Rondeau, "Le commentaire sur les Psaumes d'Evagre le Pontique," *Orientalia christiana periodica* 26 (1960): 307–48, and Rondeau, "Les commentaries patristiques du Psautier (IIIe–Ve siecles)," vol.1, Orientalia christiana analecta 219 (Rome, 1982), 121–26.

clothing and outward behavior. Further along this will be an inner "clothing" as well, so that Christ will be not only outside the Christian as act, but inside him as knowledge; as he remarks again in the Psalms *scholion*, "*Himation kyriou/gnosis alethes.*"[5]

At this level of christology, Evagrius employs a descriptive method derived from Origen, namely the doctrine of the *epinoiai.* These accompany Christ's *synkatabasis,* his accommodation or condescension to the lowly. They also mark out the path for human elevation to Christ-likeness. The scriptural and traditional titles of Christ, which continued to be employed in other fourth-century authors as well, indicated the way in which the beginning monk knew Christ. In the work on Proverbs, a Biblical book Evagrius considered to be the fundamental ethical scripture (as distinguished from the "physical" Ecclesiastes and the "theological" Song of Songs), Evagrius collected the names of Christ: vine, pastor, way, root of Jesse, living water, bread from heaven, light and life, sun of justice, *et cetera.*[6] Many of these titles recur in the *Scholia on the Psalms,* and some in the *Kephalaia Gnostika.*

Evagrius, however, not only thought of the titles of Christ as part of the divine *paideia* leading from lower conceptions to knowledge, and notions ultimately surpassed by the gnostic; he also regarded them as clues to the warfare between Christ and Satan that takes place as the Christian encounters the Word. These might be called the *epinoiai* of contradiction, and they too have their beginning in the thought of Origen. The Lord, Evagrius wrote, is a devouring fire and a lion against sinners, but light and dew for the righteous.[7] He is a hungry leopard for the negligent, a stumbling block for the unpersuaded and, in an interesting use of the term, he is *oligopsychos* against sinners.[8] Apparently Evagrius here means not "desolate," but someone with a violent soul.

5. On monastic clothing, see the introductory Letter to Anatolius in *Evagre le Pontique, Traite pratique, ou Le moine,* vol. 2, ed. and trans. Antoine Guillauont and Claire Guillaumont (Paris: Les Editions du Cerf, 1971), 484–91 (SC 171). See also *Kephalaia Gnostica,* book 5, sentence 69, 206–7, in Antoine Guillaumont, ed., *Les six centuries des "Kephalaia Gnostica" d'Evagre le Pontique* (Paris: Firmin-Didot, 1958) (PO 28.1).

6. Evagrius, *In Psalmos 103* (104): 2, and cf. ibid, 34 (35): 26: "Those baptized in Christ put him on as justice and wisdom, but those baptized in Satan put on confusion and shame (*entropē*)."

7. Evagrius, *Scholia on Proverbs,* 22, 20, in Paul Gehin, ed. and trans., *Evagre le Pontique, Scholies aux Proverbes* (Paris: Editions du Cerf, 1987), 247. On the doctrine of the *epinoiai,* see Gehin, "Introduction," 50–53.

8. *Scholia on Proverbs,* 195.

Likewise, Christ is a father and mother—father for the gnostic and mother for the monk; this, he said, was confirmed by "Christ speaking in Paul," because Paul became a father to the Ephesians and a mother to the Corinthians, whose progress was slower.[9] Eventually, and on a higher level of progress, he is friend and coheir.[10] He is at first *poimen* and next, *basileus basileuonton*—the first only temporarily, when the rational sheep need herding and protection; and the second, when the rational sheep become worthy of royal rank and Christ's own kingship is fully realized.[11]

In the *Scholia on Proverbs* and in the *Gnostikos,* one of the most important of these ethical-level titles of Christ is *philos.* Christ as friend is set against the enemy, the devil—an important connection between Evagrius's teaching and that of other Egyptian sources such as Anthony and the *Apophthegmata Patrum.* He is the "friend of the apostles," and their shared *philia* is *pneumatikê gnosis Theou.* He is friend as well because he is *kardiognostēs,* the knower of the heart.[12] "All are servants of Christ because he has conquered the world," Evagrius states in the *Psalms Scholia*; but some become friends. Furthermore, these enjoy a common likeness. "All those having knowledge of Christ are friends one with the other"; and elsewhere he asserts that where there are two friends, there is always a third, Christ. Evagrius seems to mean not that this will come about automatically, but that our knowledge of Christ depends on *philia* with him and with other monks; it is a basic commandment integral to the imitation of Christ. Moreover, Christ is profoundly *gnosis* himself, and he is "in" the gnostic in the same way that the father is "in" him.[13]

Lest the impression be given that this deepening understanding of Christ takes place solely on an individual level, it is well to recall that Evagrius wrote among and for a community in which he participated in a kind of reading-circle that considered the works of Clement and Origen, as well as the Egyptian monastic tradition, and in which the master-disciple relation was paramount. As groups, disciples did not yet depend upon an abbot, but upon the experienced monk who is, in Evagrius terminology, the *gnostikos,* a kind of ascetical classroom teacher. The *gnostikos*'s imitation of Christ was particularly crucial because he was the image of Christ who assisted others to regain their lost im-

9. *Scholia on Proverbs,* 183.

10. *Scholia on Proverbs,* 210.

11. *Scholia on Proverbs,* 120.

12. *Scholia on Proverbs,* 241.

13. *Scholia on Proverbs,* 69, 120.

ages. Some of his advice was quite concrete. For instance, he stated that monks should divest themselves of any wealth: "*Genometha penetes, hina bleposin hemas hoi tou Kyriou ophthalmoi*" is a good example of this.[14] Other passages confirm that Evagrius took poverty to be a literal requirement of the *gnostikos,* a sign of his resemblance to Christ.

The gnostic is a sign of Christ himself by becoming his living image, and by mediating the knowledge of Christ to other human intellects. In imitation of Christ, the gnostic "heals men by the aid of the Lord," Evagius writes in the *Gnostikos.*[15] He mediates knowledge belonging only to the Lord, and must die with Christ in order to understand his ways.[16] Like Christ, he must choose carefully the proper recipients of the full truth, and hide it when necessary, because not all disciples are capable of understanding the *theoria* of the scriptures.[17] For those at the level of *praktike,* the gnostic must exercise that same leniency which Evagrius ascribes to Christ as part of *synkatabasis.* This is a more external quality, an action of the gnostic to show that he, like Christ, never wavers in his love and virtue. Like the less-advanced monk, the gnostic will be engaged in combat, particularly against the temptation to anger (a teacher's irritation?) and outwardly in the battle against heretics and unbelievers. He should be an expert exegete but should not engage in disputation about God. To the gnostic, as to Christ, there attach the *epinoiai* of contradiction: the gnostic is salt for the impure and light for the pure (Mt 5:13–14). The implication is an interesting one: he is like the disciples when he is in the company of sinners, but for those on the path of virtue he is like the Lord himself.[18]

Possibly the most important description of the gnostic as Christ-like, however, is in the pair of chapters, 49 and 50, that close the *Gnostikos.* The first statement describes the change that the gnostic is expected to undergo before teaching others. It states:

> The goal of *praktike* is to purify the intellect and make it have *apatheia*: that of the *physike* is to reveal the truth hidden in all beings; but the grace of theology is to distance the *nous* from all material things and to turn it toward the First Cause.[19]

14. *Scholia on Proverbs,* 304, and cf. "Introduction," 53–54.

15. *In Psalmos* 10.

16. *Gnostikos* 33, in *Evagre le Pontique. Le Gnostique, ou a celui qui est devenue digne de la science,* ed. and trans. Antoine Guillaumont and Claire Guillaumont (Paris: Editions du Cerf, 1989), 150–51.

17. *Scholia on Proverbs,* 193.

18. *Gnostikos* 33.

19. *Gnostikos* 3, and cf. n. 3 on Matt. 5:13–14.

In the second, very terse statement, the gnostic is depicted as fixedly gazing at God the Archetype in order to show him to the fallen by means of a double reflection: "The gnostic should be looking always toward the Archetype to attempt to inscribe (*graphein*) the *eikons* without neglecting what is useful for regaining the one who has fallen (from it)." If Evagrius is recalling Gregory Nazianzen in this text, and reinterpreting Timaeus 29a, in which the Demiurge creates by gazing at the archetype, then again the gnostic is imitating the creative role of Christ the *demiurgos*. He has two levels of images in mind: the level of perfected intellect, which Christ has and which the gnostic is coming to have; and the fallen image, man, who regains the image and likeness of God through grace, mediation, and the effort to the *praktike.*[20]

With this portrait of the gnostic sketched out, it is possible to see how Christ functions, in Evagrius's thought, as a model and mediator for the gnostic, who must take on the image of Christ in order to know how to mediate it to beginners. It is interesting to read the *Kephalaia Gnostika* in the light of this doctrine, for it then seems to resemble a contemplative *enchiridion* for the gnostic instead of the exercise in speculative, cryptic theology that it has often been seen as being.

Indeed, on the basis of that work, Evagrius has been thought to have neglected the role of Christ in human salvation.[21] But everywhere in his works Evagrius insists that Christ is necessary, and necessarily as both Son of God and man. As God, he was Word, not a creature but "a precise image and true reflection of the Father's essence." It is because the Word and Holy Spirit are "direct signs of the father [that] they understand and reveal everything." Because the human mind is "their true image, and their likeness is communicated to it," it is called a "divine mind" and said to be "capable of everything."[22]

20. *Gnostikos* 49.

21. *Gnostikos* 50. See also Robin Darling Young, "Evagrius the Iconographer: Monastic Pedagogy in the *Gnostikos*," *JECS* 9.1 (2001): 53-@71.

22. In addition, see Hugo Rahner, "Die geistliche Lehre des Evagrius Pontikus," *Zeitschrift für Aszese und Mystik* 8 (1933): 21–38; Hans Urs von Balthasar, "Metaphysik und Mystik des Evagrius Ponticus," *Zeitschrift für Aszese und Mystik* 14 (1939): 31–47; and Francoise Refoule, "La christologie d'Evagre et l'Origenisme," *Orientalia christiana periodica* 27 (1961): 221–66. See Aloys Grillmeier, *Christ in Christian Tradition,* vol. 1, *From the Apstolic Age to Chalcedon (451),* 2nd ed., trans. John Bowden (Atlanta: John Knox Press, 1975), 377–84: "In Christology . . . [Evagrius] develops towards an exaggerated and eventually heretical origenism." For an alternative point of view, see Gabriel Bunge, *Briefe aus der Wuste* (Trier, 1986), 126–39.

Because the human likeness to God was lost in the fall, the human mind's restoration depended upon the incarnation of Christ as God-man, to give that direct communication of the Father that only a Nicene Christology can make possible. Commenting upon Ps 16 (LXX), "From your face my justice has gone forth," Evagrius remarks, "If the Father has given all judgment to the Son, from the *prosopon* of that one has the judgment (*to krima*) gone forth, that is, from the Son. For the *eikōn* of the Father is Christ."[23]

Furthermore, Evagrius insists in the Letter to Melania on a soteriological quite close in some respects, Gregory Nazianzen: "God was born of a woman ... in order to deliver from conception and birth ... our present conception and birth which are subject to the curse [because we have ruined our nature by our free will]."[24] In another Gregorian echo, there appears to be a *mixis* of the two natures, human and divine: It is an unspeakable marvel, Evagrius writes, "that the nature of rational beings, which because of its createdness, its having beginning and because of the changeability of its will was alien to the divine nature ... should be mingled with the nature of its creator, and in its grace will be one in Him in a all respects, without end." Evagrius goes so far as to say, however, that man "ceases to be man" because of the immortality and glory which are returned to human nature when that "likeness" to God at last arrives.[25]

Evagrius's soteriology, then, uses the terminology of *eikōn,* of *metechō/metousia,* and of *induo*—of image, of participation, and of clothing—all appropriate to pre-Nicene and neo-Nicene theology as he had it form Origen and Gregory. In the first two are described the relation between Christ and God the Father and in the third is described the relation between God and the Christian and Christ and man. Behind this soteriology is the Gospel text of John 14:1–31, where Christ states that he and the Father are "in" each other, and that he and the disciples are "in" each other; if the disciples "love me, and obey the commands I give you" they will recognize the coming Paraclete. This is possible,

23. *Ad Melaniam* 4, edited in *Evagrius Ponticus,* Wilhelm Frankenberg (Berlin: Weidmannsche Buchhandlung, 1912) (Abhandlungen der königlichen Gesellschafter der Wissenschaften zu Gottingen, Phil.-hist. Klasse. Neue Folge. Bd. XIII, n. 2), and Gosta Vitestam, "Seconde partie du traite qui passé sous le nom de 'la grande lettre d'Evagre le Pontique a Melanie l'Ancienne,' publiée et traduite d'après le manuscript du B.M. Add. 17192," *Scripta Minora Regiae Societatis humaniorum litterarum Lundensis 1963–1964* (Lund, 1964), and English trans. by Martin Parmentier in *Bijdragen* 46 (1985):2-38.

24. *Scholia in Psalmos* 16 (17.1). Cf. *Ad Melaniam* 4, 1.140: "The Word and Spirit are ... a precise image and a true reflection of the Father's essence."

25. *Ad Melaniam* 12.

Evagrius thought, only because Christ was God incarnate, and also the God-man who is visibly the image of God.[26]

The Soteriology of Philoxenos as *Imitatio Christi*

The ways in which Philoxenos has appropriated Evagrius as part of his own patristic tradition appear in texts from four major works—the *Paraenetic Mêmrê,* the *Letter to Patricius,* the fragmentary *Matthew-Luke Commentary,* and the lengthy *Commentary on the Johannine Prologue.* These, among others, show his treatment of this theme of the imitation of Christ. By this imitation Philoxenos meant the stages in an ascetic practice in which faith, wisdom, obedience, *apatheia,* and love are ordered to bring the Christian to a state in which Christ is said to be in him, and he is said to be in Christ. Such a process constitutes the revivification of the human being and reveals, ultimately, the Pauline influence upon Philoxenos—an influence, of course, shared by Evagrius.

It is useful to begin by comparing this process as Philoxenos and Evagrius present it. Here is where can be seen the differing *milieux* of the two: Evagrius the Cappadocian theologian removed to the desert, involved with spiritual discipline and theological study of Nitria, the cells, and, from some distance, the Jerusalem convent of Rufinus and Melania. Philoxenos, a scholarly monk-bishop increasingly involved in the defense of the Cyrillian christological tradition against an ecumenical council and theology interpreted as dyophysite, or even, at his most distressed moments, Jewish. It is important to note here that both wanted to argue against forms of Christian, antinomian Gnosticism—Evagrius in Egypt and Philoxenos in northern Mesopotamia.

Philoxenos, unlike Evagrius, seems never to have lived in a monastery, nor to have taken monastic vows. In Edessa, however, he entered a school devoted to the study of the Antiochene theologians, with a student life organized around quasi-monastic regulations. There he was first an adherent of a dyophysite exegesis and Christology, that of the *homo assumptus.* There he came to the Cyrillian point of view thought of as unacceptably theopaschite by its opponents: a view which allowed him to use earlier Syrian traditions despite his expressed disdain for their technical inexactitude and to come to the opinion

26. *Ad Melaniam* 12.

that only those of the orthodox, Cyrillian faith maintained the tradition of the church and the means of salvation. These two, his fervent and zealous devotion to orthodoxy and his formation in the ascetic life of an Edessan scholar, made Philoxenos throughout his career a theorist of the monastic life and an insistent promoter of Christological orthodoxy, particularly after his elevation to the see of Hierapolis/Mabbug in 485.

Despite his energetic devotion to orthodoxy, retained throughout his hectic career a strong interesting promoting the ascetic life among the monasteries of his own region and those around and to the east of Edessa. To this end he wrote mêmrê, discourses, and commentaries, as well as numerous letters. Aided, no doubt, by the scriptorium he used in his own see, throughout his career he promoted an Evagrian view of the serious Christian life. Although Philoxenos invoked the Christology of one divine nature and hypostasis, his soteriology is fundamentally that of Evagrius as well. It remains so even after Philoxenos found it necessary to repudiate in the strongest terms the interpretation of Evagrius put forward by Stephen Bar Sudaili.

In order to show this, it will be necessary to investigate two related questions repeatedly dealt with by Philoxenos: First, who is Christ in his role as our Savior? And second, what are the stages of our progressive likening to him?

The bishop of Mabbug constantly gave his Christology a Cyrillian slant by repeating the following statement or a variation of it: "Christ is God incarnate, not man divinized,"[27] and "the Son first became man and then made men sons."[28] And coupled with this concept was his insistence that Christ, man and God hypostatically united in one nature and hypostasis, grew exactly as other men do—that God participated in human life exactly as men do, and far more intensely and perfectly.

Philoxenos's soteriology generally hinges on the effects of Christ's own "growth in wisdom and stature." In an anti-Docetic passage of his *Matthew-Luke Commentary* he lays out the exact correspondence between Christ's growth and our own:

27. For a discussion of the similarity between Evagrius's thought and that of Basil of Caesarea and Gregory Naianzen, see Nicholas Geddle, "Cappadocian Elements in the Mystical Theology of Evagrius Ponticus," *Studia Patristica* 16, part 2 (1985): 373–84.

28. André de Halleux, ed. and trans., *Philoxene de Mabbog. Commmentaire du prologue johannique,* CSCO 380, 381 (Louvain, Secretariat du CSCO, 1977), 180 (178).

> If the corporeality of God is a likeness, also the benefits which have been prepared by [it] for men are likenesses. For on this account he became man, to make us sons to his Father. He was manifested a corporeal being to change us to his spirituality ... he grew in stature to bring us to completion and perfection ... he fasted and hungered and was tempted to give us victory over all the passions of sin. He conquered the Tempter in the wilderness that we might no longer be his subjects but become the masters of his contest. He endured passions and tasted death to give by his passions impassibility and to justify by his death for eternal life ... he was numbered with men to join us to the spiritual powers.[29]

This is a typical passage for Philoxenos; he consistently insists that the stages of the divine economy came about to provide a model for the Christian life—they are for humans to imitate.[30] Why, he asks elsewhere, did the Word become flesh? So that, after many sorrows and much suffering, Christians may come to be "in him."[31]

This understanding of mutual indwelling occupies an interesting portion of Philoxenos's *Commentary on the Johannine Prologue,* in which the author uses a Pauline text, as he does throughout, to understand the Johannine notion that Christ is in us, as he was in Paul:

> And if, following the witness of him who became, more than anyone else, the seer of the mysterious knowledge, he who is as he has said, likewise crucified as Christ, the power and wisdom of God, how can we not say correctly that the human aspects of God are "in power" in the image of his divine aspects? Because the power of his acts was hidden from bodily sight and made plain only to the intelligence.[32]

Philoxenos goes on to say that "it is according to this model that everyone who has received the faith in baptism and received the Holy Spirit must make it possible for Christ to live in him, but only if he has put every fleshly passion to death in himself."

In expanding upon the Adam-Christ typology of Paul, then, Philoxenos distinguishes between all men, who live after the ruination of "our first creation," and the baptized, who participate in "our last renovation" and become the *gushma,* the body of Christ.[33]

Philoxenos does not mean to convey the idea that we are divinized into

29. J. W. Watt, ed. and trans., *Philoxenus of Mabbug, Fragments of the Commentary on Matthew and Luke,* CSCO 171, 172 (Louvain: Secretariat du CSCO, 1978), 46 (40).

30. *Matthew-Luke Commentary,* 72 (62).

31. *Prologue to John,* 3–4 (3–4).

32. *Prologue to John,* 17 (16).

33. *Prologue to John,* 168–69 (166–67).

"sons of God" and likenesses of Christ in any automatic way despite the prominence, following Paul, of grace in his discussion. The most central purpose of the incarnation is not to make us merely baptized and obediently orthodox and righteous members of Christ's body the church. Rather, it is to provide an entry point for human beings into Christ's inner life of human communion with the divine, and to render us his equals "by a miracle"—top make us divine by the same process of suffering and growth in *apatheia,* tranquility, love, and contemplation as he experienced having become man "by a miracle." The human life in the body of Christ, then, actually becomes through mutual indwelling an experience of the increasing state of wisdom, contemplation, and pure, simple, intellectual life that God possessed in his "human aspects."[34]

The second question may now be taken up—that is, what are the stages in human growth in likeness to Christ? First, it should be noted that Philoxenos distinguishes sharply between three types of human life. In each state a certain type of moral life is intimately related to its corresponding type of mental and spiritual life. The first way is the way of the body, in which a person is dominated by his "natural" desires, tormented by ambition, greed, lust—the bodily vices related to the material world. In the intellectual realm, this man is completely stunted by his limitation to the use of the five physical senses. He counts the visible for reality and ignores the invisible; for him there is no interiority of objects, and no possibility of *theōria,* contemplation. This man's knowledge, which can be as vast as the analysis of the visible, material world, is attainable by the mind with no faith through a process of collection and analysis of data. It is the world of speculation, wordiness, disputation, and contrariety. If applied hypothetically to the hypothetical God, it would subject him to analysis, too. That this is a form of living death in Philoxenos's view is obvious.

Philoxenos endorses this type of knowledge for human beings as long as it does not become an end in itself, or a deceptive construction placed upon reality. Here Philoxenos reflects an already traditional view born out of the Arian controversy and visible in theological disputations before that time. He thinks of this kind of disputation as a particularly Antiochene vice, obscuring the hidden, but more real, knowledge which is gnosis. However, this kind of knowledge if of little use for monks, Philoxenos felt—they are even little aided by exegesis.

34. *Prologue to John,* 218 (216).

The two proper ways of life for Christians are those of righteousness and perfection—the second of which is the true imitation of Christ, the first, a more exterior imitation of his obedience. The second necessarily springs from the first, in that both will begin with baptism, but only in the desert will *apatheia* and love be gained. Each shares the exact attention to fulfilling the commandments—though Philoxenos could say that the commandments differed for each—but the second would continue to be dominated by the fear of God. Yet both share faith, which becomes a sense making possible perfect knowledge and the attainment, in a human being, of the knowledge and mind of Christ himself.[35]

The Letter to Patricius

The three texts discussed so far—the *Matthew-Luke Commentary,* the *Commentary on the Prologue to John,* and the earlier collection of thirteen mêmrê—all show that Philoxenos used Evagrius as an integral part of the theological tradition from which he drew for his own description of the monastic life. Evagrius, although most often unnamed in his writings, was for Philoxenos "the father" or "the Holy one." It has been seen that Philoxenos became acquainted with Evagrius during his days as a student in Edessa. His particular construction of Evagrius's soteriology shows that Philoxenos himself (like Bunge) regarded the practical and monastic works as the center of Evagrius's thought and would consequently have interpreted the more abstruse documents in the light of the former. At this point his choice of S1 or S2 version of the *Kephalaia Gnostika* becomes somewhat moot.

Yet Philoxenos's use and implicit endorsement of Evagrius's thought over a long period of time does not mean that he was unaware of illicit uses of Evagrius. Two separate letters by Philoxenos reveal that in Edessa there were monks who were invoking Evagrius as an authority for thought and behavior that were, in Philoxenos's view, badly mistaken (in one case) and completely erroneous (in the other). Those two cases are the situations of, respectively, Patricius, a monk of Edessa, and Stephen Bar Sudaili, both monks of Edessa. Their known periods of activity are separated by only fifteen years, or at the maximum thirty, de-

35. See the discussion in Chesnut, *Three Monophysite christologies,* 60.

pending on the dating of the letter to Patricius. The latter seems to have been written between 485 and 500, and the letter concerning Stephen, sent to the monks Abraham and Orestes, was almost certainly from around 515.[36] It is unknown whether Philoxenos would have continued his campaign against the kind of interpretation found in Stephen's works, because in 518 his career as bishop ended and his fatal exile under the emperor Justin began.[37]

Because the matter of Stephen has been explored by others, it can be passed over here. *The Book of the Holy Hierotheos,* which that gnosticizing monk composed pseudonymously in the late fifth or early sixth century, was an easy target for Philoxenos because he thought its use of the writings of Evagrius to be extremely wrongheaded. It also drew the ire of Philoxenos's otherwise irenic contemporary Jacob of Sarug.[38]

But Patricius of Edessa, and any other monks whom his view may also have represented, seems to have been yet another Syriac-speaking follower of Evagrius, or at least an interpreter whose views on the Greek monk stood, so Philoxenos seems to have thought, in need of thorough correction. And here again, Philoxenos can be seen to employ Evagrian soteriology, as he understood it, against a premature and overambitious approach to the monastic life. Despite the apparent concentration of the letter on the connections between the life of contemplation and its foundations in *ascesis,* the actions of Christ are always a model that Philoxenos puts forward to correct the views of Patricius.

Now Philoxenos did not write the letter without provocation. Patricius had earlier written to the bishop to ask him three questions: first, whether the monk must follow the commandments of Christ; second, whether it was necessary to flee any particular object of the passions; and third, whether the monk should give thought to the scandal he might give to the weak. Philoxenos also preserves, through direct quotation and refutation, nine assertions that Patricius put forward for episcopal approval and were probably the core of his practice, or monastic labor.[39]

36. Ibid., 87–92.

37. The *Letter to Patricius* is edited and translated in René Lavenant, *La Lettre à Patricius de Philoxène de Mabboug* (Paris: Firmin-Didot, 1963) (PO 30). For a discussion of the letter and its context, see Halleux, *Philoxène de Mabbog,* 254–59.

38. At the time of his death in Philipopolis, Philoxenos was occupied with the resistance to resurgent Chalcedonianism under Justin. See W. H. C. Frend, *The Rise of the Monophysite Movement. Chapters in the History of theCchurch in the Fifth and Sixth Centuries* (Cambridge: Cambridge University Press, 1972), 248.

39. See the letters in A. L. Frothingham, *Stephen Bar Sudaili, the Syrian Mystic, and the Book of*

It is unknown whether Philoxenos has quoted them in the order in which Patricius set them out, but the nine do divide neatly into three larger categories. In the first set, Patricius maintained that his desires were already oriented toward the love of God, to purity, and to freedom—*parrhêsia,* in the Syriac transliteration of the Greek monastic term. In the second set, he declared that his work was exegesis and spiritual reading, to write and intercede for another. In the third set, he denigrated the helpfulness of the commandments. These make an interesting catalogue, because they constitute the attributes of the *gnostikos,* the Christ-like monk who, according to Evagrius was, after himself being trained, able to act as friend, intercessor and *alter Christus* to the monks. Evagrius had drawn a portrait of the *gnostikos,* of course, in his short work of that title, and if the work was known to Patricius in Edessa, either in Syriac or in Greek, it may have been the work that the Edessan monk drew upon to legitimize, or perhaps merely to inspire, his own work.

Philoxenos responds to Patricius's query by sending the latter back to the beginning of the Evagrian path and to shift, in this particular treatment, the imitation of Christ from the model of the contemplative to that of the patient sufferer, and interestingly for Patricius the confessed bibliophile, the one whose knowledge is based not on a multiplicity of objects (books!) but upon a clear apprehension of things as they are, in the light of faith.[40]

What, then, does Philoxenos specifically recommend? He does not renounce the Evagrian thought from which Patricius, too, probably draws, but rather he reorders it so that it could function as a corrective. In doing so, he accomplished a portrait of the reformed monasticism of Philoxenos. First, Philoxenos adapts the Evagrian *imitatio Christi* to life outside the particular monastic context for which it was designed; second, he renders it discursive and didactic instead of reproducing its original, more gnomic style; and third, he emphasizes certain elements of Evagrius's teaching at the expense of others that had been unhelpful for the Edessan monk, according to Philoxenos's judgment. In doing so, he also overturned what was, apparently, Patricius's appeal to

---

Hierotheos. Leyden, 1886. They are Jacob of Sarug, "Letter . . . to Stephen Bar Sudaili," 11–24, and Philoxenos, "Letter . . . to Abraham and Orestes, Presbyters of Edessa, Concerning Stephen Bar Sudaili the Edessene," 28–48. The offending book is *Stephen Bar Sudaili, The Book of the Holy Hierotheos,* ed. and trans. F. W. Marsh (London, 1927).

40. Philoxenos responds to Patricius; three questions, in sections 3–26, 27–40, and 41–46, respectively, of the letter. The nine assertions are outlined by Lavenant in his "Analyse de la lettre," 19–21.

the antinomian texts of Paul as a justification for the quick leap from reading to *theoria* (there are some indications in the text that Philoxenos was concerned here about Gnosticism, as he had been in the case of Stephen).[41]

Philoxenos reorders Evagrius's soteriological legacy in the following ways. First, he limits Christ's grace to the period of the apostles; the salvation of the *ihidoyo,* he writes, now comes the submission of the self to laws (*puqdanê*). Ironically, Philoxenos here makes Paul an example of submission to the law, albeit the law of Christ; this apostle did not receive his visions, about which he was extremely reticent, without right actions first.[42]

"Paul," Philoxenos wrote, "recognized that some of the disciples then were abandoning the observation of the commandments and [wanted] the goodness of contemplation which comes rightly after the keeping of commands."[43] To the Colossians and the Romans both, Paul wrote that the business of the Christian was the renewal through regaining the image of God who has pity on some and hardens others. Contemplation, Philoxenos concludes, is indeed a gift of grace, but never comes before suffering and keeping the commandments, just as Jesus did.[44] Paul himself, writes Philoxenos, wishes that we would emulate the path of Christ, moving slowly and patiently through the fear of God proper to his creatures to the love of God proper to those who in some way share in the divine nature—which through imitating Christ we may do, but slowly. Like Paul, and of course like Christ in his temptations, the saints—here, the monastic *qaddishê*—asked not for wonders, but occupied themselves with keeping the commandments, allowing God then to treat them as he willed. Paul, he continued, teaches every disciple to "seek tribulations, poverty, and union to Christ's sufferings, not the wonders and high places of his kingdom."[45] Of course, the possibility of being united to Christ's suffering in the first place comes from baptism and the faith taught in subsequent catechesis—here Philoxenos is not necessarily departing from Evagrius; he had read his letter *On the Faith* and quotes it elsewhere—in that letter Evagrius certainly endorsed faith as a prerequisite for knowledge.[46] But Philoxenos makes faith a form of knowledge, even a kind of sixth sense—and this he may take from Ephrem and John Chrysostom.[47] At

41. On the imitation of Christ as sufferer, see *Patricius,* 54; pp. 62 and 65 contain cautions against "many readings."

42. *Patricius,* 68.

43. *Patricius,* 69.

44. *Patricius,* 68, 79.

45. *Patricius,* 113.

46. *Patricius,* 118.

47. *Patricius,* 54.

any rate, incorporation into Christ's body leads directly to suffering because the commandments conflict, just as they did in Christ, with the natural desires of human beings.[48]

In connection with his views on the central role of faith, Philoxenos recommends that the monk Patricius abandon excessive reading because this practice does not produce the knowledge of Christ (*yada'thâ damshihâ*).[49] Rather, "many readings," he admonishes, "produce many thoughts in the soul." They lead not to quiet, but to trouble. True, reading the scriptures is good for those in a different order (*taksâ*)—i.e. not a monastic, perhaps is living in the world. But Jesus who "wishes to give life to his members not by a gift only, but by nature," has established special rules for monks, a refinement of the commandments he gave to all Christians.[50] They are to practice hospitality toward strangers (*aksenoye,* perhaps a punning reference to himself), and this is their chief form of mortification—not visiting hospitals, distributing charity, and the like. Jesus, he adds, "gives forgiveness [to the monk] after a long and difficult penitence: [these are] rules of life, works, *praktike,* death to the whole world—then he gives to some of the righteous ones the power to heal sicknesses."[51] But this is not the end Patricius should necessarily expect—and the desire to be like Jesus in this way is likely to lead to delusions, and even fatal hallucinations.[52]

Rather, after long suffering, the monk may arrive at a true contemplation that begins with contemplation of objects and leads up to contemplation of the Trinity: a growth into Christ's own insight into the things he made, and in which he as son and creator participates. Only when suffering has yielded, following Christ, to triumphant kingship does this occur; then there is the absence of psychic suffering (*lâ hašûšûṭâ d'nâpšâ*) which is its kingdom, or *malkûṭâ*.[53]

48. Evagrius (quondam Basil), *Epistula Fidei,* in Yves Courtonne, ed. and trans., *St. Basile, Lettres,* vol. 1 (Paris, 1957), Letter 8, 22–37.

49. Ephrem and Chrysostom adopt this position in their *Hymns on Faith* and *Homilies on the Epistle to the Romans,* respectively. For Philoxenos's use of these authors, see, among other works, the *Commentary on the Prologue to John,* "Paralleles Patristiques," 258–60.

50. *Patricius,* 57.

51. *Patricius,* 84, 118.

52. *Patricius,* 111, on the monk Aswana of Edessa who "died a ridiculous death" after a hallucination prompted him to leap from a precipice.

53. *Patricius,* 118.

There may be no skipping of the steps of Christ's own incarnation and exaltation; disaster, pointless suffering, and delusion will surely result.

Much more could be said about Philoxenos's response to Patricius, and no evidence from the letter has been included here of further instances of errant monasticism in the environs of early sixth-century Edessa. But this essay has tried to point to the way in which, on one occasion, Philoxenos unselfconsciously used the soteriology of Evagrius to rebuke monastic error, seemingly based on that same author. Not much worried about Evagrius's heterodoxy, he found no contradiction between the imitation of Christ as Evagrius pictured it and the gradual, miraculous taking on of Christ's own nature as he inherited that theme from the Cyrillian tradition.

Monica J. Blanchard

9. THE SYRIAC DISCOURSES OF BEH ISHO' KAMULAYA

Purity of heart is an important concept in early Christian ascetical and monastic literature.[1] It is also an important theme in the writings of a late eighth-century East Syrian monk, Beh Isho' Kamulaya, whose writings have only recently been rediscovered. I would like to take the opportunity here to introduce the works of Beh Isho' by tracing this theme as it appears in his Syriac discourses on the monastic way of life.

Background

The Institute of Christian Oriental Research (ICOR) at the Catholic University of America owns a small Syriac manuscript which has not yet been published. Incomplete at beginning and end, it contains six discourses (*mêmrê*) on the monastic way of life, part of a collection of "Chapters of Knowledge" (*rîšê d-'îda'tâ*), and the first lines of a poem (*madrāšâ*), all of which are attributed to an East Syrian monk, Beh Isho' Kamulaya, who may have flourished in the late eighth century. Beh Isho' and his book on monastic life are mentioned in the late thirteenth-century Syriac catalogue of the library of 'Abd Isho' bar Berikha (d. 1318), also a member of the Syriac-speaking "Nestorian" Church, or Assyrian Church of the East.[2] There is no information about the other two

1. For a recent overview see Harriet A. Luckman and Linda Kulzer, eds., *Purity of Heart in Early Ascetic and Monastic Literature: Essays in Honor of Juana Raasch* (Collegeville, Minn.: Liturgical Press, 1999).

2. J. S. Assemani, *Bibliotheca orientalis clementino-vaticana, in qua manuscriptos codices syriacos, arabicos,*

works attributed to Beh Ishoʿ in the Catholic University manuscript. The manuscript is undated. The codicological evidence generally supports a date between the late ninth and early twelfth centuries.

This is the only copy of Beh Ishoʿ's works known to exist in an ancient Syriac manuscript. Twice within the past fifty years, scholars have tentatively identified Beh Ishoʿ's monastic discourses with treatises preserved in modern Syriac codexes copied around the beginning of the twentieth century in the environs of Urmia, in northwestern Iran.

In 1936 Adolf Rücker published a summary of the contents of his personal copy of a manuscript he believed to be no. 214 from the Library of the Museum Association of Urumiah (Urmi) College.[3] According to Rücker it contained *The Book of Perfection,* or seven discourses by "Berikh Ishoʿ," monk of the Monastery of Kamul at the end of the eighth century. Already in 1725 Assemani assumed that the unusual name Beh Ishoʿ, "in him is Jesus," was a misspelling of the more common name Berikh Ishoʿ, "Blessed is Jesus." Assemani suggested that Beh Ishoʿ was one Berikh Ishoʿ, East Syrian monk of the Monastery of Kamul during the patriarchate of Timothy I (d. 823).[4] Rücker, in turn, identified Assemani's "Berikh Ishoʿ" with the author of the works preserved in Urumiah College MS no. 214.[5] He situated this Berikh Ishoʿ within the general framework of better-known seventh-century and eighth-century East Syrian monastic writers such as Isaac of Nineveh, John of Dalyatha, and Joseph Hazzaya.[6]

Information about the relationship between Berikh Ishoʿ and Beh Ishoʿ can be found in the Catholic University manuscript. There Berikh Ishoʿ is mentioned by name as a fellow monk of Beh Ishoʿ in the Monastery of Kamul.

persicos, turcicos, hebraicos, samaritanos, armenicos, aethiopicos, graecos, egyptiacos, ibericos & malabaricos, ... ex Oriente conquisitos, comparatos, avectos, & Bibliothecae Vaticanae addictos recensuit, digessit, & genuina scripta a spuriis secrevit, ..., 3 vols. (Rome: Typis Sacrae Congregationis de Propaganda Fide, 1719–1728), 3.1.275.

3. Adolf Rücker, "Aus dem mystischen Schrifttum nestorianischer Mönche des 6.–8 Jahrhunderts," *Morgenland: Darstellungen aus Geschichte und Kultur des Ostens* 28 (1936): 38–54; Kashisha Oshana Sarau of Tkhoma, Kurdistan, *Catalogue of Syriac Manuscripts in the Library of the Museum Association of Oroomiah College* (Oroomiah [Urmia], Persia: n.p., 1898), 34–35.

4. On Timothy I, see Thomas Hurst, "The Syriac Letters of Timothy I (727–823): A Study in Christian-Muslim Controversy," Ph.D. diss., The Catholic University of America, Washington, D.C., 1986; and the biographical note in Harald Suermann, "Timothy and His Dialogue with Muslims," *The Harp* 8–9 (1995–1996): 263–75, esp. 267–70.

5. Kashisha Oshana Sarau gives the author's name as Mar Beh Ishoʿ Kamulaya on p. 35 of the catalog. MS no. 214 also is a modern copy, made in 1892.

6. Robert Beulay also evaluates Berikh Ishoʿ within this framework, in R. Beulay, *La lumière sans forme: introduction à l'étude de la mystique chétienne syro-orientale,* L'Esprit et le Feu (Chevetogne: Éditions de Chevetogne, 1980), 223–28.

Rücker's article and Oshana Sarau's catalog note may be the only extant sources of information about Urumiah College MS no. 214. The manuscript seems to be lost.[7]

In 1996, at the Uppsala Symposium Syriacum, Johannes Sanders announced the discovery of the works of Beh Isho' Kamulaya, under the name of Mar Bishoi, in Trichur MS16, a modern handwritten codex in the library of the metropolitan see of the Church of the East, in Trichur, Kerala, India.[8] Sanders has presented outlines of the contents of the Indian manuscript in two published articles.[9] His description shows close parallels with the contents of the ICOR manuscript. Both seem to contain the six discourses on the monastic way of life, as well as the "Chapters on Knowledge," and a poem by Beh Isho'. The Trichur codex also contains a lengthy biography of Bishoi (fols. 1–67), as he is called in that manuscript. The biography seems to be a reworking of the Syriac *Life* of one of the legendary founders of the monasteries of the Egyptian Wadi Natrun, none other than Abba Bishoi, as he is known in his Syriac guise, or in Coptic, Apa Pshoi.[10] Sanders explained the name Beh Isho' as a misunderstanding or misspelling of Bishoi.[11]

7. I have not been able to locate Adolf Rücker's personal copy of this manuscript.

8. Brief descriptions of the manuscript can be found in Edward R. Hambye, "Some Syriac Libraries of Kerala (Malabar), India: Notes and Comments," in Robert H. Fischer, ed., *A Tribute to Arthur Vööbus: Studies in Early Christian Literature and its Environment, Primarily in the Syrian East* (Chicago: Lutheran School of Theology, 1977), 35–46, see 46 (where it is identified as MS no. 23); Mar Aprem, "Syriac Manuscripts in Trichur," in René Lavenant, ed., *III° Symposium Syriacum 1980: les contacts du monde syriaque avec les autres cultures (Goslar 7-11 Septembre 1980),* Orientalia christiana analecta 221 (Rome: 1983), 355–74, see 359; J. P. M. van der Ploeg, *The Christians of St. Thomas in South India and Their Syriac Manuscripts,* Placid Lecture Series 1 (Bangalore: Dharmaram Publication; Rome: Center for Indian and Inter-Religious Studies, 1983), 136. Van der Ploeg mentions, on pp. 134–35, a provisional list of the Metropolitan's manuscripts published by Mar Aprem in "a small memorial volume, called First Anniversary Chaldean Syrian Church, Kallur 14-1-1979."

9. J. Sanders, "Introduction to the Life of Mar Bishoi (siglum MB)," *The Harp* 8–9 (1995–1996): 277–88; Sanders, "Mar Bishoi: A Unique Witness of Ascetic Life in Eastern Turkey," in R. Lavenant, ed., *Symposium Syriacum VII, Uppsala University, Department of Asian and African Languages 11–14 August 1996,* Orientalia christiana analecta 256 (Rome: Pontificio Istituto Orientale, 1998), 233–42.

10. More information about Bishoi in Syriac and Coptic can be found in Monica J. Blanchard, "Beh Isho' Kamulaya's Syriac Discourses on the Monastic Way of Life: Edition, English Translation, and Introduction," Ph.D. diss., The Catholic University of America, 2001; see appendixes (1) "English translation of the Syriac Life of Abba Bishoi," and (2) "Bio-bibliographical Note." See also Monica J. Blanchard, "The Coptic Heritage of St. Ephrem the Syrian," in Tito Orlandi and David W. Johnson, eds., *Acts of the Fifth International Congress of Coptic Studies Washington, 12–15 August 1992,* 3 vols. (Rome: C.I.M., 1993), 2.37–51; Blanchard, "Apa Bishoi and Mar Ephrem," *The Harp* (forthcoming).

11. Sanders, "Introduction to the Life of Mar Bishoi (siglum MB)," 279–80.

In the Coptic tradition, Abba Bishoi is called "the perfect one" even today, *al-rajul al-kāmil.*[12] In Syriac, the name Shamli can be understood as "perfected" or "perfect one." In two manuscripts of the Chaldean monastery of Our Lady of the Seeds near Alqosh,[13] Berikh Isho' of Kamul is identified as the disciple of Mar Shamli. Beh Isho', literally "in him is Jesus," is a perfected one (*šamlî*). Perhaps Beh Isho' is the subject of the "Discourse on the spiritual life of Mar Shamli, composed by his disciple Berikh Isho'," which appears in two Syriac manuscripts from the Chaldean monastery of Our Lady of the Seeds near Alqosh.[14]

The modern Indian manuscript may provide information about the provenance of the much older Syriac manuscript at the Catholic University of America. The Trichur copy was completed in November 20, 1900, by one "Thomas the reader, son of deacon John son of deacon Zachariah son of priest Sabro,"[15] a member of the Kellayta family of copyists and clerics for Abimelek Bar-M'naha, who later became Metropolitan Timotheos Abimelek of Trichur.[16] The East Syrian Kellayta family of copyists, teachers, and clerics, most notably Joseph Kellayta, had ties to Mar Bhishu,[17] a village some 40 km. due west of Urmia, and due east of the site of the Old Monastery of Kamul.[18] It seems that

12. Ashraf and Bernadette Sadek, *L'Incarnation de la lumière: le renouveau iconographique copte à travers l'oeuvre d'Isaac Fanous,* special issue of *Le Monde Copte* 29/31 (2000): 362.

13. Jacques Vosté, *Catalogue de la Bibliothèque syro-chaldéenne du Couvent de Notre-Dame des Semences près d'Alqoš (Iraq)* (Rome: Angelicum; Paris: Libr. Orientaliste P. Geuthner, 1929), 55 (codex CXLIX,4) and 75 (codex CC,3).

14. See note 8 on Syriac MSS 149 and 200. See also William F. Macomber, "New Finds of Syriac Manuscripts in the Middle East," in Wolfgang Voigt, ed., *XVII. Deutscher Orientalistentag vom 21. bis 27. Juli 1968 in Würzburg: Vorträge. Teil 2,* Zeitschrift der Deutschen Morgenländischen Gesellschaft, *Supplementa* I/2 (1969), 473–82, esp. 476–77, on the partial dispersion of this library's manuscripts. Regrettably, these manuscripts are not available to me, although MS 200 was still at the monastery in 1969.

15. Hambye, "Some Syriac Libraries of Kerala (Malabar), India: Notes and Comments," 46; Aprem, "Syriac Manuscripts in Trichur," 359.

16. Mar Aprem, *Mar Abimalek Timotheus: A Biography* (Trichur: Mar Timotheus Memorial Orphanage, 1975).

17. See J. Coakley, *The Church of the East and the Church of England: A History of the Archbishop of Canterbury's Assyrian Mission* (Oxford: Clarendon Press, 1992), p. 215, 239, map of the country of the Church of the East on 8–9. Details about Mar Bhishu or Mar Beh Isho' can be found in colophons and notes in Syriac manuscripts. See, e.g., the colophon of Tehran, Issayi Collection, MS 5, in Sebastian Brock, ed. and trans., *Isaac of Nineveh (Isaac the Syrian) "The Second Part," Chapters IV-XLI,* CSCO 5.554–55. Scriptores Syri 224–25 (Louvain: Peeters, 1995), 554.xxxi–xxxii. See, too, the manuscript notes in Julius Assfalg, *Syrische Handschriften: syrische, karšunische, christlich-palästinische, neusyrische und mandäische Handschriften,* Verzeichnis der orientalischen Handschriften in Deutschland, Bd. 5 (Wiesbaden: Franz Steiner Verlag, 1963), 36, 38, 40.

18. Assemani refers to the "coenobium Camulense in Gesira." The Arab geographers used this term

these two manuscripts together do constitute the rediscovery of the "Book on Monastic Life" and other works of Beh Isho' Kamulaya.

The Discourses of Beh Isho' Kamulaya

The six discourses comprise a guidebook for monks to progress in the monastic way of life. The rubricated *incipit* lines of the six discourses indicate the sequence of topics:

The first discourse which is about the splendid way of life of those who have been called to the discipline of the fear of God, earnestly longing for a life hanging upon the spiritual cross, and seeking to become sons and heirs to the holy children of light.[19]

The second discourse of Mar Beh Isho' Kamulaya about the discipline and dwelling in the cell, and the struggles in it and the "spiritual gifts" from grace that are given to the dwellers in silence.[20]

The third discourse of Mar Beh Isho' Kamulaya on the different ways of life in purity: where it comes from, its limits, and what it is.[21]

Again, the fourth discourse of the monk Beh Isho' about the entrance of the intellect to the pure place, and about the measure and level of limpid purity, the name for which is "the Promised Land."[22]

Once again, by that same Mar Beh Isho' Kamulaya, the fifth discourse, concerning the beginning of the entrance of the intellect to the place of perfection, and concerning the operations that are received from the Spirit in the place of limpid purity.[23]

---

jazira, literally "island" or "peninsula" or area between two rivers, to describe the northern area of land between the Tigris and Euphrates. These northeastern borders seem to be a little to the east of the area encompassing Tur Qardu, but they include the area of the upper Tigris in the north Siirt area and east of the middle of the river. Assemani has provided a list of references to the monastery in Syriac texts in his *Bibliotheca orientalis clementino-vaticana* 3.1.275. The East Syrian Monastery of Kamul, or Kmul, was built on the flank of a mountain east of the Tigris River in Eastern Turkey—Judi Dagh in Turkish, or Tura Qardu as it is known in Syriac. This is the same Tura Qardu as appears in place of Ararat in the Peshitta version of Genesis 8:4 and in a variety of Christian, Jewish, and Islamic sources. See M. Streck, "Djūdī," *Encyclopaedia Islamica. New Edition,* 2.573–74.

19. My translation of the Trichur MS, fol. 37v. (The Catholic University of America [CUA] MS text is difficult to read.)

20. My translation of the Trichur MS, fol. 50r–50v. (The CUA MS text is difficult to read.)

21. My translation of the CUA MS, fol. 49a–49b.

22. My translation of the CUA MS, fol. 79a.

23. My translation of the CUA MS, fol. 105b–106a.

Again, the sixth discourse of Mar Beh Ishoʿ on the work of the mind and reflection on God. What is the "prayer" that the Fathers discuss in their writings? And concerning the guarding of the heart, why do the holy Fathers have the custom, our Brother, of calling by the name "prayer" all of their virtuous ways of life and labors, whether it be the Office, or the readings, or the vigil, or the fast, or the bowing, and the rest?[24]

Purity of heart is considered in discourses three through six, and especially in discourses four and five.[25]

(79a) ... Again, the fourth discourse of the monk Beh Ishoʿ about the entrance of the intellect to the pure place, and about the measure and level of limpid purity, the name of which is "the Promised Land."[26] ... Take care of everything that concerns the good habits of "that new man."[27] (79b) You have laid the weight of it all upon my ignorance and the meagerness of my knowledge. I am too weak to show all of his graces as they are. Because the dwellers in my house still stand in a great battle with the Babylonians,[28] and the Philistines lie in wait within my bed-chambers.[29] Who can cast off from himself the weapons of his vigilance? Because the power of the Holy Spirit has not united itself with the power and portion of my soul, the Philistines fearlessly are gaining dominion over me. Nevertheless, I will advance securely on something that is beyond my measure and my power.... I have written to you those things about which you asked, as (80a) I learned it from the holy books of the Fathers, and as I heard it from the mouth of God's great one.[30] ... It is about the limpid place of the natural state of purity: both concerning the entrance of the intellect to

24. My translation of the CUA MS, fol. 119a–119b.

25. The following selections from the fourth and fifth discourses are my translations of the Syriac text of the CUA MS.

26. This typology of the Promised Land appears in the works of Isaac of Nineveh, John of Dalyatha, and Joseph Hazzaya. Robert Beulay traces it back to *Kephalaia Gnostica* of Evagrius Ponticus (1,31. 5,88. 6,45.49). See Robert Beulay, *La collection des letters de Jean de Dalyatha, mystique syrien-oriental du VIIIe siècle, Théologie historique* 83 (Paris: Beauchesne, 1990), [44], n. 17.

27. Eph 4, 24.

28. On the Babylonians as a type for gluttony and the physical passions, see Paul Harb and François Graffin, *Joseph Hazzāyā, Lettre sur les trois étapes de la vie monastique: edition critique du texte syriaque, traduction et introduction,* PO 45/2, no. 202 (Turnhout: Brepols, 1992), [102–3].

29. The metaphor of the Philistines (natural passions) keeping the Israelites (monks) from the Promised Land (stage of limpid purity) is developed in this discourse.

30. Beh Ishoʿ's guide or spiritual Father: Jesus Christ. See CUA MS, fols. 100b–101a; 106b.

that first place from which it went forth, and concerning the state of purity of the heart which is depicted as the type of the Promised Land according to the words of the Fathers.

Now briefly concerning the true limpid purity in which our Lord Christ is visible in ineffable glory. As he said in his holy Gospel: "Blessed are (80b) those who are pure in their heart, for they will see God."[31] Therefore, what is customary is not appropriate for the discerning person.[32] It is only a way to set the table for a great crowd. Because not all are nourished by bread, but among them are those who need milk according to their childlike state. Among them are those who are nourished by bread. They have a healthy stomach, which also accepts oil and wine.... (81a) And it is with regard to this, O Brother, that I write the earlier discourses. And for the upbringing of spiritual infants at this first summit[33] I put many [words] in the discourses in the form of nurturing milk to young temporal children, so that our table might be not only for the healthy, but that sustenance might be found for everyone.... (81b) ... So, my Brother, by its nature the soul is next of kin to the angels—pure, limpid discerning, rational, spiritual, the reflection of God its Creator, just as when the Creator created our father the first Adam. A voice unheard cried out in the ears of the spiritual assemblies, saying (82a) "Let us make man in our image and in our likeness."[34] Thus the glorious image of the Creator, my Brother! What deficiency is there in the Glorious One? Thus the nature of men, when from within the womb into the light of this world the pure and limpid ones are born! And if this is not the case, then consider the state of infant children and see how there is found in them no impulse knowing or feeding upon evil. See too that because of their simplicity and guilelessness they know neither cunning nor stratagems nor artifices. But when they abide in this present life ..., little by little they are transformed in the measure of their simplicity, and all of their natural beauties are changed to hateful qualities (82b) that are outside of nature.... Now each of the singles among the elect of grace forsakes the world and accepts the *schema* of the solitary way of life. They cast off the world by the contest and labors of virtuous conduct, and they arrive at their original state of purity, as it is written about each one of them in their histories—that they were made pure and straight, and they became like children metaphorically.... Behold tempo-

31. Matt. 5:8.

32. The Syriac is reminiscent of Rom. 2:18 (context, Rom. 2:17–21).

33. Greek, *akmē.*

34. Cf. Gen. 1:26.

ral children like infant babes! (84b) Behold true limpid purity and the perfection of its state.... Whoever has arrived at purity of the heart and the entrance to the natural place of limpid purity has no way to avoid tasting a little, if only as much as the tip of the little finger of one's intellect, for a little while the gifts of the Holy Spirit. For the "spirit of sonship,"[35] whose pledge we received from Baptism, dwells in us on this account.... Whenever the fog of darkness has been drawn aside (85a) and the veil of passions has been stripped from the front of the inner door of the heart, and the intellect shines with the Spirit and sees its natural place from afar, the Holy Spirit works in it there from time to time—that which we receive through Holy Baptism.

When they have entered the place of limpid purity, the Holy Spirit does not desist from working continually in their faculties. And they burn with the spirit and "tread upon snakes and scorpions and all of the power of the enemy."[36] And they heal the powers, and they walk on the water, (86a) and they "remove mountains"[37] by the living word of God. As the trustworthy promise of our Saviour and the lordly commandment of his Gospel said: "Blessed are those who accepted this *schema* of the solitary way of life, and labored diligently, and endured all of the straits, and bore the burden of the day and its heat, and overcame all of the billows and the stumbling-blocks of temptations in the harbor of the place of limpid purity. Even now they are dwelling in the new life after the resurrection, while they are still in this world; not as if they were men, but as if 'they were angels in heaven.'"[38] "For the weapons of their labor are not of the flesh, but of the Spirit of God,"[39] as the blessed Apostle Paul said.

(86b) Now since we are of the flesh, but [the Spirit] did not become flesh, we labor. When the solitary has perfected the level of bodily labors and has arrived at the place of purity from his previous abode which is the beginning of the spiritual way of life, he enters into the *theōria*[40] of Scripture and an understanding of the nature of creation. His mind meditates on these, and he ponders and

35. Cf. Rom. 8:15.

36. Cf. Luke 10:19.

37. Cf. 1 Cor. 13:2.

38. Cf. Matt. 22:30; Mark 12:25. The Savior's promise is a reference to the Beatitudes, Matt. 5:3-12. See too E. A. Wallis Budge, trans., *The Paradise of the Holy Fathers ... translated out of the Syriac with notes & introductions,* 2 vols. (1907; repr., Seattle, Wash.: St. Nectarios Press, 1984), 2.285–286.

39. Cf. 2 Cor. 10:4.

40. Greek, *theōria.* For translations of "contemplation," "vision," and "divine vision," see *The Ascetical Homilies of Saint Isaac the Syrian, translated by the Holy Transfiguration Monastery,* trans. Dana Miller (Boston: Holy Transfiguration Monastery, 1983), cx–cxi.

investigates night and day until they give way, and his intellect is refined from its denseness and is enlightened. The vision of his understanding expands indefinitely with the light of the *theōria* of their natures. Its sight surpasses without impediment everything in heaven and on earth and above heaven and below the deepest depths. (87a) Swiftly, by the simple light of his nature, as if by a flash of lightning, he now departs from the first summit of the measure of bodily nature, and he begins to arrive at the border of the second summit, the discipline of the mind, and the second measure which is that of natural life. Since his knowledge is still of the body, he gazes with its structure at the entire *theōria* at which the intellect gazes. Because until the inner door of the heart is opened from within, it is the *theōria* that reaches what is within the heart by means of its light and brightness, drawing to itself the vision of the intellect from the appearance outside, and by *theōrias* recalling and immersing it in a contemplative structure. The intellect of its own accord strives after the vision (87b) of the *theōrias,* and it constructs and fashions an entire *theōria* which it seeks as a giver of grace to itself. For when the heart has been purified from within and it recalls the light of grace noetically, after this, not of its own accord, the intellect pursues the vision of the *theōrias.* But the *theōria,* shining forth from within, gathers the intellect unto itself and works it with its simple light. Like the nature of the heart of the earth in springtime shoots sprout forth forcibly, along with fruits and flowers of every kind. In this way too the pure heart from which the veil of passions has been stripped, forcibly emits and brings forth new offshoots of grace. And the beauty of all the *theōrias* is radiant in the noetic light....

(88a)... Our spiritual Fathers also call the door of the heart "the Promised Land." Just as that Promised Land is plentifully abundant with corporeal goods, so too this mystical Land of Promise is purity of heart, abundantly rich in good things of good color. Just as the Philistines used to dwell in that Promised Land and prevent the sons of Israel from entering and inheriting that land, and from enjoying the good things in it, so too the spiritual Philistines—evil intentions and passions and demons—stand between us and the inner door of our heart, keeping us from entering (88b) that spiritual place, the temple of our soul, and keeping us from [enjoying] the spiritual goods that are laid up there. For as much as the intellect of its own accord strives after the vision of the *theōrias* in the place of the heart by itself, still it does not have dominion in the Promised Land, but roams at the edge and goes round the circuits....

(89a) … Because when the heart has been made pure and the veil of darkness of the passions has been stripped from it, the Holy Spirit works continually in the faculties of man. It is within our habitation and the house and dwelling-place of our heart. …

(91a) … Immediately at the opening of that place a little door is unlocked so that with a push and a squeeze the intellect just barely is able to enter within it. And when it has entered there within the inner chamber of the heart, which is the pure place of which the Fathers speak, the man sees his image and soul, resembling the radiance of the moon, which the Fathers call the precious sapphire and the color of the hue of heaven.[41] He perceives his soul to be a child, verily a little childishly prattling baby. …

(93a) … Now the little gate I mentioned above, it is opened within by the man, by which means the intellect enters inside the place of the heart, which is the pure natural place. The shining image of the soul like a clear mirror is visible there. This is the "narrow gate" mentioned by our Saviour in his Gospel: "Narrow is the gate and straight is the way that leads to life. And few are those who find [it]."[42] And, "Wide is the gate and broad is (93b) the way that leads to destruction, and many are those who enter by it."[43] But this also, "Behold, the kingdom is within you."[44] He means this same one, and the same one, the "treasure of life" that is mentioned in the hidden reading, he proclaimed it the "pearl of great price,"[45] by which the needy merchants are enriched. So likewise the blessed Apostle Paul said about it: "We have this treasure in an earthen vessel for the greatness of its power is from God."[46] He and the Fathers call it "the pure natural place." Now one calls it, "the pneumatic stage," and another calls it "the purity of the heart," and another calls it "the place of the soul's spiritual existence." There are those who name it (94a) "the incorporeal nature within us," and those who call it our "new man."[47] It is entirely the form of light, the form of the image of the Skillful Creator.

Now the righteous ones in the [Old Testament], I mean the prophets and the nation of the house of Israel, they used to call the natural place "the place of

41. This imagery, which also appears in the writings of Joseph Hazzaya and John of Dalyatha, seems to be Evagrian. See Beulay, *La collection des letters de Jean de Dalyatha,* [104–5, n. 7], [252–55]; Harb and Graffin, *Joseph Hazzāyā,* [130–31]. Cf. also Ezek. 1:26; 10:1.

42. Cf. Matt. 7:14.

43. Cf. Matt. 7:13.

44. Luke 17:21.

45. Cf. Matt. 13:46.

46. 2 Cor. 4:7.

47. The Apostle Paul. See Eph. 4:22-24.

God." Because all of the prophets used to stand in this pure, natural place: Moses and Isaiah and Daniel and Ezekiel and the rest of the eye-witnesses of those veiled writings in the Old [Testament] concerning the coming of the King's anointed one, and by whatever means it was seen by them. Also as the Apostle Paul said, "In manifold and in all ways (94b) God spoke with the Fathers by the prophets from the first."[48] So prophecy and prediction of some sort are granted to all who are deemed worthy of entrance to the pure natural place. So when you see these marks in yourself and you perceive them, O Brother, know truly that you have entered the natural place and you have arrived at the measure of the natural state. And you are ready to be sustained by the good things of the Promised Land—milk and honey and spiritual manna, instead of the labors and vexations which you endured throughout the entire time of your contest—hunger and thirst and the severity of battles and trials.

Milk is mentioned because of the *theōria* of the exalted bodies, for (95a) it appears first in the vision of the soul. And the soul is nurtured with it like milk until it is weaned. Honey is mentioned because of the incorporeal *theōria*. This is the vision of the angels of light. It appears after the *theōria* of the corporeals shines in the soul. And spiritual manna is likened to the *theōria* of the Holy Trinity, by which the intellect is sustained in the place of spirituality. It is the Promised Land, the pure natural place. These are the good things which I mentioned above. Therefore everyone who has not already entered this pure natural place is deprived of the Promised Land.... (95b) ... Guard the *taksâ* my Brother, and it will work in the vineyard of our heart night and day.... (105a)

... Behold the heaven within you if you are pure, and you will see the angels in it when they shine forth, and their Lord with them and within them. For although our Lord Christ, who is in the joyous light, is in every place, he is so in a way that cannot be comprehended. Now it is said that he resides in heaven and it is his dwelling place. And if our heart is a second heaven when it is purified from the passions, (105b) then too our Lord Christ's dwelling place is there. Therefore of necessity it is required that we continually depict the form of our intellect in its gate, that inner one that is for our good, until compassion opens for us that inner gate of heaven, and our Lord in his manifestation that is visible in them as the offshoots of his rays of light in the state of limpid purity. He transforms the barren to rejoicing ones. Because he truly is the comfort

48. Heb. 1:1.

of the mourners. For to him is the glory, and may he gladden us with his sight and his love. Amen.

Jesus Christ in the Pure Heart: Selections from the Fifth Discourse

(114a) … For truly Christ our Saviour is the light of life, the great sun of righteousness.[49] (114b) In that place of the state of spirituality the light of his glorious countenance shines forth on the discerning intellect that is sanctified by the operation of the Holy Spirit. Here is made known to the intellect the contemplative faculty (*theōrētikē*): the declaration of the mystery of the Holy Trinity in an insight and at the same time in a vision for him from the mystery as it is given by it to the understanding. When the intellect mixes with Christ and Christ mixes fully with the intellect in a vision of limpid purity, then God becomes man and man God. It is not the case that he is different in union and spirit. For with his immersion in the sea of light he becomes self-existent and boundless. The speech of the spirit is heard by the son of the spiritual (115a) body of the intellect, as he says—the self-existent one who became man, and Jesus who became God. In uniting he is not inseparable and beyond. For he is true, self-existent God who is without beginning, Father everlasting who is forever. Here the secret intellect knows him, and it muses upon and searches out the power which is in him.… But the son is separate and without beginning, and also with him eternally. He was begotten beyond times and worlds and desires. Equal with him in nature, not less than him in his being. He is the Spirit who proceedeth, and the force from the Father, and his pure life. He too is everlasting, and he is self-existent, that is, without beginning, one (115b) eternal *ousia* who is raised up from three *qnômê.* Neither void nor divided, neither *qnômê* without *ousia* nor *ousia* without *qnômê.* For *ousia,* according to nature, I say, exists in three equal *qnômê*: the unbegotten Father and the begotten son and the Spirit who proceedeth—one nature, one might, one power, one lordship.… And of his own will the Eternal, Everlasting One condescended to dwell in our body, while not being altered from what he is.… (116a) … He became our hidden changed one, and an invisible one. But since he willed in his love to delight

49. Cf. Mal. 3:20.

in those endowed with reason in the plan of his mysteries and in the vision of his glory, Jesus Christ our Lord took the son of man and he dwelt in him in a union inseparable and for ever. And he made for him a dwelling-place, and his appearance was concealed in a dull image[50] .... (116b) ... For not only one of the *qnômê* of the Godhead dwells in Christ our Lord, but the entire Godhead in three *qnômê* willingly abided and dwelt in the humanity of our Lord, and his *qnômâ* gleamed in the light and in the ineffable glory of the Holy Trinity.

Beh Isho‘'s words on the union of man and God might have presented a problem for Patriarch Timothy I, who excommunicated John of Dalyatha, Joseph Hazzaya, and John of Apamea at the synod of 786/787.[51] The distinctive and unusual name Beh Isho‘, "In him is Jesus," is also provocative in the context of Beh Isho‘'s writings. The name is so well-suited to Beh Isho‘'s own teachings that one wonders if he chose it himself, and if Beh Isho‘ might be known to us by other name as well; perhaps the Mar Shamli of the manuscripts from the Chaldean monastery of Our Lady of the Seeds near Alqosh.

50. Cf. Heb. 1:3?

51. A French translation (from Arabic) of the proceedings of the Synod can be found in Beulay, *La lumière sans forme,* 229–31.

Shawqi Talia

10. ODE TO JOY

ܩܢܝ ܚܟܡܬܐ ܘܒܟܠܗ ܩܢܝܢܟ ܩܢܝ ܣܘܟܠܐ. ܚܒܒܝܗ̇ ܕܬܪܡܪܡܟ
ܪܫ ܚܟܡܬܐ
ܕܬܝܩܪܢ. ܘܬܬܠ ܒܪܫܟ ܐܬܘܬܐ ܕܪܘܚܬܐ ܘܟܠܝܠܐ ܕܫܘܒܚܐ
ܘܟܦܘܝܗ̇
ܬܣܒܟ.

—Proverbs 4:6–9

The genesis of this *soġīṭā* was the presentation of a festschrift[1] to Fr. Sidney Griffith, professor of Semitic languages at the Catholic University of America. Dr. Monica Blanchard, of the Institute of Christian Oriental Research at the university, kindly invited this writer to preface the presentation with an introduction.[2] It was, indeed, an honor and a privilege to do so. Professor Griffith has been a colleague and a friend for more than three decades.

Scholars and readers of Syriac studies and Christian Arabic literature are well apprised of Professor Griffith's contribution in these two fields. His erudition in

1. The venue for this presentation was a reception given by Beth Mardutho: the Syriac Institute, at the closing of the Fourth North American Syriac Symposium, held at Princeton Theological Seminary, July 9–12, 2003. This was, indeed, a most propitious and auspicious occasion to make this presentation. The word *soġīṭā* is used here not in the classical Syriac mode but only in its aesthetic acclamation and versification. Since this word is a Syriac appellation for an occasional poem that extols and praises a person or an event—Saint Ephraim being the exemplar of this style—we have elected to give it this rubric. Given the spirit of this occasion, the poem is presented hereby as a *soġīṭā*.

2. This writer extends his deep appreciation to Monica Blanchard for her gracious invitation to make the introductory remarks before the presentation of the festschrift to Professor Griffith and for including it in this publication.

the field of early Christian studies, especially of the Syrian Church, has deepened our understanding and appreciation of its ecclesiastical and literary heritage, as well as bringing to light opaque theological and doctrinal developments of the Christian Orient. His research in the field of Christian-Muslim dialogue in the formative years of Islam has expanded our understanding of the nature of this intellectual interlocution that took place between these two religions.

But his examination of these two disciplines is appreciated not only for its intellectual rigor and perspicacity but also for bringing hope and heart to those who belong to the Syrian Church. We whose mother tongue is Neo-Aramaic and whose liturgical language is still sung in that mellifluous, classical Syriac, irrespective of church affiliation, see in his chrestomathy a consolation and a catharsis.[3] The future of this church in its native land is, sad to say, very dim, perhaps in its twilight. In consequence of his enlarging the horizon of Syriac studies, the Syrian Church, in all of its denominations, is now engaged in an ecumenical dialogue with the Western churches and in an interdenominational one. This new dialogue has brought a prospect of an ecclesiastical harmony and the promise of a theological concord within the Syrian Church. His love for this Oriental Church, seen through his copious writings, has brought hope that this ancient church, which has produced so many luminaries from Saint Ephraim to Aphrahat, the Persian sage, will be sustained and survive in its motherland. Scholars of Syriac and Christian Arabic, among them Professor Griffith, are a perpetual fount of assurance. This church, whose language was spoken by our Lord, is endeavoring not to disappear in its homeland.

On such an occasion the expected thing is to proffer salutary words in praise of the honoree. So when Dr. Blanchard invited this writer to preface the presentation. the first instinct was to make a felicitous sentiment to the gathering at this reception.[4] However, after some rumination on the nature of the remarks, and it was obvious what they should be, thoughts turned to the ancient Semites, asking, "What would they do?" Historically, on such an occasion the subject of the celebration would be feted with a poem, a *soḡīṯā* or a *tešboḥtā,* if you please. This tradition has been an honored one among the ancient Semites and is still practiced by their modern descendents. It was in this spirit that this

3. Churches using the classical Syriac in their liturgy are the Assyrian Church of the East, the Chaldean, the Maronite, the Syro-Malabar, the Syro-Malankar, the Syrian Catholic, and the Syrian Orthodox.

4. See note 1.

writer elected to compose a poem celebrating the presentation of a volume to Professor Griffith. It is presented here as a token of deep respect and affection.[5] But it is not only this writer who is presenting this poem on this special occasion. For it is also the Syrian Church, with its multidenominational communicants, its churches, monuments, monasteries, and convents, who are partaking in this festive presentation. They all sing, "Thank you for being a *Ruḥā Bassimtā 'u Bēt Yulpānā.*"

The poem is written in the Neo-Aramaic dialects of the villages and hamlets of the plains of Mosul (ancient Nineveh), of northern Iraq. Specifically, it is the dialect of the town of Tel-Kape,[6] situated eighteen miles north of Mosul. The vernacular of this area, called Surath (i.e., Syriac), is one of a large subgroup of dialects historically referred to as Neo-Aramaic. To the student of Semitic philology, these dialects are of paramount importance, for each dialect exhibits its own peculiarities—linguistic, historical and sociocultural. And while some research has been done in these dialects, very little study has been done on their relationship to Aramaic and classical Syriac. Furthermore, political and religious reasons have hindered any serious field research in the different dialects. Most of the research has centered on a descriptive grammar of a particular geographical area or a village.[7] A serious philological study of these dialects is still the hope of students of Syriac.

In the last fifty years these dialects have absorbed many foreign words, thus greatly diluting the historical integrity of the Neo-Aramaic. Furthermore, emigration has emptied many of the villages that speak Neo-Aramaic. Hence there is an urgent need to study these dialects. Their survival, like the presence of Christianity in the land of its birth, is at stake.

The number of those speaking the different dialects of Neo-Aramaic has been declining since the first decade of the twentieth century. Two major events have had a profound effect on these dialects and those who speak them. The

5. Owing to the restriction of time at this reception, a much shorter version of this poem was read there. The full text is presented here.

6. The Iraqi census of 1961 showed a population of 7,307, all belonging to the Chaldean Catholic rite. Today, due to economic reasons, internal conflicts, and three international wars, the number is around 3,000, one-fifth of them Muslims.

7. Due to the difficulty of doing linguistic field work in the villages of these dialects, most of the research for the descriptive grammar is done through the use of an "informant," usually far away from the geographical area. Clearly, the further away from these towns, the less chance of accurate linguistic information reaching the researcher.

first was the genocide against the Christians of the Ottoman Empire, specifically the Armenians and Syrian Christians.[8] While the former suffered the most, the latter suffered enough casualties to cause the second catastrophic event. This was the emigration from areas where the many massacres took place, resulting in a depopulation of most villages of their Christian communities. Most of the immigrants were dispersed throughout the Arab world, with a large number emigrating to the West, especially the United States. The political and religious unrest of the past fifty years has accelerated this migration. Among immigrants whose native language is Neo-Aramaic, there is a tendency to marginalize it, since the language of their adopted country is the medium of communication. For the first generation of these immigrants, Neo-Aramaic has become an anachronism. Its only relevance to them is the fact that it is related to classical Syriac, the liturgical language of their respective churches.

Today, Neo-Aramaic (i.e. vernacular Syriac) is spoken in the following geographical areas:

1. West Neo-Aramaic, spoken in Ma'lūla (Christians) and Jubba'dīn and Bakh'a (Muslims), three communities situated thirty-five miles northeast of Damascus, Syria.

2. Ṭūrōyō: Spoken in Ṭūr 'Abdīn and the area near Mardin, in northeast Turkey.

3. East Neo-Aramaic, often called Assyrian (Āṭurāyā) or Chaldean, spoken in the Christian villages of Kurdistan,[9] Lake Urmia in Iran, and the plains of Mosul, in northern Iraq.

4. Immigrants who now reside in the West, especially the United States, and a small minority of their first generation.

5. Jewish communities of northern Iraq, most of whom migrated to Israel after its establishment in 1948.

Historically Neo-Aramaic has been an oral vernacular. It has not been formally taught in schools, and has produced a limited religious and secular liter-

8. The Neo-Aramaic speaking communities that experienced the many massacres between 1910-25 were situated in Ṭūr 'Abdīn and Mardin (Turkey), and Iraqi Kurdistan and Mosul (Iraq). They included Assyrians, Chaldeans, Syrian Catholics, and Syrian Orthodox.

9. Historically, a geographic area bounded by northern Mesopotamia (modern Iraq), northeast Turkey and northwest Iran.

ature. There have been some printed liturgical compositions, with distribution limited to priests and deacons. Some occasional pieces are published in religious publications, such as festal poems, eulogies, or specific communal commemorations. Early in this century there were a few attempts to publish newspapers, but they did not come to fruition. The only Neo-Aramaic-speaking communities that have produced a substantial literature are the Chaldean town of Alkosh,[10] thirty-five miles north of Mosul, and those of Lake Urmia in Iran. The latter were far more successful in producing a fairly extensive and varied literature, including newspapers and books.[11] Given the occasional theme of this paper, no attempt is made to discuss the descriptive grammar of this Neo-Aramaic vernacular, nor its historical relationship to classical Syriac. Hopefully, such a work will be presented in a different venue.

The poem is presented herewith in the Syriac script, following as much as possible a phonetic transcription. However, where a word has gone through only a minor consonantal shift, such as *ara* (earth) for classical *ar'a,* we have given the classical and not the vernacular. Nevertheless, in the transliteration we have been faithful to the phonetics of the vernacular in order to give the reader a full appreciation for the orthographic and syntactical shift from classical Syriac to this dialect of Neo-Aramaic. The English translation mirrors the style and spirit of the Neo-Aramaic of the poem. It is the Neo-Aramaic (i.e., vernacular Syriac) which this writer learned at home and from the literati in this dialect in Iraq and the United States.

1 ܫܠܡܐ ܒܟܘܢ، ܒܫܡܐ ܕܒܒܐ ܘܒܪܘܢܐ ܘ ܪܘܚܐ ܕܩܘܕܫܐ ܬܠܬܐ ܕܡܫܝܚܝܘܬܐ
ܗܘܐ ܐܢܫܐ ܕܒܥܬ ܡܫܬܘܬܐ ܗܕܐ ܟܠܗ ܦܨܚܘܬܐ ܐܠܗܝܬܐ

2 ܐܬܪܝ ܫܡܝ ܟܠܕܘ ܘ ܐܬܘܪ ܘ ܒܝܬܢܗܪܝܢ ܘ ܢܝܢܘܐ ܘ ܦܘܪܬ ܒܒܕܝܢ ܘ ܐܘܪܗܝ
ܟܠܠܗ ܟܠܗ ܫܠܡܘܬܐ
ܫܡܘ ܟܠܢ ܒܗܕܐ ܠܟܠܐ ܬܘܚܐ ܒܪܝܟܐ ܗܕܐ ܡܨܝܚܘܬܐ ܘ ܘܦܪܚܬܐ ܫܠܡܘܬܐ

10. See Geoffrey Khan, *The Neo-Aramaic of Qaraqōš* (Leiden: Brill, 2002), 8.

11. L. Yaur, "A Poem in the Neo-Aramaic Dialect of Urmia," *Journal of Near East Studies* 16 (1957): 73.

3 ܢܘܚܐ ܘ ܢܝܚܘܬܐ ܒܒܗܘܢ. ܒܠܥܕ ܕܗܘܕܐ ܒܠܘܫܬܐ ܕܓܒܒܐ ܘ ܡܕܝܫܘܬܐ
ܫܒܐ ܕܗܒܗܘܢ ܬܠܥܝܐ ܕܡܘܪ̈ܝܐ ܡܥܒܕܢܐ. ܒܪ̈ܫܦܢܝܐ ܐܝܠܐ ܘܐܠܦܐ
ܕܦܓܥܢܘܬܐ

4 ܒܫܘܪܬ ܠܒܢܝܐ ܐܘܪܗܝܐ. ܐܪܒܥܐ ܢ̈ܘܡܐ ܘ ܢ̈ܘܡܬܐ ܫܡܠܝ ܦ̈ܐܠܐ ܘ
ܒ̈ܢܝܬܐ
ܗܘܠܐ ܡܠܦܢܘܬܐ ܘ ܡܡܠܠܘܬܐ ܘ ܡܠܬܐ. ܟܠܠ ܬܘܫܥܐ ܡܠܝܫܘܬܐ ܘ
ܢܘܪܬܐ

5 ܕܢܚܐ ܐܘܬܗܘܢ ܬܒܠ. ܒܢܘܒܗܘܢ ܥܒܠ ܣܡܡܬܐ ܕܢܥܡܬܘܬܐ ܪܒܬܐ
ܦܪܢܐ ܘ ܗܟܠܐ ܕܡܦܩܢܘܬܐ ܕܐܘܪܢܐ ܕܢ̈ܫܐ ܦܪܠܐ. ܘ ܦܪܘܪܘܬܐ
ܥܠܝܡܘܬܐ

6 ܠܒܠܐ ܕܐܡܪܢܗܘܢ ܢܣܐ ܟܠܗܐ ܕܠܒܐ ܕܝ ܐܢܐ ܫܘܪܝܐ ܕܐܬܪ ܦܪܡܬܐ
ܒܪܬܐ ܕܡܪܐ ܐܕܝ ܘ ܡܪܐ ܡܪܝ ܐܝܠܐ ܒܡܢܝܘܬܐ ܘ ܕܢܠܘܬܐ ܘ
ܥܡܘܡܘܬܐ

7 ܒܕ ܥܡܘܢ ܠܥܐܡ ܕܡ ܐܪܒܥܐ ܒܙ̈ܘܬܐ ܘܒܢܘܡܪ̈ܬܐ
ܒܢܡܡܬܐ ܢܘܬ ܡܢ ܐܪ̈ܝܐ ܕܢ̈ܪܐ ܡܓܪܝܐ ܘܗܘܐ ܠܦ̈ܘܡܬܐ

8 ܕܢ̈ܬܐ ܘ ܡ̈ܬܬܐ ܐܝܠܐ ܒܒܒܢܐ ܕܢܥܡܢܐ ܒܐܘܠܝܬܐ ܘ ܐܒܠܘܬܐ
ܐܢܫܐ ܕܡ ܙܠ ܘ ܠܐ ܒ̈ܪܬܐ ܦܥܠܐ ܫܒ̈ܘܬܐ ܕܫ̈ܘܡܬܐ ܘ ܡܘܬܐ

9 ܐܠܐ ܚܘ ܒܗܕܐ ܗܕܐ ܡܢܗܘܢ ܠܦܒܢܐ ܘ ܒܫܡܥܐ ܘ ܡܦܝܣܢܐ. ܡܬܒܥܢܘܬܐ
ܒܠܝܫܘܬܐ
ܬܠܠ ܒܠ ܡܢ ܦܪܢܐ ܘ ܪܢܘܥܐ. ܒܡܕܝܢܬܐ ܠܡܕܝܢܬܐ ܡܢ ܐܪܒܥܐ ܒܪ̈ܬܐ
ܦܬܘܬܐ ܡܠܝܬܐ

10 ܡܠ̈ܝܢܐ ܘ ܡܦܩܢܘܬܐ ܘ ܬܠܡܝ̈ܕܐ. ܒܗܢܝܐ ܘ ܒܠܒ̈ܢܐ. ܐܢܫܐ
ܕܢܡܡܬܐ
ܫܡܥܐ ܡܢܐ ܙܒܢܪܐ ܘ ܫܢ ܪ̈ܒܐ ܐܝܠܐ ܡܪܐ ܡܕܒܪܢܘܬܐ ܘ ܬܪܒܝܬܐ

11 ܬܕ̈ܦܝܣܢ ܒܐܝܣܘܢ ܪܒܐ ܗܕܢܐ ܒܪ ܐܢܫܐ ܢܘܪܐ ܕܡܬܢܗܪܢܘܬܐ
ܥܢܝܐ ܐܝܠܐ ܘ ܦܫܐ ܡܡܡܒܐ. ܦܠܝܚܐ ܘ ܡܬܡܪܒܝܢܐ ܘ ܡܪܐ ܕܦܠܘܚܘܬܐ

12 ܐܠܗܐ ܕܝܗܒ ܠܟܠܐ ܚܝܐ ܒܝܕܐ ܦܪܝܫܬܐ ܘܪܒܝܐ ܕܫܦܝܪܘܬܐ ܕܚܕܘܬܐ
ܐܠܘܦ ܠܒܢܝܐ ܕܒܪܘܢ ܡܫܝܚܐ ܡܫܬܪܝܢܐ ܘ ܡܫܝܚܐ ܬܕܡܘܪܬܐ ܐܝܬ ܒܪ
ܡܫܝܚܘܬܐ

13 ܡܢ ܟܬܒܐ ܐܠܗܐ ܕܝܠܟܝܐ ܘ ܒܪ ܕܘܝܕ ܡܪܝܐ ܕܢܫܐ ܕܢܫܝܬܘܬܐ
ܐܬܠܬܐ ܥܡ ܕܐܦܪܝܡ ܘ ܡܘܫܐ ܘ ܦܪܘܦܠܐ ܘ ܐܫܥܝܐ ܢܒܝܐ ܡܪ̈ܬܐ
ܡܘܗܒܬܐ

14 ܫܒܝܚ ܠܟ̈ܬܒܐ ܡܪܢܐ ܠܐ ܡܢ ܡܡܠܠܐ ܕܡܫܡܠܝܘܬܐ ܕܗܘܪܒܬܐ
ܪܒ ܦܪܝܩ ܒܢܐ ܕܝܠܗ ܦܬܘܪܐ ܠܒܢܝܐ ܟܠܗܘܢ ܕܐܬܪ̈ܬܐ ܕܡܫܝܚܐ ܘ ܕܢܫܝܘܬܐ

15 ܡܪܐ ܐܦܪܝܡ ܐܡܪ ܗܟܢ ܕܡܒܪܘܢ ܗܘܐ ܡܫܡܪܐ ܡܪܐ ܒܗܘܢܬܐ ܡܫܝܚܘܬܐ
ܬܫܒܘܚܬܐ ܬܡܗܐ ܒܢܐ ܕܝܠܗ ܠܒܢܝ ܐܝ ܕܢܘܗܪܐ ܘ ܣܠܘܩܬܐ

16 ܐܫܘܢ ܦܪܝܩ ܬܘܠܝ ܘ ܡܢܝ ܐܢܝ ܒܢ̈ܝܐ ܫܡܥ ܠܗ ܫܘܐܠܐ ܟܠܐ ܫܘܐܠܐ
ܒܠܚܘܕܘܬܐ
ܟܠܠ ܡܡܫܪܐ ܡܢ ܟܪ̈ܒܝܗܝ ܐܝܬ ܡܢ ܠܡܢܘܬܐ ܐܬܬܪܐ ܕܡܢ ܙܘܢܐ
ܕܘܪܫܬܐ

17 ܐܡܪ ܗܘܐ ܐܢܐ ܐܝܟ ܡܫܡܫܢܐ ܕܒ̈ܝܬܐ ܦܪܝܫܬܐ ܘ ܡܪܝܢܐ ܕܡܫܝܚܐ ܡܪܐ
ܕܫܠܝܛܘܬܐ
ܕܪܥܠ ܟܠܗ ܪܘܚܐ ܠܒܢܝܐ ܡܕܝܢ ܐܪܡܝܐ. ܬܕܡܘܬ ܡܠܦܢܐ ܬܐܫܝܬܘܬܐ

18 ܘ ܗܘܐ ܡܘܡܝܐ ܘ ܚܕܐ ܘ ܡܘܡܐ ܬܪܝ ܕܡܘܠܟܢܐ ܕܡܘܪܬܘܬܐ ܘ ܪܚܡܘܬܐ
ܪܒ ܦܪܝܩ ܦܫܠܐ ܡܦܫܘܩܐ ܒܗܘܪܬ ܬܦܘܪܝܢܐ ܕܐܟܠܝܢ ܦܬܪܐ ܕܐܘܪܝܚܐ ܘ
ܐܘܪ̈ܚܬܐ

19 ܘ ܡܢܝ ܐܠܗܐ ܚܬܐ ܟܪܘܒܝ ܦܪܝܩ ܫܡܥܘ ܠܗ ܐܢܬ ܡܢ ܦܪܘܫܐ ܘ ܡܪܐ
ܕܝܒܪܬܐ
ܡܠܬܐ ܕܒܪܟܐ ܡܫܝܚܐ ܗܘܝ ܡܠܦܢܐ ܘ ܡܬܬܒܢܐ ܘ ܬܪܓܡܢܐ ܕܡܠܬܐ

20 ܐܡܪ ܐܫܘܢ ܐܘ ܒܢ ܫܡܥܢܐ ܘ ܦܬܪܐ ܬܐܡܪܐ ܐܬܝ ܚܝܐ ܫܘܐܠܐ ܟܠܐ
ܗܘܪܬܐ
ܠܒܢܘܢ ܐܝܠܐ ܢܦܫܐ ܐܘ ܟܠܒܐ ܘ ܡܢ ܡܢ ܦܬܪܐ ܒܗܕܐ ܠܒܢܐ ܗܘܐ ܡܪܐ
ܡܬܠܘܬܘܬܐ

21 ܒܪܘܟܐ ܕܐܪܥܐ ܘ ܒܫܡ̈ܝܐ ܘ ܣܘܪܝܐ ܡܫܪܝ. ܬܗܕܪܐ ܡܢܝܠܝܐ ܘ ܟܪ
ܣܘܦܣܛܘܢܐ
ܡܚܠܐ ܕܬܪܝ. ܐܠܗ ܒܪܒܐ ܡܫܝܚܐ. ܐܠܗ ܩܕܡܝܐ ܘ ܫܠܡܐ ܕܒܠܡܘܬܐ

22 ܢܝܚܬܗ ܟܕ ܗܘܐ ܒܪܘܚ ܒܐܘܪܫܠܡ ܡܒܪܟܬܐ ܡܕܝܢܬܐ ܕܘܝܕܝܬܐ
ܡܠܟܠܐ ܘ ܡܦܘܫܩܠ ܠܒܢܝܐ ܕܝܢ ܐܪܡܝܐ ܒܡ ܕܐܬܝܐ ܠܡܚܠܐ ܕܡܘܕܝܘܬܐ

23 ܕܪܘܠܐ ܐܣܘܡ ܠܡܠܘܬܐ ܕܪܒܢܐ ܕܟܒܫ̈ܬܐ ܕܝܣܘܣܐ ܘ ܕܒܝܢܘܬܐ
ܒܢܝܢܘܬܐ
ܡܪܝܐ ܕܐܦܪܘܛ ܝܚܡܐ ܘ ܐܦܪܝܡ ܦܪܝܐ ܘ ܒܪ ܓܠܒܐ ܡܪ̈ܐ ܓܡܝܐ ܘ
ܡܡܡܘܬܐ

24 ܘܢܝܐ ܗܘܐ ܘ ܚܘܬܠ ܪܒ ܫܘܚ ܚ̈ܘܬܐܚ ܘ ܦܪ̈ܝܐ ܘ ܢܪ̈ܝܐ ܘ ܡܪܝܫܐ ܕܠܡܠܘܬܐ
ܡܚܡܐ ܒܡܘܪܬ. ܠܒܢܐ ܕܡܢ، ܫܚ ܒܠܒܢܐ ܛܝܡܘܬܐ. ܚܠܠ ܡܦܫܘܩܘܬܐ

25 ܡܫܬ̈ܠܝܐ ܕܪܘܛܝܢܘܬܐ ܬܘܠܐ ܐܚܪ ܡܢ ܒܢ̈ܝ ܘ ܡܢ̈ܬܐ. ܬܘܠܐ ܒܡܣܘܪܬܐ ܐܣܟܘܠܐ. ܡܢ ܦ̈ܢܐ ܘ ܡܢ ܒܠܕ̈ܢܐ. ܛ̈ܦܣܐ ܕܛܪܘܬܐ ܕܡܫܡܫܢܘܬܐ

26 ܡܢ ܥܡܠܐ ܫܡܡܬܐ ܐܘ ܐܫ̈ܢܬܐ ܐܘ ܫ̈ܢܬܐ. ܘ ܫܠܡܘܬܐ ܪܘܚܢܬܐ
ܒܡܬ ܕܢܘܠܦܢܐ ܦܥܠ ܛܛ ܡܪ̈ܒܝܢܬܐ ܕܢܡܚܢܐ ܘ ܡܪ̈ܒܝܐ ܕܛܘܒܢܘܬܐ

27 ܬܒ ܪ̈ܬܘܬܐ ܕܡܢܚ̈ܢܬܐ ܐܬܐ ܐܬܐ ܢܘܗܪܐ ܕܡܫܠܡܢܘܬܐ ܘ ܡܫܠܡܢܘܬܐ
ܕܡܫܠܡܢܘܬܐ
ܘ ܣܘܡܬܐܘܗ̇ ܐܠܐ ܢܝܫܢܘܬܐ ܘ ܡܢܘܪܐ ܬܒܢܝܢ ܕܦܘܫܬܐ ܘ ܡܡܡܘܕܝܬܐ

28 ܥܪܒ ܕܠܡܠܘܬܐ ܕܠܒܢܐ ܐܪܡܝܐ ܐܬܐ ܘ ܕܐܠܝܛܘܣܘܦ ܕܝܡܡܬܐ
ܬܠܝ̈ܕܐ ܬܠܐ ܒܡܪ̈ܝܬܐ ܬܪܫܡܐ ܡܢܘܗܝ ܦܪܢܐ ܘ ܦܪܢܐ ܘ ܬܪܓܘܡܬܐ

29 ܐܠܗܐ ܐܘܠܘܫ ܫܦܪ ܘ ܡܘ̈ܣܬܐ ܒܡܣܡܡܘܬܐ ܘ ܣܚ ܐܚܐ ܪܒܬܐ ܒܡܣܪܐ ܠܡܠܬܐ
ܡܪܐ ܡܫܡܠܢܐ ܘ ܦܪ̈ܢܐ ܕܒܢܬܐ ܗܘܐ ܒܡܘܗܝ ܟܠܠ ܒܢܐ ܕܡܫܡܫܢܘܬܐ
ܕܢܒܘܬܐ

30 ܡܪܐ ܐܦܪܝܡ ܗܘܐ ܕܒܘܬܠ ܡܡܒܪܐ ܘ ܡܪ̈ܝܐ ܐܠܐ ܒܪܘܗܝ ܦܝܫܚ ܬܘܪ
ܒܬܘܪܬܐ
ܘ ܡܢ ܛܠܘܗܝ ܫܡܥܐ ܘ ܐܦܪܐ ܐܫܚ ܐܠܗܐ ܕܐܢܫܐ ܕܒܘܪܐ ܕ ܣܘܪܬ ܘ
ܣܘܪܬܬܐ

31 ܙܗܝܘܬܐ ܕܦܝܠܘܣܘܦܝܢ ܐܝܠܐ ܫܘܒܚܐ ܟܠ ܐܝܟ ܐܝܟܘܬ ܫܡܫܐ ܕܙܕܝܩܘܬܐ
ܬܘܚܐ ܕܗܘܕܝܐ ܡܦܬܘܢ ܫܝܢܬܐ ܒܫܝܢܬܐ ܘ ܡܠܘܢ ܐܪܥܐ ܕܡܠܟܘܬܐ

32 ܡ̈ܠܟܐ ܗܘܠܝܐ ܐܡܪܘܢ ܒܗܪܐ ܘܡܫܐ ܒܪ ܬܠܝܐ ܠܪܦܘܢ ܒܚܫܬܐ ܕܡܠܦܢܘܬܐ
ܒܪ ܦܠܘܢ ܬܠܡܝܕܐ ܠܐܣܟܘܠܐ ܕܬܠܡܝܕܐ ܠܘܝܐ ܐܣܟܡܐ ܕܪܘܚܢܘܬܐ

33 ܒܪ ܐܢܫܐ ܘ ܒܪ ܚܠܡܐ ܡܬܚܠܡܘܢ. ܗܘܝܢ ܫܘܠܐ ܚܠܠܬܐ ܘ ܡܫܬܘܕܝܢܘܬܐ
ܐܝܟ ܠܥܝܢܐ ܕܬܚܘܬܐ ܡܫܘܫܠܘܬܢ. ܬܬܚܙܝܢ ܐܝܟ ܡܒܥܝܢܐ ܕܡܫܘܚܬܐ

34 ܐܝܠܐ ܗܪܐ ܘܗܘܐ ܒܪܝܐ ܐܝ ܕܐܝܬܐ ܘ ܡܫܬܝܐ ܒܗܪܐ ܐܪܥܐ ܕܒܪܝܬܐ
ܬܠܝܬ ܕܐܡܪܝܢ ܬܫܘܚܢ ܚܝܐ ܘ ܥܠܡܐ ܗܪܐ ܐܝܠܐ ܘܗܘܐ ܕ ܦܘܫܚܬܐ

35 ܒܪܬܘܢ ܕܒܪܬܝ ܟܝ ܡܫܬܝܐ ܫܚܝܐ. ܫܡܝܐ ܕܚܡܐ ܠܝ ܡܬܪܚܡܢܘܬܐ
ܐܚܝܐ ܫܦܝ̈ܪܐ ܡܠܟܐ ܕܒ ܠܡܘ ܗܠܒܝ ܐܝܠܐ ܬܕܗܘܢ ܫܦ̈ܝܪܐ ܕܡܬܚܝܠܢܘܬܐ

36 ܟܝ ܦܬܓܡܐ ܡܠܘܬ ܬܗܪܐ ܐܝܢܐ ܢܗܝܐ ܘ ܫܪܝܐ ܕܡܫܬܘܐ ܕܐܬܝܠܦܘ܀
ܕܡܬܚܕܬܘܬܐ
ܡܫܪܪ ܡܟܝܠ ܢܡܡܐ ܕܢ̈ܫܐ ܘ ܘܘܪ ܫܝܢ̈ܝܐ ܕܒܘܢܝܘܬܐ ܬܕܪܬܐ ܗܕܪܬܐ

37 ܠܝ ܒܗܡܘܢ ܡܟܝܠ ܘܢ. ܐܬܘܢ ܒܫܡܝܐ ܐܝܠܐ. ܬܠܬ̈ܘܬܐ ܘܠܘܢ ܢܗܘܪܬܐ
ܠܐ ܐܚܝܐ ܠܗܘܢ ܐܝܟ ܒܬ̈ܘܬܐ ܩ̈ܕܡܝܐ ܐܠܗܐ ܒܫܡܝܐ ܒܚܝܪܐ ܒܝܫܘܬܐ

38 ܗܘܐ ܗܪ ܒܠܘܫܐ ܕܝ ܒܪܬܐ ܘ ܡܚܝܦܢܐ ܒܡܠܝ ܐܢܫܐ ܕܡܬܚܝܬܐ
ܬܫܘܝܬܐ ܕܒܪܝܐ ܚܕܝܘܬܐ ܠܐ ܡܥܢܬܘܢ ܠܐ ܐܠܗܘܢ ܘܡܫܚܘܢ ܠܐ ܕܗܘܐ ܕ ܗܘܪܬܐ ܘ ܠܐ
ܒܠܝܘܬܐ

39 ܗܪܐ ܙܒܢܐ ܫܦܝܪܬܐ ܒܬܪܝܢ ܐܝܠܐ ܕܪܘܚܐ ܕܡܫܘܪܬܐ ܘ ܐܢܫܘܬܐ ܘ
ܦܠܘܚܐ ܕܡܫܒܚܘܬܐ
ܠܐܠܐ ܠܐ ܕܗܘ ܒܡܬܪܘܢ ܘ ܐܬܪܘܢ ܬܠܝܬ ܕܐܡܪܘܢ ܕܒ ܗܕܝ ܒܠܗܐ ܕ
ܦܘܫܚܬܐ

40 ܐܝܠܐ ܒܢܝܐ ܕܐܬܚܪܬܘܢ ܝܠܝ ܝܘܡܐ ܫܘܡ ܒܚܠܡܐ ܘ ܡܬܚܫܒܢ ܘܗܘܪܘ
ܒܪܚܡܘܬܐ
ܡܬܚܝܢܐ ܒܡܬܠܝ ܚܢܬܐ ܫܘܡ ܐܫܐ ܫ̈ܢܝܐ. ܒܬܪ ܡܪܘܡ ܗܠܝ ܚܢܝܐ ܘ ܫܠܡܐ
ܠܚܝܢܘܬܐ

1. Peace be upon you. In the name of the Father and the Son and the Holy Spirit: Trinity, the life-giving,
   May the partakers gathered at this banquet be full of heavenly blessing.

2. Mesopotamia is my home, also Assyria, Chaldea, Nineva, Ṭūr ʿAbdīn and Edessa, all much becoming,
   Harken to me, tonight we sing to a humble man a song and a poem most discriminating.

3. Tranquility and serenity be with all of you, this gathering of teaching and schooling,
   Your devotion to the language of the faithful of the Syrian Church is a comely ornamenting.

4. For days on days we heard discourses in the tongue of Edessa, ecclesiastical sayings and many a teaching,
   A harmony for the soul they were, exhortations, eloquences, and responses, all illuminating.

5. You are a luminary unto us, from you we have received wisdom most edifying,
   Readings from the Epistles, with recitation and rumination, all an exposition, on the way of life revealing.

6. To you assembled here I, son of ancient Assyria, say this heart of mine is grieving,
   Church of Mār Addāi and Māri is abandoned, she is in pain most tormenting.

7. When hearing Aramaic, this tongue of ours, in liturgy and chanting
   fervently, day unto day, from our eyes tears like unto rain come flowing.

8. Monasteries and towns of these lands are crying in suffering, in lamentation, and mourning,
   Their people have departed, and their churches have become ruins of the dead and the dying.

9. But see, on this blessed day, pleasant and indeed elating, this splendrous assembling,
   From every city, from near and afar, of this good inhabited earth, we come into this gathering.

10. Teachers, commentators, and students, religious and secular—all in wisdom knowing,
Some are young, others are doyens, all given to perspicacity and reflecting.

11. Joyful that we may be in our brother, Rabbi Sidney, a flowing river of precepting,
A man of goodwill he is, a venerable priest, a philosopher well cultivated for discerning.

12. One day, at a blessed moment, God put into his heart an exhortation to witnessing:
"Come learn the language of my Son the Messiah, the Shepherd and Giver of life, and betake disputing."

13. Then God of Ages, and the Son of David, they who bestow the kingdom everlasting,
With Saint Ephraim, Jacob of Serug, and Isaac of Nineveh, all learned ones, they were in a seating.

14. Praise be their names spoke, "O meek ones, faithful in your Christian believing,
The language of Aramaic, ancient tongue of the bright land of the East, Rabbi Sidney desires its mastering."

15. Saint Ephraim said, "Let us to this honored Christian priest put a questioning
That we may ascertain whence he wishes to examine this tongue so sweet and illuminating."

16. Rabbi Sidney, our brother sat with these blessed ones and to their questions humbly took to listening,
Said one and all, "Of this ancient language of Assyria, how much are you in knowing?"

17. Answered he, "I am a priest of the Holy Church, and in Christ the Ruler is my emulating,
The Holy Spirit put into my heart the language of the children of Aram, that mankind I go teaching."

18. It was a day then two, and there was a reverential and spiritual perusing
In Syriac, precepts of the Good News, the Book of Life, Rabbi Sidney took to commenting.

19. Then the Almighty spoke again, "Listen to me my son, O sagacious one, you who are comprehending,
Christian Arabic do teach and also of this tongue be translating and composing."

20. Said our brother, "Our Heavenly Father and Hope of Mankind, about Arabs I have a questioning:
Is your tongue Arabic or Chaldean, and who among the Syrians is in this language worthy of acclaiming?"

21. The Creator of heaven, the moon and the stars answered him, he who is given to praying and philosophizing:
"Christian Arabic is my other tongue, one ancient and beautiful in writing.

22. But do you know in the holy city of Jerusalem, the City of David, when my son was residing,
In this Aramaic tongue of ours he tutored the Jews who to the temple came, and so was His preaching."

23. A year, then, many a year, books of the Church Fathers, some secular, others on natural law he sat examining,
Teachings of Aphraḥāt the Sage, Saint Ephraim, and Bar Ṣalībī, holy ones given to reflecting.

24. In time Rabbi Sidney wrote books, lessons, and annotations, all given to explicating,
Some in the language of Our Lord, others in Arabic, all given to elucidating.

25. Men and women, students of Christianity, did come with him visiting,
Scholars, some were priests, others were laymen, all *topoi* of excellent reasoning.

26. My brothers and sisters, from him they heard wisdom, spiritually uplifting,
Daily this house of learning was a place of guiding and a teaching most venerating.

27. To the heirs of the Church of the East you are a shrine for a veritable and imbued instructing,
To the children baptized in the Truth your ordination is a light and a consecrating.

28. Your erudition in Syriac is a beacon, to the people you are a profound dialectician when preaching,
Disciples gather with you in classes, listening to your reading and also the interpreting.

29. May God give you days and years harmonious, and life of hope long enduring,
Christ who bestows life, and saints of the church, be with you every moment of scholarly deliberating.

30. Saint Ephraim, composer of *maymārs* and commentaries, is jubilant in you, his joy overflowing,
Love and honor to you, we the children of the Syrian Church are saying.

31. Your virtuous work is a grace, for us you are righteousness shining,
May the Holy Spirit guard you, hour unto hour, and upon you the promised land be granting.

32. Angels were with you on the day they escorted you to that house of learning,
When you became a student at Catholic University, your priestly attire wearing.

33. Religious and laymen bless you, from you they heard oratory, also reasoning,
Writings of the Church fathers you have explicated, your expounding to your brethren is inspiring.

34. Blessed be this special day, this day of sixty-plus-five since coming into being,
We say to our brother, "Pax Christi and amity," this is a day of celebrating.

35. Dear priest, in your divine liturgy lift us in your offering, that we see God's merciful granting,
We are sinners before the Son of the Good One, hoping to be at the right hand sitting

36. Our Savior guard this prophetic one, as the truth of the Good News he is re-illuming,
Send the Spirit of life before him, make his ministry for the Church a serving.

37. We stand before you and say, "Gracious you are for putting in our hearts enlightening,"
not only we, but our forefathers too, now beholding, down from heaven beaming.

38. Let this gathering be a blessed one, and may it be for all a source of mediating,
Mercy of the First Born be upon you, keep your love for the language of Syriac abiding.

39. We compose this song, a pleasing one, a token of appreciation and collegiality, a labor of loving
This evening is nigh, let us chant and pronounce, a Festschrift to Rabbi Sidney we come bearing.

40. The time has come to bid each other farewell. Sing to the Messiah a song of praising,
May God gather us seven times more, hear us Our Lady, let peace and tranquility be eternally lasting.

Bibliographical References

The following bibliography is included as a reference for readers who are interested in the comparative philology of Neo-Aramaic dialects, as well as Semitic philology.

Blanc, Haim. *Communal Dialects in Baghdad.* Harvard Middle Eastern Dialects Monographs 10. Cambridge, Mass.: Harvard University, 1964.

Contini, R., F. A. Pennacchietti, and M. Tosco, eds. *Semitica Serta Philologica Constantino Tsereteli Dictata.* Turin: Silvio Zomarani, 1993.

Fiey, Jean M. *Assyrie Chrètienne: Contribution à l'Etude de l'histoire et de la gèographie ecclesiastiques.* Beirut: Institute de Lettres Orientales de Beyrouth, 1965–69.

Heberman, Robert. *The Syntax and Semantics of Verb Morphology in Modern Aramaic. A Jewish Dialect of Iraqi Kurdistan.* American Oriental Series 69. New Haven, Conn.: American Oriental Society, 1988.

———. "The History of Modern Aramaic Pronouns and Pronominal Suffixes." *Journal of the American Oriental Society* 108 (1998): 557–75.

———. "Reconstructing Pre-modern Aramaic Morphology: The Independent Pronouns." In *Studies in Neo-Aramaic,* edited by W. Heinrichs, 79–88. Harvard Semitic Studies Series. Atlanta: Scholars Press, 1989.

———. "The Chaldean Aramaic of Zakho." In *Semetica Serta Philologica,* edited by Contini, Pennacchietti, and Tosros, 115–26.

Hetzorn, Robert D. "The Morphology of the Verb in Modern Syriac (Christian Colloquial of Urm)." *Journal of the American Oriental Society* 89 (1969): 112–27.

Jastrow, Otto. *Die Mesopotamisch-Arabischen Qōltu-Dialect.* Band I. Phonologie and Morphologie, Abhandlungen für die Kunde des Morgenlandes 43/4. Wiesbaden: Franz Steiner, 1978.

———. "Tikrit Arabic Verb Morphology in a Comparative Perspective." *Al-Abhath* 31 (1983): 99–110.

Khan, Geoffrey. *A Grammar of Neo-Aramaic. The Dialect of the Jews of Arbel.* Leiden: Brill, 1999.

———. "Quelques aspects de l'expression d''etre' en neoaraméen." In *Langues des Diaspora. Langues et Contact,* edited by Anaïd Donabédian, 139–48. Faits de Langues de Linguistique 18. Paris: Ophrys, 2001.

———. *The Neo-Aramaic Dialect of Qaraqosh.* Leiden: Brill, 2002.

Krotkoff, George. *Neo-Aramaic Dialect of Kurdistan: Texts, Grammar and Vocabulary.* American Oriental Society 64. New Haven: American Oriental Society, 1985.

Maclean, Arthur John. *Grammar of the Dialects of Vernacular Syriac.* Cambridge: Cambridge University Press, 1895.

———. *A Dictionary of the Dialects of Vernacular Syriac as Spoken by the Eastern Syrians of Kurdistan, North-West Persia, and the Plain of Mosul.* Oxford: Clarendon, 1901.

Mingana, Alphonse. *Clef de langue araméenne ou Grammaire complete et pratique des deux dialects syriac occidental et oriental.* Mosul: Imprimerie des Péres Dominicains, 1905.

Mutzafi, Hezy. "The Neo-Aramaic dialect of Maha Khtaya d-Baz: Phonology, Morphology and Texts." *Journal of Semitic Studies* 45, no. 2 (2000): 293–322.

Nöldeke, Theodor. *Grammatik der Neusyrischen Sprache am Urmi-See und in Kurdistan.* Leipzig: T. O. Weigel, 1868.

Polotsky, Hans. "Studies in Modern Syriac." *Journal of Semitic Studies* 6 (1961): 1–32.

———. "Eastern Neo-Aramaic. B. Zakho." In *Aramaic Handbook,* edited by Franz Rosenthal, ii.1, 73–77; ii.12, 104–11. Porta linguarum Orientalium. 4 parts. Wiesbaden: Harassowitz, 1967.

Rhétore, Jean. *Grammaire de langue Soureth. Mosul.* Imprimerie des Péres Dominicains, 1912.

Rubba, J. "Forms Derived from Verbal Roots in Tisqoopa Modern Aramaic." In *Semitica Serta Philologica,* edited by Contini, Pennacchietti, and Tosco, 273–87.

Sabar, Yona. "From Tel-Kēpe in Iraqi Kurdistan to Providence, Rhode Island: The Story of a Chaldean Immigrant to the United States of America in 1927." *Journal of the American Oriental Society* 98, no. 4 (1978): 410–15.

———. "A Folktale and Folk Songs in the Christian Neo-Aramaic Dialect of Tel-Kēpe

(Northern Iraq)." In *Semitica Serta Philologica,* edited by Contini, Pennacchietti, and Tosco, 289–97.

Sachau, Edward. *Skizze des Fellichi-Dialect von Mosul.* Abhandlungen der Königlischen-Preussischen Ackademie der Wissenschaften zu Berlin. Berlin, 1895.

Sara, Solomon. *A Description of Modern Chaldean.* Janua Linguarum. Series Practica 213. The Hague–Paris: Mouton, 1974.

———. "Feminine Gender in Modern Chaldean. Form and Function." In *Studies in neo-Aramaic,* edited by W. Heinrichs, 45–52. Harvard Semitic Studies. Atlanta: Scholars Press 1990.

———. "Marked Gender in Modern Chaldean [ta/Θa] Suffix." In *Semitica Serta Philologica,* edited by Contini, Pennacchietti, and Tosco, 229–308.

Socin, Albert. *Die Neu-arämaischen Dialect von Urmia bis Mosul. Text und Übersetzung.* Tubingen: Laupp, 1882.

Tsereteli, K. "The Aramaic Dialect of Iraq." *Annali dell'Istituto Universitario Orientale di Napoli* S. 22 (2000): 245–50.

BIBLIOGRAPHY OF THE WORKS OF SIDNEY H. GRIFFITH

The following works are cited frequently in the bibliography and are abbreviated as indicated:

ACMP	Griffith, Sidney H. *Arabic Christianity in the Monasteries of Ninth-Century Palestine.* Brookfield, Vt.: Ashgate, 1992.
BCTA	Griffith, Sidney H. *The Beginnings of Christian Theology in Arabic: Muslim-Christian Encounters in the Early Islamic Period.* Burlington, Vt.: Ashgate, 2002.
Encyclopaedia of the Qur'ān	McAuliffe, Jane Dammen, ed. *Encyclopaedia of the Qur'ān.* 2 vols. Leiden/Boston/Köln: Brill, 2001, 2002.
Oxford Dictionary of Byzantium	Kazhdan, Alexander P., et al. *The Oxford Dictionary of Byzantium.* New York: Oxford University Press, 1991.
Religion in Geschichte und Gegenwart	Betz, H. D., et al., eds. *Religion in Geschichte und Gegenwart: Handwörterbuch für Theologie und Religonswissenschaft,* 4th ed. Vol. 1. Tübingen: J. C. B. Mohr (Paul Siebeck), 1998.

General Studies in the Christian Near East

"The Prophet Muhammad, His Scripture and His Message, According to the Christian Apologies in Arabic and Syriac from the First Abbasid Century." In *La vie du Prophète Mahomet: Un colloque organizé par le Centre de Recherche d'Histoire des Religions, Université des Sciences Humaines de Strasbourg, 23–24 octobre 1980,* edited by Toufic Fahd, 99–

146. Bibliothèque des Centre d'Études Supérieures Spécialisés. Paris: Presses Universitaires de France, 1983. Reprint in *ACMP.*

"Jews and Muslims in Christian Syriac and Arabic Texts of the Ninth Century." *Jewish History* 3 (1988): 65–94.

"Muhammad and the Monk Bahīrā: Reflections on a Syriac and Arabic Text from Early Abbasid Times." *Oriens Christianus* 79 (1995): 146–74. Reprint in *BCTA.*

"Arabia." In *Encyclopedia of Early Christianity,* 2nd ed., edited by Everett Ferguson, vol. 1, 98. New York: Garland, 1997.

"From Aramaic to Arabic: The Languages of the Monasteries of Palestine in the Byzantine and Early Islamic Periods." *Dumbarton Oaks Papers* 51 (1997): 11–31. Reprint in *BCTA.*

"Bahīrā-Legende." In *Religion in Geschichte und Gegenwart,* 1:1064.

Parry, Ken, David J. Melling, Dimitri Brady, Sidney H. Griffith, and John F. Healey, eds. *The Blackwell Dictionary of Eastern Christianity.* Oxford: Blackwell, 1999.

"The Handwriting on the Wall: Graffiti in the Church of St. Antony." In *Monastic Visions: Wall Paintings in the Monastery of St. Antony at the Red Sea,* edited by Elizabeth S. Bolman, 185–93. New Haven, Conn.: American Research Center in Egypt/Yale University Press, 2002.

Studies in Syriac

Ephrem

"Ephraem, the Deacon of Edessa, and the Church of the Empire." In *Diakonia: Studies in Honor of Robert T. Meyer,* edited by Thomas Halton and Joseph P. Williman, 22–52. Washington, D.C.: The Catholic University of America Press, 1986.

"Ephraem the Syrian's Hymns 'Against Julian': Meditations on History and Imperial Power." *Vigiliae Christianae* 41 (1987): 238–66.

"Images of Ephraem: The Syrian Holy Man and his Church." *Traditio* 45 (1989–90): 7–33.

"'Faith Seeking Understanding' in the Thought of St. Ephraem the Syrian." In *Faith Seeking Understanding: Learning and the Catholic Tradition. Selected Papers from the Symposium and Convocation Celebrating the Saint Anselm College Centennial,* edited by George C. Berthold, 35–55. Manchester, N.H.: Saint Anselm College Press, 1991.

"'Singles' in God's Service: Thoughts on the *Ihidaye* from the Works of Aphrahat and Ephrem the Syrian." *The Harp* 4 (1991): 145–59.

"The Image of the Image Maker in the Poetry of St. Ephraem the Syrian." In Studia patristica 25, edited by Elizabeth A. Livingston, 258–69. Leuven: Peeters, 1993.

"Faith Adoring the Mystery": Reading the Bible with St. Ephraem the Syrian. Père Marquette Lecture in Theology 1997. Milwaukee: Marquette University Press, 1997.

"A Spiritual Father for the Whole Church: The Universal Appeal of St. Ephraem the Syrian." *Hugoye: Journal of Syriac Studies* 2, no.1 (1998). http://syrcom.cua.edu/hugoye/

"The Marks of the 'True Church' According to Ephraem's *Hymns against Heresies.*" In *After Bardaisan: Studies on Continuity and Change in Syriac Christianity in Honour of Professor*

Han J. W. Drijvers, edited by G. J. Reinink and A. C. Klugkist, 125–40. OLA 89. Leuven: Uitgeverij Peeters en Departement Oosterse Studies, 1999.

"Setting Right the Church of Syria: Saint Ephraem's Hymns against Heresies." In *The Limits of Ancient Christianity: Essays on Late Antique Thought and Culture in Honor of R. A. Markus,* edited by William E. Klingshirn and Mark Vessey, 97–114. Ann Arbor, Mich.: University of Michigan Press, 1999.

"'Spirit in the Bread; Fire in the Wine': The Eucharist as 'Living Medicine' in the Thought of Ephraem the Syrian." *Modern Theology* 15 (1999): 225–46.

"The Thorn among the Tares": Mani and Manichaeism in the Works of St. Ephraem the Syrian." In Studia patristica 35, edited by M. F. Wiles and E. J. Yarnold, 395–427. Leuven: Peeters, 2001.

"Christianity in Edessa and the Syriac-Speaking World: Mani, Bar Daysan, and Ephraem; the Struggle for Allegiance on the Aramean Frontier." *Journal of the Canadian Society for Syriac Studies* 2 (2002): 5–20.

"St. Ephraem the Syrian, a Spiritual Teacher for Today." *The Maronite Voice* 9, no.5 (2003): 6–8, 12.

"Syriac/Antiochene Exegesis in Saint Ephrem's Teaching Songs *De paradiso*: The 'Types of Paradise' in the 'Treasury of Revelations.'" In *Syriac and Antiochian Exegesis and Biblical Theology for the Third Millennium,* edited by Robert D. Miller, 27–52. Piscataway, N.J.: Gorgias Press, 2008.

Other

"Chapter Ten of the Scholion: Theodore Bar Kônî's Apology for Christianity." *Orientalia christiana periodica* 47 (1981): 158–88.

"Theodore Bar Kônî's Scholion: A Nestorian Summa Contra Gentiles from the First Abbasid Century." In *East of Byzantium: Syria and Armenia in the Formative Period. Dumbarton Oaks Symposium, May 9–11, 1980,* edited by Nina Garsoïan, Thomas Mathews, and Robert Thomson, 53–72. Washington, D.C.: Dumbarton Oaks, 1982.

"'Abdīshō' Bar Berīkā." In *Oxford Dictionary of Byzantium,* 1:4.

"Chronicle of 819." In *Oxford Dictionary of Byzantium,* 1:444.

"Chronicle of 1234." In *Oxford Dictionary of Byzantium,* 1:444.

"Chronicle of Edessa." In *Oxford Dictionary of Byzantium,* 1:444–45.

"Dionysos of Tell Mahrē." In *Oxford Dictionary of Byzantium,* 1:628–29.

"Elias Bar Shināya." In *Oxford Dictionary of Byzantium,* 1:686.

"Gregory Abū 'l-Faraj [Bar Hebraeus]." In *Oxford Dictionary of Byzantium,* 2.878–79.

"John of Ephesus." In *Oxford Dictionary of Byzantium,* 2:1064.

"Joshua the Stylite." In *Oxford Dictionary of Byzantium,* 2:1076.

"Michael I the Syrian." In *Oxford Dictionary of Byzantium,* 2.1362–63.

"Paul of Kallinikos." In *Oxford Dictionary of Byzantium,* 3:1608.

"Romance of Julian." In *Oxford Dictionary of Byzantium,* 3:1805.

"Sergios of Reš'aina." In *Oxford Dictionary of Byzantium,* 3:1879–80.

"Syriac Literature." In *Oxford Dictionary of Byzantium,* 3:2000–2001.

"Disputes with Muslims in Syriac Christian Texts: From Patriarch John (d. 648) to Bar Hebraeus (d. 1286)." In *Religionsgespräche im Mittelalter/Religious Disputations in the Middle Ages. 25th Wolfenbütteler Symposion, 11 to 15 June 1989,* edited by Bernard Lewis and Friederich Niewöhner, 251–73. Wolfenbütteler Mittelalter-Studien 4. Wiesbaden: Otto Harrassowitz, 1992. Reprint in *BCTA.*

"Monks, 'Singles,' and the 'Sons of the Covenant': Reflections on Syriac Ascetic Terminology." In *ΕΥΛΟΓΗΜΑ: Studies in Honor of Robert Taft, S.J.,* edited by E. Carr, S. Parenti, A. A. Thiermeyer, and Elizabeth Velkovska 141–60. Studia Anselmiana 110, Analecta liturgica 17. Rome: Centro Studi S. Anselmo, 1993.

"Julian Saba, 'Father of the Monks' of Syria." *Journal of Early Christian Studies* 2 (1994): 185–216.

"Asceticism in the Church of Syria: The Hermeneutics of Early Syrian Monasticism." In *Asceticism,* edited by Vincent L. Wimbush and Richard Valantasis, 220–45. New York: Oxford University Press, 1995.

Review of Andrew Palmer, trans., *The Seventh Century in the West-Syrian Chronicles* (1993). *Speculum* 72 (1997): 544–45.

"Syria, Syriac." In *Encyclopedia of Early Christianity,* 2nd ed., edited by Everett Ferguson, vol. 2, 1100–102. New York: Garland, 1997.

"The Life of Theodore of Edessa: History, Hagiography, and Religious Apologetics in Mar Saba Monastery in Early Abbasid times." in *The Sabaite Heritage in the Orthodox Church from the Fifth Century to the Present,* edited by Joseph Patrich, 147–69. OLA 98. Leuven: Peeters, 2001.

Studies in Christian Arabic

Theodore Abu Qurrah

"The Controversial Theology of Theodore Abû Qurrah (c. 750–c. 820): A Methodological, Comparative Study in Christian Arabic Literature." Ph.D. diss. (directed by R.M. Frank). The Catholic University of America, 1978.

"Some Unpublished Arabic Sayings Attributed to Theodore Abū Qurrah." *Le Muséon* 92 (1979): 29-35.

"Theodore Abū Qurrah's Arabic Tract on the Christian Practice of Venerating Images." *Journal of the American Oriental Society* 105 (1985): 53–73. Reprint in *ACMP.*

"Free Will in Christian Kalām: The Doctrine of Theodore Abū Qurrah." *Parole de l'Orient* 14 (1987): 79–107. Reprint in *ACMP.*

"Theodore Abu-Qurra," with Alexander Kazhdan. In *Oxford Dictionary of Byzantium,* 3.2041.

Theodore Abū Qurrah: The Intellectual Profile of an Arab Christian Writer of the First Abbasid Century. Annual Lecture of Dr. Irene Halmos Chair of Arabic Literature, 1992. Tel Aviv: Tel Aviv University, 1992.

"Theodore Abū Qurrah's *On the Veneration of the Holy Icons*: Orthodoxy in the World of Islam." *Sacred Art Journal* 13 (1992): 3–19.

"Muslims and Church Councils: The Apology of Theodore Abū Qurrah." In Studia patristica 25, *Papers Presented at the Eleventh International Conference on Patristic Studies Held in Oxford, 1991. Biblica et apocrypha, orientalia, ascetica,* edited by Elizabeth A. Livingstone, 270–99. Leuven: Peeters, 1993. Reprint in *BCTA.*

"Reflections on the Biography of Theodore Abū Qurrah." *Parole de l'Orient* 18 (1993): 143–70.

"Faith and Reason in Christian *kalām*: Theodore Abū Qurrah on Discerning the True Religion." In *Christian Arabic Apologetics during the Abbasid Period (750–1258),* edited by Samir Khalil Samir and Jørgen S. Nielsen, 1–43. Studies in the History of Religion 63. Leiden: Brill, 1994.

"The View of Islam from the Monasteries of Palestine in the Early 'Abbāsid Period: Theodore Abū Qurrah and the Summa Theologiae Arabica." *Islam and Muslim-Christian Relations* 7 (1996): 9–28.

A Treatise on the Veneration of the Holy Icons Written in Arabic by Theodore Abû Qurrah, Bishop of Harrān (c. 755–c. 830 A.D.). Eastern Christian Texts in Translation 1. Louvain: Peeters, 1997.

Other

"Comparative Religion in the Apologetics of the First Christian Arabic Theologians." *Proceedings of the PMR Conference: Annual Publication of the Patristic, Mediaeval and Renaissance Conference* 4 (1979): 63–87. Reprint in *BCTA.*

"Habīb ibn Hidmah abū Rā'itah, a Christian *mutakallim* of the First Abbasid Century." *Oriens Christianus* 64 (1980): 161–201. Reprint in *BCTA.*

Review of Michael Hayek, *'Ammar al-Basri: Apologie et controversies* (1977). *Journal of Near Eastern Studies* 39 (1980): 243–44.

Review of Hans Putnam, *L'église et l'Islam sous Timothée I (780-823): Étude sur l'église nestorienne au temps du premiers 'Abbasides avec nouvelle edition et traduction du dialogue entre Timothée et al-Mahdi* (1977). *Journal of Near Eastern Studies* 39 (1980): 243.

"The Concept of al-Uqnūm in 'Ammār al-Basrī's Apology for the Doctrine of the Trinity." In *Actes du premier congrès internationale d'études chrétiennes (Goslar, 11–13 septembre 1980),* edited by Samir Khalil Samir, 169–91. OCA 218. Rome: Pontificium Institutum Studiorum Orientalium, 1982.

"Eutychius of Alexandria on the Emperor Theophilus and Iconoclasm in Byzantium: A 10th-Century Moment in Christian Apologetics in Arabic." *Byzantion* 52 (1982): 154–90. Reprint in *ACMP.*

"'Ammār al-Basrī's Kitāb al-Burhān: Christian *kalām* in the First Abbasid Century." *Le Muséon* 96 (1983): 145–81. Reprint in *BCTA.*

"The Arabic Account of 'Abd al-Masīh an-Nağrānī al-Ghassānī." *Le Muséon* 98 (1985): 331–74. Reprint in *ACMP.*

"The Gospel in Arabic: An Inquiry into Its Appearance in the First Abbasid Century." *Oriens Christianus* 69 (1985): 126–67. Reprint in *ACMP.*

"Stephen of Ramlah and the Christian Kerygma in Arabic in Ninth-Century Palestine." *Journal of Ecclesiastical History* 36 (1985): 23–45. Reprint in *ACMP.*

"Greek into Arabic: Life and Letters in the Monasteries of Palestine in the 9th Century: The Example of the Summa Theologiae Arabica." *Byzantion* 56 (1986): 117–38. Reprint in *ACMP.*

"A Ninth Century Summa Theologiae Arabica." In *Actes du deuxième congres international d'études arabes chrétiennes (Oosterhesselen, septembre 1984),* edited by [Samir] Khalil Samir, 123–41. OCA 226. Rome: Pontifical Institute for Oriental Studies, 1986. Reprint in *ACMP.*

"Anastasios of Sinai, the Hodegos, and the Muslims." *Greek Orthodox Theological Review* 32 (1987): 341–58.

"Dionysius Bar Salībī on the Muslims." In *IV Symposium Syriacum 1984: Literary Genres in Syriac Literature (Groningen-Oosterhesselen, 10–12 Septembre),* edited by H. J. W. Drijvers, R. Lavenant, C. Molenberg, and G. J. Reinink, 353–65. OCA 229. Rome: Pontifical Institute for Oriental Studies, 1987.

"Free Will in Christian Kalām: Moshe Bar Kepha against the Teachings of the Muslims." *Le Muséon* 100 (1987): 143–59.

Review of Rashid Haddad, *La trinité divine chez les théologiens arabes* (1985). *Theological Studies* 48 (1987): 176–79.

"The Monks of Palestine and the Growth of Christian Literature in Arabic." *The Muslim World* 78 (1988): 1–28. Reprint in *ACMP.*

"Anthony David of Baghdad, Scribe and Monk of Mar Sabas: Arabic in the Monasteries of Palestine." *Church History* 58 (1989): 7–19. Reprint in *ACMP.*

"Bashīr/Bēsēr: Boon Companion of the Byzantine Emperor Leo III: The Islamic Recension of his Story in Leiden Oriental MS 951(2)." *Le Muséon* 103 (1990): 293–327. Reprint in *BCTA.*

"The First Christian Summa Theologiae in Arabic: Christian kalām in Ninth-Century Palestine." In *Conversion and Continuity: Indigenous Christian communities in Islamic Lands Eighth to Eighteenth Centuries,* edited by Michael Gervers and Ramzi Jibran Bikhazi, 15–31. Papers in Mediaeval Studies 9. Toronto: Pontifical Institute of Mediaeval Studies, 1990.

"Free Will in Christian Kalām: Chapter XVII of the Summa Theologiae Arabica." In *Lingua restitute orientalis: Festgabe für Julius Assfalg,* edited by Regine Schulz and Manfred Görg, 129–34. Ägypten und Altes Testament 20. Wiesbaden: Harrassowitz, 1990.

"Islam and the Summa Theologiae Arabica, Rabī' I, 264 A.H." *Jerusalem Studies in Arabic and Islam* 13 (1990): 225–64.

"Agapios of Hierapolis." In *Oxford Dictionary of Byzantium,* 1.35.

"The Apologetic Treatise of Nonnus of Nisibis." *Aram* 3 (1991): 116–38. Reprint in *BCTA.*

"Eutychios of Alexandria." In *Oxford Dictionary of Byzantium,* 2.760.

"Yabh Allāhā III." In *Oxford Dictionary of Byzantium,* 3.2213.

Arabic Christianity in the Monasteries of Ninth-Century Palestine. Collected Studies 380. Brookfield, Vt.: Variorum, 1992.

"Images, Islam, and Christian Icons: A Moment in the Christian/Muslim Encounter in Early Islamic Times." In *Le Syrie, de Byzance à l'Islam, VIIe-VIIIe Siècles. Actes du Colloque International. Lyon—Maison de l'Orient Mediterranéeen, Paris—Institut du Monde Arabe, 11–15 Septembre 1990,* edited by Pierre Canivet and Jean-Paul Rey-Coquais, 121–38. Damascus: Institut Français de Damas, 1992.

"Holy Land History from the Archive of Old South Palestinian Arabic Texts." *Cathedra for the History of Eretz Israel and Its Yishuv* 69 (1993): 57–78. In Hebrew.

"Mayfa'ah: Un sito dimenticato della primitive tradizione islamica." In *Umm al-Rasas/ Mayfa'ah I: Gli Scavi del Complesso di Santo Stefano,* edited by Michele Piccirillo and Eugenio Alliata, 51–54. Studium Biblicum Franciscanum Collectio Maior 28. Jerusalem: Studium Biblicum Franciscanum, 1994.

"Michael, the Martyr and Monk of Mar Sabas Monastery, at the Court of the Caliph 'Abd al-Malik: Christian Apologetics and Martyrology in the Early Islamic Period." *Aram* 6 (1994): 115–48.

"The Kitāb Misbāh al-'Aql of Severus al-Muqaffa': A Profile of the Christian Creed in Tenth-Century Egypt." *Medieval Encounters: Jewish, Christian and Muslim Culture in Confluence and Dialogue* 2 (1996): 15–42. Reprint in *BCTA.*

"The Muslim Philosopher al-Kindi and His Christian Readers: Three Arab Christian Texts on 'The Dissipation of Sorrows.'" *Bulletin of the John Rylands University Library of Manchester* 78 (Special issue on the "Church of the East: Life and Thought") (1996): 111–27. Reprint in *BCTA.*

"Abū Rā'ita, Habīb Ibn Hidma." In *Religion in Geschichte und Gegenwart,* 1.92-93.

"'Ali Ibn Sahl Ibn Rabban Aṭ-Ṭabarī." In *Religion in Geschichte und Gegenwart,* 1.299.

"'Ammār al-Baṣrī." In *Religion in Geschichte und Gegenwart,* 1.413.

"Apologie des Kindī." In *Religion in Geschichte und Gegenwart,* 1.632–33.

"Arabisch-christliche Literatur." In *Religion in Geschichte und Gegenwart,* 1.699–70.

"Bibelübersetzungen. I. Übersetzungen in Antike Sprache. 5. Übersetzungen ins Arabische." In *Religion in Geschichte und Gegenwart,* 1.1498.

"Christians, Muslims, and Neo-Martyrs: Saints' Lives and Holy Land History." In *Sharing the Sacred: Religious Contacts and Conflicts in the Holy Land, First-Fifteenth Centuries C.E.,* edited by Arieh Kofsky and Guy G. Stroumsa, 163–207. Jerusalem: Yad Izhak Ben Zvi, 1998.

"What Has Constantinople to Do with Jerusalem? Palestine in the Ninth Century: Byzantine Orthodoxy in the World of Islam." In *Byzantium in the Ninth Century: Dead or Alive? Papers from the Thirtieth Spring Symposium of Byzantine Studies, Birmingham, March 1996,* edited by Leslie Brubaker, 181–94. Society for the Promotion of Byzantine Studies Publications 5. Aldershot, Hampshire: Ashgate/Variorum, 1998.

"Eutychius of Alexandria (Sa'īd b. Betrīq)," with the editors of *Encyclopedia Iranica.* In *En-*

cyclopaedia Iranica, edited by Ehsan Yarshater, 9:77–78. New York: Bibliotheca Persica Press, 1998.

"The Monk in the Emir's Majlis: Reflections on a Popular Genre of Christian Literary Apologetics in Arabic in the Early Islamic Period." In *The Majlis: Interreligious Encounters in Medieval Islam,* edited by H. Lazarus-Yafeh et al., 13–65. Wiesbaden: Harrassowitz, 1999.

"Christians and Christianity." In *Encyclopaedia of the Qur'ān,* 1.307–16.

"Church." In *Encyclopaedia of the Qur'ān,* 1.335–36.

"'Melkites,' 'Jacobites' and the Christological controversies in Arabic in Third/Ninth-Century Syria." in *Syrian Christians under Islam: The First Thousand Years,* edited by David Thomas, 9–55. Leiden/Boston/Köln: Brill, 2001.

"Gospel." In *Encyclopaedia of the Qur'ān,* 2.342–43.

The Beginnings of Christian Theology in Arabic: Muslim-Christian Encounters in the Early Islamic Period. Collected Studies 746. Burlington, Vt.: Ashgate, 2002.

Yaḥyā ibn 'Adī, The Reformation of Morals: A Parallel English-Arabic Text Translated and Introduced. Eastern Christian Texts 1. Provo, Utah: Brigham Young University Press, 2002.

"Answers for the Shaykh: a 'Melkite' Arabic Text from Sinai and the Doctrines of the Trinity and the Incarnation in 'Arab Orthodox' Apologetics." In *The Encounter of Eastern Christianity with Early Islam, edited by* E. Grypeou, Mark Swanson, and David Thomas, 277–309. (Boston, Mass.: Brill, 2006).

The Church in the Shadow of the Mosque: Christians and Muslims in the World of Islam. Princeton, N.J.: Princeton University Press, 2007.

"Die Kirche im Schatten der Moschee: Christen und Muslime in der islamischen Welt." *Pro Oriente Jahrbuch* (2007): 24–45.

"Christians, Muslims and the Image of the One God: Iconophilia and Iconophobia in the World of Islam in Umayyad and Early Abbasid Times." In *Die Welt der Götterbilder,* edited by Brigitte Groneberg und Hermann Spieckermann, 347–80. New York, N.Y.: Walter de Gruyter, 2007).

"From Patriarch Timothy I to Hunayn ibn Ishāq: Philosophy and Christian Apology in Abbasid Times; Reason, Ethics, and Philosophy." In *Christian and Muslims in Dialogue in the Islamic Orient of the Middle Ages,* edited by Martin Tamcke, 75–98. Beirut: Orient-Institut/Würzburg: Ergon Verlag in Kommission, 2007.

"Bediüzzaman Said Nursi and Louis Massignon in Pursuit of God's Word: A Muslim and a Christian on the Straight Path." *Islam and Christian-Muslim Relations* (2008): 5–16.

"John of Damascus and the Church in Syria in the Umayyad Era: The Intellectual and Cultural Milieu of Orthodox Christians in the World of Islam." *Hugoye* 11 (2008).

"Crosses, Icons, and the Image of Christ in Edessa: The Place of Iconophobia in the Christian-Muslim Controversies of Early Islamic Times." In *Transformations of Late Antiquity: Essays for Peter Brown,* edited by Philip Rousseau and Manolis Papoutsakis, 63–84. (Burlington, Vt.: Ashgate, 2009).

"Christians under Muslim Rule." In *Early Medieval Christianities, c. 600-c.1100,* edited by

Thomas F. X. Noble and Julia M. H. Smith, 197–212, 687–90. Cambridge: Cambridge University Press, 2008.

"Patriarch Timothy I and an Aristotelian at the Caliph's Court." In *The Christian Heritage of Iraq*, edited by Erica C. D. Hunter, 38–53. Piscataway, N.J.: Gorgias Press, 2009.

Interreligious Dialogue and Spirituality

"W. H. C. Frend and the 'Rise of Christianity'" (review of Frend, *The Rise of Christianity*, [1984]). *Journal of Religion* 66 (1986): 431–36.

Review of D. S. Wallace-Hadrill, *Christian Antioch: A Study of Early Christian Thought in the East* (1983). *Catholic Historical Review* 75 (1989): 123–24.

"Thomas Merton, Louis Massignon, and the Challenge of Islam." *The Merton Annual* 3 (1990): 151–72.

"The Descendants of Abraham." *CUA Magazine* 3, no. 2 (Summer 1991): 18–21.

"Christians and Muslims." *The Priest* 47, no. 7 (July 1991): 13–15.

"Henri Hyvernat (1858–1941) and the Beginning of Syriac Studies at The Catholic University of America," with Monica Blanchard. *Aram* 5 (1993): 181–96.

"Kenneth Cragg on Christians and the Call to Islam." *Religious Studies Review* 20 (1994): 29–35.

Review of Bat Ye'or, *Chrétientés d'Orient entre jihâd et dhimmitude* (1991). *Speculum* 69 (1994): 419–20.

Review of Douglas Burton-Christie, *The Word in the Desert: Scripture and the Quest for Holiness in Early Christian Monasticism* (1993). *Journal of Religion* 75 (1995): 114–15.

"Sharing the Faith of Abraham: The 'Credo' of Louis Massignon." *Islam and Christian-Muslim Relations* 8 (1997): 193–210.

"'As One Spiritual Man to Another': the Merton-Abdul Aziz Correspondence." In *Merton and Sufism: The Untold Story. A Complete Compendium*, edited by Rob Baker and Gray Henry, 101–29. Louisville, KY: Fons Vitae, c1999.

Ph.D. Dissertations and Masters Theses Advised at the Catholic University of America

Amar, Joseph Philip. "The Syriac Vita Tradition of Ephrem the Syrian." PhD diss., 1988. Partially published as "Byzantine Ascetic Monachism and Greek Bias in the Vita Tradition of Ephraem the Syrian," *OCP* 58 (1992): 23–56.

Garland, Amy Galli. "An Arabic Translation of the Gospel According to Mark." M.A. thesis, 1979.

Hurst, Thomas Richard. "Letter 40 of the Nestorian Patriarch Timothy I (727–823): An Edition and Translation." M.A. thesis, 1981.

Hurst, Thomas Richard. "The Syriac Letters of Timothy I (727-823): A Study in Christian-Muslim controversy." Ph.D. diss., 1986. Partially published as "The Epistle-Treatise: An

Apologetic Vehicle. Letter 34 of Timothy I." In *IV Symposium Syriacum 1984: Literary Genres in Syriac Literature (Groningen-Oosterhesselen, 10–12 Septembre)*, edited by H. J. W. Drijvers, R. Lavenant, C. Molenberg, and G. J. Reinink, 367–76. OrChrAn 229. Rome: Pontifical Institute for Oriental Studies, 1987.

Martinez, Francisco Javier. "The Syriac Apocalypse of Pseudo-Methodius: Critical Edition and English Version." M.A. thesis, 1982.

Martinez, Francisco Javier. "Eastern Christian Apocalyptic in the Early Muslim Period: Pseudo-Methodius and Pseudo-Athanasius." Ph.D. diss., 1985. Partially published as "The Apocalyptic Genre in Syriac: The World of Pseudo-Methodius." In *IV Symposium Syriacum 1984: Literary Genres in Syriac Literature (Groningen-Oosterhesselen, 10–12 Septembre),* edited by H. J. W. Drijvers, R. Lavenant, C. Molenberg, and G. J. Reinink, 337–52. OrChrAn 229. Rome: Pontifical Institute for Oriental Studies, 1987.

Mathews, Edward G., Jr. "Isaac of Antioch, 'On Solitaries, Mourners and Hermits': A Translation and Commentary." M.A. thesis, 1987. Partially published as "'On Solitaries': Ephraem or Isaac?" *Le Muséon* 103 (1990): 91–110.

Talia, Shawqi N. "The Fatimid Caliph al-Hâkim's Treatment of Christians According to the History of Yahya ibn-Sa'îd al-Antâkî." M.A. thesis, 1980.

Talia, Shawqi N. "Bûlus al-Bûši's Arabic Commentary on the Apocalypse of St. John: An English Translation and Commentary." Ph.D. diss., 1987.

Taylor, Richard Andrew. "An Analysis of the New Testament Citations in the Sermo de Domino Nostro of St. Ephrem Syrus." M.A. thesis, 1985.

Taylor, Richard Andrew. "An Analysis of the Syriac Text of the Book of Daniel." Ph.D. diss., 1990. Partially published as "The Peshitta of Daniel: Questions of Origin and Date." In *VI Symposium Syriacum 1992. University of Cambridge, Faculty of Divinity, 30 August–2 September 1992*, edited by René Lavenant, 31–42. OrChrAn 247. Roma: Pontificio Istituto Orientale, 1994. Substantially published in *The Peshitta of Daniel.* Monographs of the Peshitta Institute 7. Leiden: Brill, 1994.

Blanchard, Monica J. "Beh Isho' Kamulaya's Syriac Discourses on the Monastic Way of Life: Edition, English Translation, and Introduction." Ph.D. diss., 2001.

Horn, Cornelia B. "Beyond Theology: The Career of Peter the Iberian in the Christological Controversies of Fifth-Century Palestine." Ph.D. diss., 2001.

Editorial Projects

Aram. The Aram Society for Syro-Mesopotamian Studies. Oxford. Member of the U.S. and British Academic Boards, 1988–present.

Bulletin of the Royal Institute for Inter-Faith Studies. Published by the Royal Institute for Inter-Faith Studies in Amman, Jordan. Member of the Editorial Board, 1999–present.

The Comprehensive Aramaic Lexicon. Hebrew Union College and Johns Hopkins University. Associate editor, 1985–1988.

Corpus scriptorum christianorum orientalium (CSCO). The Catholic University of America and The Catholic University of Louvain. Member of the Consultative Board, 1978–present.

Early Christian Texts in Translation. Peeters, Leuven. Co-editor, 1997–present.

Hugoye: Journal of Syriac Studies. Published by the Syriac Computing Institute at the Catholic University of Ameria, with a mirror site at the Peshitta Institute, Leiden. Member of the Editorial Board, 1998–present.

Islam and Christian-Muslim Relations. Centre for the Study of Islam and Christian-Muslim Relations, Selly Oaks College, Birmingham, England, and the Center for Muslim-Christian Understanding, Georgetown University, Washington, D.C. Consultant editor, 1990–present.

Journal of Early Christian Studies, Johns Hopkins University Press. Associate editor, 1993–present.

The Library of Early Christianity. The Catholic University of America Press. Member of the editorial board, 1996–present.

Medieval Encounters: Jewish, Christian and Muslim Culture in Confluence and Dialogue. Brill, Leiden. Member of the editorial board, 1995–present.

Monographs of the Peshitta Institute, Leiden. Member of the editorial board, 1998–present.

ðIKMA: Revista de Estudios Cristianos/Journal of Christian Studies. CEDROC, Beirut, Lebanon, and Universidad de Córdoba, Spain. Member of the Advisory Board, 2002–present.

CONTRIBUTORS

Joseph P. Amar is professor of Syriac and Arabic at the University of Notre Dame.

Gary A. Anderson is professor of Old Testament/Hebrew Bible at the University of Notre Dame.

Monica J. Blanchard is curator of the Semitics/Institute of Christian Oriental Research Library at the Catholic University of America.

Sebastian Brock is professor emeritus in Syriac Studies at the University of Oxford.

Robin Darling Young is associate professor of theology at the University of Notre Dame.

Alexander Golitzin is professor of theology at Marquette University.

Susan Ashbrook Harvey is Willard Prescott and Annie McClelland Smith Professor of Religious Studies at Brown University.

Michael J. Hollerich is professor of theology at the University of St. Thomas.

Francisco Javier Martínez is the Bishop of Córdoba, Spain.

Kathleen McVey is Joseph Ross Stevenson Professor of Church History at Princeton Theological Seminary.

Shawqi Talia is lecturer in Arabic and Islamic Studies at the Catholic University of America.

To Train His Soul in Books: Syriac Asceticism in Early Christianity was designed and typeset in Garamond by Kachergis Book Design of Pittsboro, North Carolina. It was printed on 60-pound House Natural Smooth and bound by Sheridan Books of Ann Arbor, Michigan.